ONE MAN'S WAR

ONE MAN'S WAR

AN ACTOR'S
LIFE AT SEA
1940-1945

RICHARD BEALE

BLOOMSBURY

Published by Conway
An imprint of Bloomsbury Publishing Plc
www.bloomsbury.com

50 Bedford Square
London
WC1B 3DP
UK

1385 Broadway
New York
NY 10018
USA

First published 2015
© Richard Beale, 2015
© Illustrations Richard Beale, 2015

British Library Cataloguing-in-Publication Data
A catalogue record for this book is available from the British Library.

ISBN: HB: 978-1-8448-6333-4
ePDF: 978-1-8448-6330-3
ePub: 978-1-8448-6334-1

10 9 8 7 6 5 4 3 2 1

Typeset in Joanna MT Std by Deanta Global Publishing Services, Chennai, India
Printed and bound in Great Britain by CPI Group (UK) Ltd, Croydon CR0 4YY

To find out more about our authors and books visit www.bloomsbury.com.
Here you will find extracts, author interviews, details of forthcoming
events and the option to sign up for our newsletters.

Contents

List of illustrations

1. My Mother, Constance Beale.
2. My parents on their wedding day, just a few hours after peace was declared at the end of the First World War.
3. My Father, Harry George Beale, left, on his favourite horse, Paddy.
4. The ill-fated HMS *Hood*. She was sunk with great loss of life a few days after I was aboard as relief 'washer-up' in the wardroom pantry.
5. Introducing Simon to the Navy.
6. Me in naval uniform with Simon.
7. Simon, a special dog.
8. Me at Gibraltar Airport, about to leave in search of eggs.
9. My first command, motor launch (HDML) 1070 leaving Sheerness.
10. Left, Morris Drake (Quack) and me in the centre, beside a Beau fighter. Later, Quack became a High Court judge: The Hon. Sir Morris Drake DFC.
11. Ljerka Ebenspanger, aged seven at Fasano, Italy.
12. HDMLs leaving harbour.
13. My last command, ML 135 underway off Bari.
14. The bridge wheel of ML 135.
15. Mentioned in dispatches.

Foreword

People write books for various reasons, some for fame, some for money, some for solace and many for a mixture of all three. I wrote One Man's War out of a feeling of indignation!

One morning in the early spring of 2014, I became aware of something missing in my life. For forty-two years as an actor I had read and learned other people's words. Was it not time to set down a few words of my own, for better or for worse?

The thought tapped at the door of my consciousness for several weeks until it opened, and the decision was made.

What was to be the subject? The theatre was rejected as being over-published already. Sailing, and life in post-war Britain, also seemed inadequate and I doubted my ability to make them interesting. That left the war. Here was a ready-made series of events that only needed recall.

The first pages were written in a bed and breakfast establishment, an ideal place for the task as it held no distractions, and was sufficiently boring to keep my mind on the job.

By the time I returned to my newly decorated cottage enough momentum had been gathered to continue the process. Events unfurled in my memory like a roll of film, and the book began to write itself.

One Man's War became a day-by-day account of one man's part in the 1939–45 war against Hitler. The action ranges over the

North Sea, the Western Approaches and, to a greater extent, the Mediterranean and the Adriatic.

In the early chapters and at the end I have tried to give glimpses of England at the time, and of home life when on leave.

Apart from the outset, I have omitted many references to the calendar, although I must have been aware of dates when writing up the log. Events became part of a continuum in which happenings led from one to the next in a chain, ending in the cessation of hostilities in 1945.

I particularly thank Roger Kirkham for carrying out the arduous task of typing my hand-written manuscript and transferring it to a CD. Very special thanks to my daughter Anya for all her help and encouragement.

One Man's War is dedicated to the memory of all who died that we may live, and to the memory of my two brothers who also served at sea.

CHAPTER 1

From Finchley
to the *Arethusa*

1940–41

'Stand in line. No talking!'

Having delivered this ultimatum, the Petty Officer retired to his corner and renewed his acquaintance with a mug of tea and half a pork pie.

My war started in Finchley, which is a bit like saying 'the earthquake started next door.' To be precise, it began in the Territorial Army Drill Hall in Finchley. It was late spring 1940 and unusually hot. A long queue of callow young men stretched the full length of the hall. Each had a rather pathetic-looking cardboard box hanging around his neck by a piece of string, which contained the civilian gas mask. Somehow the box and the string added to the callowness of the scene.

A strong smell of sweat, backed by a faint odour of carbolic, hung in the air like a cobweb. The front of the line faced a blank wall with a door near the centre. From time to time this door would open and a uniformed figure would emerge and beckon to the young man at the front of the queue to enter.

Eventually my turn came. I went through the door to be faced by a long table behind which sat a three-ring Royal Navy (RN) Commander, flanked by a Lieutenant Commander and a Lieutenant. I was questioned about my family, my friends, my hobbies, my school, what books I had read and my favoured sports until at last, the 'thousand dollar question' was put to me by the senior officer. He raised his eyes until they were level with mine and, looking hard at me, asked quietly,

'Why do you wish to join the navy?'

I was unprepared for this, and thought wildly of various answers. Should I spout some rubbish about love of the sea, about admiring the Senior Service, or invent some nautical family connections? No, because I was basically a truthful young man of nineteen and, after what seemed like five minutes, said, 'Well, sir, if I have to die I would rather die at sea than in a trench.'

That's torn it, I thought. That's the end of that. I'll be told to go home and wait to be called up by the army. It was at the time of the so-called 'Phoney War' and as yet no one had felt the effects of hostilities. Maybe I would never be called. I waited while their heads came together and conferred in private. At last the commander turned to me and said, 'Subject to a satisfactory medical you will be accepted.' Then the floor gave way beneath me, and a hundred days of hopes and dreams came flooding to life.

'Thank you, sir, I will do my best,' I said.

'That's all we ask, proceed,' he replied, and he pointed to one of two doors, one leading to a temporary sick bay, and the other to the outside world.

The sick bay walls were decorated with posters bearing cheerful messages about disease, mostly of the venereal kind. There was some rudimentary equipment and a nurse. My pulse was taken, my height measured, my chest and heart were sounded and then finally a sample of urine was required. I was given a small hospital bottle, but, on account of the three hours I had been in the building, this container proved most inadequate. The bottle filled too rapidly, and I was rushed over to a sink to complete the operation. The nurse giggled. This was an unpromising start to my naval career. I was then taken to an annex housing a desk, two filing cabinets and a Chief Petty Officer who was having his tea. He put aside a ham sandwich, gulped down the last of his mug, and commenced a long recitation designed to give the 'new boy' some idea of what to expect in the weeks to come. The gist of which was that I was to return home to wait for further instructions. I was also not to go abroad, or leave my present address, engage in careless talk, or give up my job before receiving a call-up notice.

Six weeks later I received instructions to report to HMS *Collingwood* at Fareham, in Hampshire; a rail warrant was enclosed. Goodbyes were said, tearfully in the case of my Mother and manfully by my Father. We shook hands and he wished me luck. Men did not embrace in those days. Then came a surprise: my two younger brothers, who were still at school, presented me with a magnificent dressing case in soft calf leather bearing a label inscribed Swain & Adney, Park Lane, London. They had sold their most treasured possession, an electric train set, which had been built up over the years and covered the loft floor. It was hard to remain calm and in control in the face of such generosity.

HMS *Collingwood* proved to be a large training camp, consisting of some twenty huts surrounding a parade ground. Each hut housed twenty-four trainees. The hut was lined with twelve double bunks, six on each side. Life in the camp was in the main uneventful, if not to say boring. We drilled, learned to sail a cutter, learned to row whalers – which are the lifeboats carried in the waists of cruisers and larger vessels – we were taught sailor's

3

knots and splices, with each followed by more drilling on the parade ground.

The food there was reasonable. But it was said that the tea and cocoa were laced with some stuff called 'Rumoy' which was supposed to inhibit sexual desire. There was a good NAAFI (Navy, Army and Air Force Institutes facility) where you could supplement the diet with bacon and beans, and buy Cadbury quarter-pound chocolate bars for tuppence a time.

We were allowed shore leave from which men would often return still bleeding from a session with the local tattooist. On arrival we had been issued with two suits of bell-bottom trousers, two caps, pants, shirts and collars, plus a hammock and kitbag. A drunken evening so often ended with a tattoo. The chap in the bunk above me had several tattoos done in a ring around his neck, and his open sailor collar revealed spots of blood oozing from every design.

Only one event of note occurred in my time at Collingwood. There was considerable rivalry among the huts. From time to time a raid would take place, usually at night, the object of which was to remove some important object, like a bed or a lavatory chain, from the appointed victims. In one of these affairs I was struck on the head with a piece of wood. Two stitches from the camp doctor were needed, and I have the scar to this day.

I was fortunate in having an aunt and uncle who lived nearby in Bournemouth. I was able to stay with them at weekends instead of making the long trips back to London and Hertfordshire. If I'm honest, the real reason for going to my relations' house was my cousin Eileen. She was a very pretty girl of sixteen. She would sit next to me in the back of my uncle's Vauxhall during visits to the New Forest and other beauty spots. At such times the 'Rumoy' in the cocoa did not seem to be having much effect.

The weeks at Collingwood eventually wore to a close. I was glad when it was over. Somehow the training had made me feel more like a Boy Scout than a sailor. One needs to be in daily touch with the sea to feel part of Britain's great naval history.

Chatham Barracks was my next stop. This was where trainees waited for a ship, or another shore establishment. Our rank by that time was that of Ordinary Seaman. At Chatham we did nothing but march around the square to the shouted orders of a Petty Officer. The place had originally been built to house just two thousand men, but during my time there it was said that there could be fourteen thousand bodies waiting for a draft to somewhere else. The place was really a holding ground where chaos reigned. I was there for three weeks, and quickly discovered that it was only necessary to carry some papers around, looking busy, to avoid drills.

The worst part of Chatham Barracks was the tunnel below the establishment. By this time air raids had begun and the huge numbers of men staying there were marshalled nightly into this dungeon. Here one might avoid death by explosives, but would possibly suffer respiratory damage from the foetid atmosphere. Smoking was allowed, which, alongside the overcrowding and the stench, made the air below the barracks unbearable.

I did find a way to avoid this ordeal. At Chatham the 'inmates' were divided into four watches designated by colour: yellow, red, blue and white. One colour watch was allowed ashore each night. On leaving the gate you showed your card briefly to the guard, and proceeded into the town. You did not have to report back until 8am the following morning. Therefore every fourth night you were free of the awful 'tunnel'.

I noticed that the guard was changed every night, and it would be unlikely they would remember faces. Consequently, I was able to buy a card for each watch from men who were leaving. I never knew how they managed to avoid giving up their watch colour at the main gate office when they finally left. It cost me several weeks' NAAFI money, but was definitely worth it. In Chatham town there was a comfortable seamen's mission where you could buy a bed for the night for a shilling, and a substantial meal for another shilling. One night as I was leaving the main gate, an army pick-up truck hurtled round the corner, and slowed down to avoid a bus. I signalled him for a lift and he shouted, 'Jump in.' I landed on the running board, and climbed into the cab. At this point the driver accelerated dramatically, not to say dangerously, and I bellowed into his ear, 'Why so fast?'

He shouted back, 'Got an unexploded bomb in the back, taking it out to chalk pit where I'll deal with it!' My war was now beginning in earnest.

Not long after that I fell in love with a little nude dancer, who was appearing at the Chatham Music Hall. She was part of a professional review and, wearing only a spangled G-string, she danced into my dreams.

Two days later, along with two others, I received my movement orders. I was drafted to a small barracks at Rosyth and had to wait there for the arrival of the light cruiser *Arethusa*.

Then came one more instance of a changing life. Those about to be drafted had to display all their kit for inspection. All clothes issued, plus hammocks and shaving gear, had to be placed on the deck to be checked by a Petty Officer to make sure nothing had been lost or stolen. Like the simple fool that I was, I had placed my beautiful dressing case among the rest of the gear. After inspection I left the room to visit the lavatory. When I returned the room was empty, and my dressing case was missing. I went at once to the 'Jaunty' (Master-at-arms) and reported the loss. He laughed,

'You'll learn, my lad, you will learn!'

For weeks I mourned the loss, not for the sake of the case itself, but because it had been the result of a huge sacrifice by my two younger brothers, who were still at school and who would no longer be able to enjoy something they had known for most of their young lives. The loss of innocence for all of us was beginning.

The time at Rosyth Barracks was short. The *Arethusa* failed to return to Rosyth and went instead to Portsmouth, to where I was then re-routed. I was to report aboard the *Arethusa* at 10.00am the following day, and a rail warrant was enclosed. Now, this was more like it. 'Report aboard *Arethusa*.' This sounded properly naval to me and was the first real leap into the life at sea ahead.

Going south to Porthsmouth, on a somewhat slow train, I discovered that it stopped at Harpenden and St Albans, where my parents lived. I reckoned that by getting off at St Albans, I could spend a few hours at home, catch an early train to London, and still be in Portsmouth by 10.00am. It was cutting everything a bit fine, but it could be done. Alas the best laid plans ... I fell asleep near Harpenden, woke suddenly at the next station, thought we had reached St Albans and so I got off. But I was six miles from home. It was 11.00pm and I had to walk the whole way, arriving at 1.00am. My parents were glad to see me of course, but worried by the risk I had taken. Mother fried me an egg and some bacon, and tried to pretend that it was breakfast time, not 3.00am. After only two hours at home, my Father drove me to the station, and somehow I got aboard *Arethusa* at the appointed time.

That journey to Portsmouth was a step back into the past. For the first time since leaving home, I felt a twinge of homesickness. The countryside slipped by ablaze in sunshine and I was transported back to childhood and my school days. The suburbs gave way to open fields and farmsteads that reminded me of the country around our house in Hertfordshire. I realised that I had had a privileged upbringing, and parents who had created an elegant home out of nothing.

My Father had served in the Royal Flying Corps during the First World War and married my Mother while on leave, on the day after the armistice was signed. He joined a small firm of photo-engravers in Holborn, London and, by sheer hard work became the managing director and later, the owner of the business. Over a ten-year period he built the company up to become an important player in the print world, employing sixty craftsmen.

We had a lovely home set in three acres of land, out of which he created a garden with a swimming pool and tennis court. Beyond the court there was an orchard and a spinney of tall trees. As children we used to play there and make campfires – which were strictly forbidden. We were never spoilt but made to work both outside and inside the house. One of my jobs was to empty and clean the pool using a long broom and a bucket of strong chlorine. At the age of twelve, with the help of my middle brother, Tony, I cut turf from the paddock and laid a lawn around the pool while my parents were away on a short, and rare, holiday in Devon. For most of the time we had a live-in maid, later to become a mother's-help, and it was one of these girls who was left in charge of the house and us boys.

The house itself had once been a stable block and groom's quarters on a country estate, which was ideal for conversion into a large and comfortable home. Father planned all the work, which was carried out by builders under his direction. He retained part of the stabling where he kept two horses, and from the age of six we were taught to ride.

While my Father climbed the ladder of success, we lived in a number of houses and I was sent to a number of different schools. Two of these were harsh boarding schools that were not in the top rank, but aped the manners of those that were. I attended the first at the age of eight, where as a new boy I was bullied, which happened to all new kids, and beaten by prefects and forced to fight my corner in the junior common room. However, being the son of my Father, and used to hard knocks, I gave as good as I got.

At my second boarding school I was beaten repeatedly as before, but this time more severely and with canes. Here, the prefects seemed to have unlimited power. I finished my third term by carving my initials on the school gateway which, unknown to me at the time, was a memorial to the old boys who had died in the First World War. Nevertheless, I was 'sacked' for my actions.

In desperation, I suppose, I was then sent to St George's School in Harpenden, a few miles from what became our family home. This establishment was run on Christian principles, and was co-educational. There were flowers in the classrooms, large playing fields, and a wonderful atmosphere of gentle family life, where boys and girls of all ages mingled together as if they were brothers and sisters. I gave no more trouble. I tried to contribute to the organisation by starting a tradition whereby the junior sixth form gave a drama entertainment in the gym each year. I was awarded my colours in the first rugby fifteen, but failed to learn anything of use academically, apart from a deep love of literature. I was then thirteen years old. All of these 'mind pictures' flooded through my brain as the train rattled on towards Portsmouth. Gradually they receded as houses and telegraph poles began to appear, and I started to concentrate on what lay ahead.

Before leaving Rosyth I had entrusted my hammock and kit bag to the railway authorities, to be delivered to the left luggage department at Portsmouth. This was a common procedure at the time because servicemen were moving round the UK in the course of reaching their billets.

It was 8.30am when I arrived, and the station buffet was open. I ate another breakfast and then, hoisting my hammock onto the left shoulder and wedging the kit bag under the right arm, I set off for the docks. In spite of the early hour, the town was alive and on the move. Squads of men were being marched from place to place, shops were open and military vehicles constantly passed me on the way.

Arethusa was alongside, and the sight of her made my heart beat faster. Here was the object of all my hopes and dreams. She was sleek and grey. The sentry on duty at the gangway signalled to another to take me to the Bosun's office. I was signed on, given a place to stow and sling my hammock, and shown my place at a table in the seamen's mess. After the rough and tumble of *Collingwood*, and the organised chaos of Chatham barracks, this ship exhibited an air of quiet purposeful activity. Occasionally an announcement would come from the loudspeakers or a Bosun's pipe would sound, signalling some part of the ship's routine.

Arethusa was a light-cruiser, built in Chatham dockyard, and one of four similar vessels famous for being the first warships that had plates that were welded together rather than riveted, which was the normal method of construction. Many sailors were sceptical about this way of assembling the hull, and some thought that the flexing of the sides in high seas might open the welds. Consequently, they became unfairly known as the 'Chatham gash-boats'. No such calamity occurred, and the four ships served continually throughout the war. Two of the others were named the *Calypso* and the *Curacoa*, but I forget the name of the fourth. *Curacoa* later became an important part of operations in the Adriatic, of which more later.

Life soon settled down in this steel world of guns, metal and scrubbed wood. I learned to chip away rust, to paint, to scrub and help fire a 'Multiple Pom-Pom'. This was an eight-barrelled weapon firing two-pound shells at speed. My action station was as a 'layer'. I controlled the down movement of the barrels, while the other member of the weapon's two-man crew controlled the movement from side to side. The Gunnery Officer and the Chief

Gunner's Mate were friendly, purposeful men who did their best to make sure that we would be of use during an engagement. There were two of these weapons, one on each side amidships in the waist, so far as I remember. There were two turrets, each housing a pair of six-inch guns. Throughout the ship there was a constant hum of generators and a warm smell of hot oil, which was not unpleasant. One night, while off watch, I awoke in my hammock to notice that another sound had joined that of the generators, and that a slight vibration of everything was present. I peered through a porthole to see nothing but water. We were at sea in calm weather and one more stage in my war was about to start.

We patrolled the North Sea and the Western Approaches. We escorted convoys, and sometimes anchored in Scapa Flow, where shore leave was given to those off watch. One afternoon I roamed the bare hills and valleys that surrounded Scapa Flow. When I looked down at the anchorage the sea appeared almost black in this cold northern land. Surf broke against rocks and gleamed fiercely white against the dark water. I turned, and marched on towards what appeared to be a small house set in an area of green where sheep were grazing. Loud cries were coming from the building and when I looked though one window I saw a bloodstained figure in the midst of a mass of bleating sheep. The man was cutting their throats one by one, and flinging the twitching carcasses onto a heap in the corner: a sickening sight that has never left me.

On returning to the landing stage I was picked up by the liberty boat, and taken back aboard still thinking of the awful sight I had witnessed. However, this experience was quickly replaced by another, but one that was ludicrous, rather than horrifying.

I was sent aboard a battle cruiser, to replace a galley hand who was off sick. In retrospect i think it was HMS *Hood* of which more, a little later. She was anchored nearby. I was to be there as 'relief washer-up' in the wardroom galley.

It was 8.00pm and a party was in progress in the ward room. I could hear shouts and laughter and the sound of small bells. I opened the small serving hatch and looked through. An amazing sight met my eyes. Officers were bicycling round the wardroom table, ringing the handlebar bells and hurling darts at pictures, which were framed but without any glass. One Lieutenant was climbing out of a ventilator shaft. The object of the exercise seemed to be to pick up a dart from the pile on the table, and then throw it at a picture, in one movement, while steering the bike with the other hand.

Suddenly someone threw a dart at a portrait of King George, piercing his left eye. There was an immediate hush and the senior officer present called for silence and dismounted his bike.

'Oh! Not intended at all, bad show. That's enough now, gentlemen.'

With that they wheeled their bikes quietly out and dispersed. It was only later that I was able to laugh at this scene. At the time I was, using a modern term, 'gobsmacked' that such 'hallowed' individuals as these officers could behave like us lesser mortals.

Fortunately for me I was only there for that one night. Not long after that evening, the Hood was sunk by the German battleship, Bismarck, with a loss of 1415 officers and men. There were only three survivors.

Two days later, now back aboard the Arethusa, we were on our way to Iceland in company with the mine layer Agamemnon which, according to the buzz below decks, was to lay mines off the approaches to the main harbours of Iceland. The weather was atrocious. The scuppers were awash with sick, and the skipper had to be lashed to his chair on the bridge. The swells were so deep that the Agamemnon, only two cables on our starboard beam, was disappearing in the troughs. I never knew whether the operation had been successful or not, and this was always the case. Lower decks were rarely kept informed of events at that early stage of the war, though the situation improved as hostilities expanded.

One day, some two weeks after this operation, I was called to see the officer of the watch and told that I was to be made a 'CW Candidate'. I was given a white band to wear round my cap instead of the ship's ribbon, and informed that I would, in due course, be sent for training as an officer. Of course this would depend upon not blotting my copybook in the meantime. Commission and Warrant (CW) candidates were traditionally given the most unpleasant jobs. There were two of us and the other CW was made 'captain-of-the-heads'. This meant that he was in charge of the seamen's lavatories, and had to keep them clean. This man turned the situation to his own advantage by keeping the place spotlessly clean and hanging notices that said, in essence, 'Leave this place as you would wish to find it.' He also installed a table near the entrance upon which were a selection of magazines. I have no idea how he managed to get hold of these, or from where. These additions to the heads were eventually discovered by the authorities and removed.

CHAPTER 2

✳

Getting into action

1941

My next operation of note was my first experience of enemy fire and my introduction to real hostilities. Somewhere in the North Sea we were told to prepare for a night of action. All lights were extinguished, and absolute silence was maintained. Shoes were removed, and only the faint sound of one engine at slow ahead was audible.

We crept up Bergen Fiord on a pitch-black night with the object of laying mines off the harbour mouth. I was at my action station on the multiple 'Pom-Pom' and all guns on the ship were at the ready. The sea was calm. You could feel the silence and the tension as we crept up the centre of the approach to Bergen Harbour. The hills and mountains on either side were just visible as black shapes that kept disappearing entirely as low cloud intervened. Presently, the dim lights of Bergen Town became visible, and the faint outline of a harbour wall showed uncertainly ahead. At times all would vanish in a drift of mist. A few minutes after the last sighting I felt the ship beginning a slow turn. This must be it, I thought, and waited to hear the splash of the first mine. It never came. Instead there was a bright orange flame and clouds of white smoke lit the sea astern. We finished the turn at high speed and fled from the scene at thirty knots. Guns opened up from both sides of the fiord, but it is very difficult to hit a ship moving at speed on a dark night. We became conscious that shells were landing around us, and our six-inch guns began to speak. The Gunnery Officer came past and checked on our state of readiness.

'Shall we answer the fire, sir?' I asked him.

'Yes, of course,' he replied. 'Where you see a flash, aim at that!'

Somehow we cleared the fiord without being hit. I heard the engines shutting down to a more normal cruising speed as we headed for the UK and home. We were never told officially what had happened, but the story on the mess deck was that a signalman coming up from the wireless room with a signal for the skipper had stumbled and fallen onto the smoke-float release button. This seemed a likely explanation. After all, what else could account for the catastrophe? You may wonder why we were not detected before reaching Bergen Harbour. The answer lies in the primitive nature of all detection apparatus in the early days of the war. Radar was not perfected, there was no GPS, radio signals could not be accurately located and Bergen was a remote place.

It was not long after this that I was drafted to HMS *King Alfred* to train for a commission. This establishment was based at Lancing College, Hove. The routines reminded me of *Collingwood*, and seemed to be a long way from what war was all about. We were taught the finer points of seamanship, officer behaviour and duties. But the main instruction was in the art of navigation and how to obtain a position from the sun by sunsights. It was usual to take an average of six readings owing to the movement of small vessels in a seaway. We were taught chart work by pedalling around a field on 'stop me and buy one' ice cream carts. On the flat top in front of the rider there would be a chart and a parallel reader. Using a hand-held compass we would take bearings of surrounding objects and landmarks, then fix our position, which would be marked on the chart.

I cannot say that I enjoyed *King Alfred* or that I learned very much, being an indifferent navigator with only just enough ability to get by. There was also the ever-present anxiety about passing the final exam. To be failed and returned to service as a rating was unthinkable. The exam at the end of our term was difficult, especially in relation to celestial navigation. I managed just enough marks to get by and was passed. The relief was immense, particularly as a few candidates had been failed. The results were announced on the notice board, and celebrations for the successful began as soon as shore leave permitted. In company with a few friends I went 'on the town', sampling wine bars and ending at a bistro-type restaurant where, among other things, I ate oysters washed down with sweet Sauterne: not a dish to be recommended!

As a result of this spree I fainted next morning at divisions and fell flat on my face during the Lord's Prayer. I was taken to the sick bay where I spent a week suffering a form of oyster poisoning. They later told me that at times my temperature had reached a hundred and four degrees. After seven days I recovered sufficiently to return to Lancing and finish the course.

Three days before leaving *King Alfred*, we were asked to state a preference for the branch and kind of vessel we wished to join. I chose MTBs (motor torpedo boats) and to my delight was allotted a place at HMS *St Christopher* at Fort William, Scotland. This was the training base for MTBs and motor launches (MLs). There followed a week's leave, and the purchase of a uniform and officer's kit. We were given enough money to buy two uniforms and ancillary gear, at the famous services outfitter Gieves & Co., in Bond Street. I managed to save a little cash by going to Simpson's, in the Strand, instead. I was now the proud possessor of one gold wavy-ring on each sleeve, denoting that I was a Sub-Lieutenant RNVR (Royal Naval Volunteer Reserve). RNVR officers rose to high positions during the war and, although they never equalled the regular RN, they often commanded some of the smaller naval vessels and served as first Lieutenants and Gunnery Officers in larger warships.

After making my purchases, I went home for the remaining six days, and while there I received a signal extending my leave for another ten days until a place at *St Christopher* became vacant. This was wonderful luck. It enabled me to settle into family life again for a short period, and to renew some old friendships. I swam in our pool, played some tennis with my Father, and set about making contact with school-day friends and members of the rugby club. My Father had only just recovered from a bombing injury. His works were opposite Smithfield Meat Market in Farringdon Road. The raids on London had just begun and Smithfield was one of the first targets to be hit. The blast shattered the windows of his office. He was taken to hospital with a dozen glass splinters in his face and neck, but, amazingly, his eyes were not damaged. He returned to work the same day.

Among the friends I was able to see was a school-time girl friend, for whom I had a passion at that time. At the end of the first week at home I reached her by phone, having tried her house several times. She was at a women's college in Oxford and, to my amazement, she agreed to spend an afternoon and evening with me. I had dreamed of this at *King Alfred*, and it almost became my *raison d'être*. I had visualised escorting her down the aisle to a seat at the Playhouse, with the house lights shining on my one gold ring and brass buttons. I had thought of it at nights and during the boring parts of instruction.

Now it was actually going to happen. I drove to Oxford in my Mother's Austin Ten using part of her precious petrol allowance.

Arriving at midday, I parked near the college and gave my name to the gatekeeper. A phone call was made and Diana appeared almost at once. Diana, or Collie as we called her at school, as her surname was Collbeck, came towards me showing real pleasure at seeing me. I could not believe it. She was actually delighted to meet me again and spend time with me. How lucky can you get? She was wearing a loose cotton summer dress through which one could see the outline of her slim figure. Collie was an athlete, and in her last term at school, was made Victrix Ludorum for her track and field achievements. Naturally fair, straight hair framed the honey-coloured skin of her face and neck and her brown legs ended in small brown feet thrust into sandals revealing toes lightly touched with pink. All the days and nights aboard *Arethusa*, in barracks, and at *Collingwood*, slipped from me as if they had never been, and I was back in the joyful days of youth. During the time between school and war I worked in my Father's firm and had always remained constant in my devotion to Collie, though I saw her only rarely. This afternoon and evening would make up for all that.

'Henry! How lovely to see you!' Henry was my nickname at school, and to hear it again was another flash into the past.

She kissed me lightly on the cheek and stars fell around me. Was I conscious or dreaming?

'Collie, have you had lunch?' I asked.

It appeared that she had, and I had lost all appetite for food, though it did remain for something else. We decided to go on the river, and then have dinner before going to the Playhouse where I had booked two stalls for Shakespeare's *Much Ado About Nothing*. A prescient title as it transpired.

At the boathouse all the punts and rowing boats were out. A pity, as I fancied myself at punting, having done a certain amount in peacetime. 'I've got a canoe left, sir, and that's all I've got,' said the boatman. 'She's a bit dusty, but that's no count. I'll have her ready in half an hour.'

We sat on the bank and watched craft passing up and down and listened to the buzz of bees and summer insects among the reeds. It was a hot afternoon by the river, and the war seemed far away.

'Ready now, sir.' There was a splash and our canoe was steadied against the landing stage by John, the boatman. We stepped aboard carefully as canoes are not very stable, but once you sit down they are as steady as any other small boat. We each took a paddle and set off. Collie was clearly in her element. I felt hot in my uniform but dared not remove my jacket for fear of capsizing us. I could not decide what to do with my cap as the bottom of the canoe had filled with a little water so I kept it on my head. In the centre of the river it was much cooler, and I began to enjoy the motion of the boat and the scene about us. Colleges, libraries and the honey-coloured stone buildings of Oxford slid astern, giving way to summer meadows and tree-lined banks. I turned round once to look at Collie. She was one big smile.

'Wonderful, Henry, wonderful!' she said. 'Let's see if we can beat this boat behind. It's catching us.'

We redoubled our efforts and lengthened the gap. I judged that the current against us would be less nearer the bank, and so headed that way. It certainly did make a difference, and we left the other boat far behind. 'Well done, Henry, that was a good idea, it made all...' said Collie. Then, disaster! We hit a submerged tree trunk and overturned. My cap floated away, and we had to be rescued by some civilians in a punt. At least my cap and the canoe were rescued, as they floated back the way we had come. Between shouts of laughter, our rescuers told us that they would return the canoe to the yard as they were going back there themselves. Someone on the bank was heard to remark, 'If this is the navy in operation, the country is in a bad way.'

Collie and I struggled up the bank and collapsed in a wet heap on the grass. I looked at this wonderful girl expecting to see distrust, if not anger, but she was shaking with laughter and would not hear of blaming me. What a girl. For the moment I forgot my own position.

Then, one by one, the problems came into view. There was my sodden uniform. We were at least three miles from the town centre with no change of clothes and seats booked at the theatre for that night. The list went on and on. Suddenly I had an idea, and shouted to the people towing our canoe, but they were just rounding a bend on their way back to the boatyard and too far distant to hear. There was nothing for it but to walk.

Collie was a lovely sight. Her summer dress clung to her slim body, water dripped from her hair and settled in glistening droplets about her neck, and she seemed to be enjoying the moment and the prospect before us. On the other hand, I was a miserable object. An angry man in a sodden uniform, and his Majesty's naval uniform at that. We set off and I had no idea of what to do next. Heads turned as people passed us, and there was an occasional giggle. I tried to disguise my identity by taking off the jacket, but it was heavy and wet, so I put it on again, thinking it might dry sufficiently to be of use later on. Not a chance. I soon realised that there was no chance of this, but kept it on anyway as a defiant gesture to the world about us. It was at this point that I made a vow that somehow, God knows how, I would take Collie to dinner, and keep our date at the Playhouse.

'Collie, do you have friends in your house who have brothers?'

'Yes, why, Henry?'

'Well, I thought they might sometimes leave a change of clothes with their sisters, should they come straight from the office on a visit.'

'Brilliant idea, Henry, yes, of course,' she said. 'I know several girls whose brothers, and boyfriends, change in their rooms quite often. We can borrow some and can change in my room.'

I relaxed and started to look forward to the evening. After all, the disaster might have compensations in more ways than one.

Alas, it was not to be. Fate had not done with me yet, it seemed. We had been walking for an hour and were close to the college, when I noticed the time. It was five past six by the clock above the main gate.

'Oh! Henry, we are too late. No men are allowed in the college after six pm.' This was a strict rule in those days.

'What shall we do Henry?' For the first time the girl looked troubled. This was my spur, the kick on the backside that I deserved.

'Don't give it a thought. Leave it to me. I'll manage somehow. Go in now before you catch cold. Get dry and meet me at 7.15,' and I named a bistro. I kissed her on the cheek and marched off full of a determination that had no foundation. The men's outfitters that I knew was closed, and prolonged ringing of the bell failed to bring anyone to the door. I wandered on, the recent boast fading, lost, into unreality. I was passing Balliol College and noticed a man pruning a rose bush and another sitting on a bench reading. It was to this man that I addressed myself.

'Excuse me, sir.' He looked up.

'Good God! I say, old man, what happened?' Here was a Christian, a gentleman, a rose among thorns. He did not laugh, but looked concerned as I described the afternoon, and what I hoped would be an evening at the bistro and Playhouse. He was charity itself. 'Follow me, old man,' and he led me into the building and to his rooms and a bath.

After a bath he fitted me up with a change of clothes, and sent me on my way, wishing me luck at the gate. I took down his name and promised to send back everything, properly laundered and pressed, within a few days. It takes one young man to understand and really appreciate another. My luck had changed and I walked quickly to the bistro. If I hurried I could keep my promise to be there by 7.15pm. Only my shoes reminded me of how wet I'd been, as these I could not change. No matter, wet feet were a small price to pay. My Mother's car was fairly nearby, and I dumped the wet things on the floor. I had removed my wallet and a few other things from the pockets, and partially dried them in front of an electric fire in my new friends' room. The notes and chequebook were still damp but usable.

Collie and I arrived almost at the same time, and her amazed comments were most flattering. 'Henry, I never thought you would be here. How on earth did you do it? You look fine.' I glanced at my reflection in a small mirror, and was appalled at the sight. If I looked fine then the world had changed. I could be mistaken for someone selling matches, or even a rat-catcher. However, the meal really was fine. We ate lamb cutlets, with new potatoes, asparagus and garden peas, followed by summer pudding with cream. A bottle of house red completed the meal.

We were just in time for *Much Ado*, but the house lights did not illuminate my one gold ring and brass buttons. Instead they revealed a pair of flannel trousers that were too short, and a tweed jacket that was too long. I cannot remember a single word, a single line or scene from the play. Future plans occupied me entirely. I was determined to keep the shameful facts of the afternoon a secret from my family, one humiliation being sufficient for the day. We said goodbye at the college, kissed and parted, waving as the distance between us increased.

I have realised since that the catastrophe on the river meant only excitement and fun to this girl, something that any undergraduate would recount later, to raise a laugh.

To me, however, it was a shocking affair, and I was not yet ready to laugh. The drive home in the small hours was by contrast utterly peaceful. A warm starlit night enclosed the land and only the music of the engine broke the silence. No drone of planes, no sound of bombs in the distance and practically no traffic disturbed this journey home, giving no hint of the life to come. I put the car away as quietly as I could, and placed the wet clothes in an outside lavatory that was seldom used. It was 3.00am and no one stirred.

There were still five days left of my leave and I planned to take everything to the dry cleaners in St Albans and, if possible, wash and dry my shirt and pants myself. It would be difficult to do this unnoticed, but I could think of nothing else. The girl at the cleaners solved everything. She was so delighted by my account of the capsize that she took over completely. She washed and dried my shirt and pants herself. The uniform was cleaned and valeted and the situation restored to normal.

The day after the end of my leave found me on the train for Scotland and Fort William. I arrived late in the afternoon and was immediately struck by the grandeur of the place. HMS *St Christopher* was situated at the edge of a loch bounded by hills and mountains, the largest of which was Ben Nevis. The base consisted of a large country house, attended by a number of military style huts and outbuildings. A landing stage completed the scene. Groups of MTBs, MLs and harbour defence motor launches (HDMLs) were moored close to the stage and two MLs were alongside. My spirits rose and my heart beat faster at the sight. I was shown to a cabin shared by three other men, and told that dinner would be served in the mess at 7.30 sharp and that latecomers would not be served. The food throughout my stay at the base was of a high standard and there was always a choice between fish and meat at dinner.

At *St Christoper*, we were taught to handle the boats at sea, to moor, to anchor, and to bring alongside. We were also taught how to maintain a state of 'being in all respects ready for sea' by knowing everything about the craft, the engines and the armament. Every boat crew included one engineer, usually a Chief Petty Officer, who was in charge of the engines at all times.

An MTB was 75 feet long and powered by three Rolls Merlin engines driving three screws. They could, in calm weather, reach a speed of 40 knots. They carried two torpedo tubes, one each side of the foredeck, and several mountings for small arms and Oerlikon 'point-fives'.

An ML was 125 feet long and in some cases mounted a Bofors cannon on the foredeck. This was a formidable weapon capable of shooting down an aircraft, and dealing with E-boats, which were the German equivalent to MLs. On the afterdeck were mountings for two sets of twin Oerlikons and two sets of twin-point fires. They carried twelve depth charges, and anti-submarine detection (Asdic). They were powered by two Hall-Scott Defender engines, each developing 650 hp and burning 100 octane aviation fuel, of which the tanks held 3000 gallons. They had a top speed of 21 knots. They were used for escorting convoys, patrolling sea lanes and clandestine operations off enemy coasts. HDMLs were 75 feet in length and powered by two Gardner, Gleniffer or Thornycroft engines, which gave the boats a top speed of fourteen knots. Gardners were considered to be the most reliable of the three makes. The HDMLs carried a two-pounder gun on the foredeck; twin-strip Lewis guns mounted either side of the bridge, and twin 'point-five' mounts on the afterdeck; also eight depth charges, and Asdic. They were used for patrolling sea lanes and approaches to harbours and, occasionally, for escorting convoys.

I was disappointed to be assigned to an HDML. However, I was lucky to be there at all and was determined to do my best. A week before the end of the course, I climbed Ben Nevis on my free Sunday. I believe it took me six hours and was told that the locals did it in four, running most of the way. Three quarters of the way up a girl passed me wearing shorts and T-shirt. When I reached the top she was finishing her lunch. The flat area at the top was snowbound. I walked to the edge to look down.

'Stop! Stand still!' She stretched out an arm and pulled me gently back to the middle. I had stepped on a snow-filled crevice that would have collapsed and sent me to the bottom.

On my last day free from all further classes and disciplines, I walked down to the jetty to take a last look at the boats and the mountains beyond. There I met two interesting men in conversation. One was Allan Villiers, who taught us aircraft recognition. He was an amazing man who had sailed in square-riggers, and claimed to know the Messerschmitt family who made the famous fighter-planes. He spoke of Willie Messerschmitt and why the planes were the shape they were. The older man was a Major, a member of a team that was training in the hills. One of their tasks was to reach a destination in London, with only a map, a compass, a knife and a bag of rice. No money was allowed, and no extra clothes. They had to travel alone. I reckoned that the navy was a cushy number after hearing that.

I had been appointed First Lieutenant of the HDML1070 based at Sheerness. Her then commander was under scrutiny for bad ship handling and incompetence. I had been aboard for only ten days, when the base commander sent for me to ask my opinion of my commanding officer. I thought very carefully before answering, 'Well, sir, I would prefer to serve under someone else.'

Within a week he was replaced by an Australian Lieutenant, a man of few words but entirely competent. It was clear that this officer was destined for higher things. After a month he left, and

I was given command. This was unexpected, and it took me a day or two to realise that I was actually in command of my own ship. The whole ship's company was given shore leave while the vessel was serviced and engines overhauled. I went home for a week, and enjoyed the congratulations of my family and some home-cooked food. My Mother presented me with a cocker spaniel puppy, the last of a litter of six. I named him Simon. I shall tell more of him later.

On my return to Sheerness I found 1070 alongside, with Basil Knight aboard. He had been appointed First Lieutenant, and the crew was to arrive the following day. Basil was a man of great good humour, with a witty turn of phrase. He was an excellent navigator, but an incompetent signaller with an Aldis lamp and a poor ship handler. However, we got on very well for I was no better at signalling than him. Fortunately we carried a wireless operator who was efficient at using an Aldis lamp.

At this point I should describe the layout below deck, and the crew. The total complement was fourteen people. Eleven seamen, one of whom was the wireless operator, plus the cook, were housed in the foc'sle, where they each had a bunk. Moving aft, next came the galley, and abaft that the engine room.

The Cox'n, usually a leading seaman or Petty Officer (PO), shared a small cabin with the engineer, the most senior person on board after the officers. He was always a Chief PO in my experience. This cabin, and the wireless room opposite, were under the quarter deck and next to the small wardroom which had bunks for two officers, with separate heads (toilet) and washbasin.

The upper deck armament has been described. It was an example of how unprepared we were at the outset of hostilities. The two-pounder on the foredeck was a museum piece, and the Lewis machine-guns belonged to the First World War. Only the twin-point fires could be considered adequate. However, our main job was anti-submarine work, and the location of mines dropped from aircraft. Each night, when not on patrol, we would anchor out in the estuary and keep watch. The time and position of any mines dropped had to be noted and reported immediately.

One morning a few days after I had assumed command we received a signal from the Base Commander. This was an officer of almost Olympian importance from our point of view. He was a four-ring RN Captain in charge of the base, all ships operating in the estuary and with jurisdiction over anything entering or leaving the estuary. His title was Senior Officer Thames Local Defence Force, known by us as 'Subtle Duff'.

Apart from a flotilla of HDMLs, there were at least another twelve ships of assorted sizes that comprised the force. Each morning half the force left the port of Sheerness, to anchor in established positions or to patrol the approaches to the Thames. The following morning the other half would relieve them. The work was intensely boring unless someone spotted a mine being dropped. The base arranged regular leave for all personnel. A signal from 'Subtle Duff' informed me that he would be coming aboard at 5.00pm the next day. This was the signal that every CO (commanding officer) dreaded, and it happened to every new arrival. The Base Commander's name was Cordeaux, and it was said that Captain Cordeaux had a medical degree as well as his exalted rank and title. A rumour current at the time was that he had saved a man's life by freeing him from a trapped position by an amputation. The ship on which he was present in his capacity of Examining Officer had hit a mine with considerable loss of life.

The next forty-eight hours will be etched in my mind until I die. When I look back now I wonder that I was allowed to survive as a CO. At exactly 5.00pm the Captain's launch was alongside, and the Cox'n piped him aboard. So far, so good. We had swept the orange peel off the deck, and the ship and its crew looked reasonably clean. I led him down to our small wardroom where Basil Knight ordered tea through the voice-pipe. When it arrived the Steward was naked to the waist, with the arms of his overall tied round his middle, a horrible sight. That was compounded by Basil saying, 'I'm sorry, sir, that we have no lemon.'

I never knew whether he was sincere, or being ironic. After tea we slipped our mooring and headed for the open sea to our anchoring position. Cordeaux stood beside me on the bridge. Once we were underway I lost my apprehension and felt reasonably normal again. We anchored without trouble, and I ordered slow astern on one engine after the anchor had touched bottom. This was to help the plough shape of the CQR to bite into the mud. When the chain led straight ahead and was taut, it meant that the anchor was holding. I went to make sure of this as was my custom. Once more it was so far, so good. It was by then 8.00pm. The cook served up a reasonable meal that the Captain ate without comment but, according to Basil, he seemed to enjoy. I remained on the bridge keeping watch with a hand-bearing compass and binoculars. I ate my dinner in situ. It was a quiet night, with small broken waves running before a force three easterly wind. The Captain appeared as I was swallowing the last of the stew, and ordered all small arms to be fired. The gunnery hands went to their posts and big trouble began.

The 'point-fives' fired normally, but the stripped Lewis on starboard side jammed. The rating wrestled with the magazine, trying to get it to turn. Suddenly there was an explosion, and a bullet ripped through the deck just below the gunwale, narrowly missing Cordeaux's feet. The damage to the ship's side was minimal, being far above the waterline, and the small hole could be easily plugged. However, the damage to my confidence was considerable. I waited for the 'human explosion', but it never came. Instead the Captain ordered me to up anchor and patrol northward to Harwich and beyond. We proceeded at eight knots, and nothing occurred to take my mind off the horror that had just taken place.

We had been underway for about an hour when 'Subtle Duff' ordered the wheelhouse to be blacked out, with navigation to be carried out blind from thereon. Screens were put up, but one was missing. Once again, Basil made an apology.

'I'm sorry sir, but we have never had that one. It's been ordered for sometime, I believe.' Almost before he finished speaking, a seaman appeared waving it triumphantly. 'It was in the tiller-flat, sir, under some cordage.'

It was clear to me that this must be the end. The two weeks of command had been enjoyable, but it was all over now. What I most hoped for was that I would not lose my commission as well as my command.

The night wore on. It was 1.00am and we were north of Harwich when Captain Cordeaux offered to relieve me on the bridge. I had been there for eight hours. Was this another pitfall, another trap to walk into? The answer was, almost certainly, yes. 'Thank you, sir, but I prefer to remain in charge.' 'In charge of what?' he said. I wondered if it was to be in charge of a vessel that was soon to be handed over to someone else. Ah, well, I thought. I must make the most of the time I have left and behave according to King's rules and regulations. Then something happened that was to have a bearing on the future, although I did not realise its importance at the time. The Base Commander took his cap off, and slowly placed it on the shelf that housed the engine room telegraph. He looked straight at me and nodded his head. This was a signal that the offer was 'off the record' and that I might take advantage of it without censure.

'Thank you, sir,' I said. 'I will get my head down for a spell in the wheelhouse. Please call me at once for any reason whatever.' It was a calm night. The steady throb of the engines and the sound of the bow wave coursing down the ship's side acted like a drug, and I was asleep within seconds.

In spite of the troubles and tensions of the past hours, I must have been asleep for about thirty minutes, perhaps longer, I don't know, but suddenly I sat upright and, without thought, bolted through the hatch and on to the bridge. Pushing Cordeaux aside, I shouted down the voice-pipe to the helmsman below, 'Starboard twenty, midships, steady as you go! Slow both!'

We were in a minefield. Very slowly we made our way back to the swept channel and safety. I cannot explain what caused me to wake up and take action. There was nothing whatsoever to suggest that we were in a heavily mined area, but we were, nevertheless. Was it some sort of miracle? Had I extra-sensory powers? Or was it just luck? I shall never know. The rest of the night passed without incident or any comment from 'Subtle Duff'. Much later in the war, and in another part of the world, another miracle occurred, but that one had nothing to do with me.

Later the Captain ordered me to return to base. He did not refer to anything that had happened, which rather increased my pessimism and gloomy thoughts.

As we entered harbour, one more minor horror occurred. The Captain ordered Basil to signal to one of the Defence Force and request the CO to report to his office as soon as possible. Knowing that Basil was hopeless with a signal lamp, I engaged the Captain in conversation, trying to prevent him from checking the signal, as I had no doubt that he would be able to read the signal from the audible clicks made as the shutter moved. Basil was sending some indecipherable nonsense and, out of the corner of my eye, I could see the other vessel constantly flashing R (repeat). It all came to an end as Cordeaux stepped into his barge, and was carried ashore. The moment he was out of sight, Basil had the dinghy launched, and I knew full well what this was for. He wanted to pass the message by hand before Cordeaux could reach his office.

For me the next few weeks passed in a state of determined gloom. I pushed aside any possibility of reprieve. I would lose my command at least, and that would be that. Routine patrols and mine watching continued in boring succession, one after the other, one after the other…

To my surprise, 1070 was given two days' 'general leave' like every one else in the force, and when our turn came I went home deciding, while on the journey, to tell the family nothing of my disgrace. No point making life worse before it was unavoidable. It was on this weekend that I got to know the puppy, Simon and to fall in love with him. He was highly intelligent – at least I thought so – for he learnt to walk at heel in two days. When the time came to leave I was torn. Should I take him, or leave him in the care of my Mother who was adamant that he should be left in the place that he knew? I decided to take him. After all, I could not be in worse trouble than I was already, and I knew of a trawler in the force that had a dog, and of HDMLs that had cats.

On the way back to Sheerness I was prepared for any puddles that Simon might leave on the floor of the carriage, but he behaved himself impeccably, which boded well for his future on board.

The countryside flashed by, and the smell of hay drifted through the window. It was harvest time, but in the skies above the Battle of Britain was beginning. As well as the early exploratory raids, in one of which my Father had been wounded, London and its approaches were now experiencing heavy attacks by large numbers of bombers, both by day and night. A few evenings later I counted more than fifty planes in one flight heading towards the city, and aerial battles could be seen daily. I wondered then, as I do now, if we will ever fully appreciate our debt to the fighter pilots, and the RAF in general.

The train arrived exactly on time (an example of the normality that still existed over much of the country). If you discounted the bombers, it was hard to believe that we were at war. My Father still worked, teashops were open and theatres were packed.

However, as I walked along the wall, the sight of the masts and funnels of the many wrecked ships that littered the sea beyond the harbour reminded me that the navy had a huge task ahead. The country had to be fed and the sea lanes kept open. Most of those wrecks had been caused by mines, so perhaps one should not grumble about the boring anchor watches.

I had left 1070 alongside. Simon and I arrived at the same time as some of the crew. Basil Knight, and the other watch, had remained aboard and it was now their turn for leave. Simon was an instant success. He delighted the crew by his sunny nature and sporting outlook. He would chase anything that moved, and never tired of playing the fool. He spent as much time in the fo'c'sle as he did with me in the wardroom, but he always slept on the end of my bunk. The sailors taught him to use the prow of the boat for his lavatory, it being constantly awash when we were at sea. In harbour or at anchor a bucket of seawater sufficed. He learned his 'duty' very quickly, as he did walking to heel.

I was truly relieved by the attitude of the sailors. Had they not welcomed Simon, life for the dog and myself would have been difficult on a small ship. As it was, he was made an honoured member of the ship's company.

The other watch returned two days later, and patrols and anchor watch routines resumed. It was my practice to deliver my anchor watch and patrol reports by hand soon after entering harbour. For this purpose it was necessary to go alongside. Simon would jump ashore and follow me round the base. Although whenever he saw a cat he was off like a rocket, I let him do it, reckoning the exercise to be good for him.

The weeks passed by and yet there was no summons to the Base Commander's office, or a signal to attend a Court Martial. I began to believe that I had a future in the navy. In one cheeky gesture I applied to join a destroyer, or an MTB, but heard nothing. The summer was sliding imperceptibly into autumn. The days were still quite warm, but the temperature was dropping, especially in the afternoons. It was on such a day that I was to receive another blow, this one perhaps more damaging than anything that had gone before.

We were mooring alongside for me to go ashore with Simon, and hand in my report. Usually the dog always knew when it was time to go ashore, and he would be on deck waiting his chance to jump. But this day he was not on deck, and so I called his name several times. There was nothing, no dog. The entire ship was searched. Nothing. I cannot describe my feeling at the time; words cannot do it justice.

Without hope, or a care for the authorities in the Watch Tower, I turned the ship round and headed back out to sea and our anchor watch position of the night before. Simon had slept on my bunk during the night, so he must have fallen over the side some time after first light. Simon was practised at walking the deck, even in a seaway, so it was likely that he could not resist chasing a seagull that had swum too near us. In the commotion of raising the anchor he was not missed. The sea was glassy calm and, with the binoculars, one could see the surface for long distances. Nothing! We reached our position and scanned the water in all directions. Nothing!

I was not surprised, only deeply saddened. I turned the boat back on to the course for Sheerness, but had not completed the turn when Basil shouted, 'What's that?' Pointing at something, he handed me the glasses. The flicker of hope died as I looked. A pair of seagulls it seemed, just idling on the water, some two hundred yards away. Nevertheless I headed towards them, and the two bumps began to look more like small pieces of seaweed. Suddenly the truth exploded through the binoculars and into my brain. It was Simon! His nose was just above the water with the top of one ear showing.

Very, very carefully I eased the boat alongside. A small wave would have sent him under and probably to his death. A seaman stretched full length over the side, with another sailor holding his ankles. He fished Simon out and onto the deck, where he lay exhausted but breathing. Both his eyes were closed and he did not move for a long time.

Some two hours later, as we were nearing the harbour entrance, he opened both eyes and started panting, and by the time we were inside, he was standing and shaking his sodden coat. Simon had somehow kept himself afloat for at least five hours. From that time on, every member of the crew would have defended the dog with his life. He was a hero.

The next few hours passed in a dream. Everything that had happened, especially the serious rescue and recovery, seemed unreal. I went ashore to the base, expecting more than just a reprimand for leaving harbour without permission. But there was nothing. What on earth were the Watch Tower and the XDO doing? XDO stands for 'Extended Defence Officer' and it is his role to monitor all vessels entering or leaving. I handed in my report some four hours late. Nothing! When I returned Simon was not on the deck.

'Where is he?' I asked the guard at the gangway.

'The Wrens took him, sir. They have got him in their quarters.'

Apparently the story had travelled. I went to the 'Wrenery', as we called their quarters, and enquired about my dog.

'He's in the common room, sir, I'll take you there.'

I entered to be greeted by an amazing sight. Simon was lying in front of a log fire. He had been bathed, shampooed and scented. A ribbon bow was around his neck and a half chewed bone lay close by.

He wagged his tail when he saw me, as if to say, 'I've got a cushy number here.'

I have often wondered since how, with so much death and destruction around, one could expend so much emotion on a dog? I have no answer. The fact remains that Simon was a special dog and I have never had, or wanted, another one.

Autumn passed into winter, with nothing happening that was worth a report. The equinoctial gales came and went, and that winter proved to be the coldest I can ever remember, apart from 1947. On several days, seawater froze on the guardrails. Duffle coats were drawn from the base, and parcels of knitted socks and scarves began to arrive from anxious mothers. The daylight air raids grew less, but the night-time attacks continued.

During one weekend's leave I met a school friend who had served in the British Expeditionary Force (BEF), and was rescued at Dunkirk. He told me that when he was disembarking in Calais at the outset, cranes were lifting tanks and armoured vehicles from the holds of ships. But, when the sirens sounded for lunch, the tanks were left hanging in the air over the Calais docks, while the French dockworkers went to lunch. At the time the German army was breaching the Maginot line.

On another weekend, a week or two before Christmas, I made an attempt to improve my image with Collie, which had been somewhat dented by the affair at Oxford. Knowing she would be at home on Christmas vacation, I telephoned and invited her to come with me to the 'Varsity' Match at Twickenham. She accepted with more than just politeness. She radiated warmth and pleasure, and I seriously began to think of marriage one day, if she would have me. This time I borrowed my Father's car to make up for the 'rat-catcher' appearance at the theatre. It was a Daimler Fifteen Sports Saloon and, in my foolish innocence, I thought it would impress her.

There are a number of entrances all around Twickenham rugby ground, as all rugby fans know, and on this afternoon every one of them had a long queue waiting. I looked at my watch, and joined the one that seemed a little shorter than the others. We moved slowly forward, and eventually passed into a brick-built hut that looked similar to the others. It was a men's lavatory and people must have been surprised, to say the least, to see Collie standing in line among the male rugby fans! She married a doctor in the end, and no wonder.

The boring patrols and anchor watches continued into the spring until, one day in March, deliverance arrived in the form of an order from the base. HDML 1070 and two others were to store ship, take on fuel, service all weapons and prepare for sea. A further signal arrived, instructing me to draw charts for a northward passage to the Clyde. Now Basil came into his own. He was an expert at laying courses, which he did with great care and precision, and I believe he gained pleasure from the work.

Late one afternoon, we shook the dust of Sheerness from ourselves and from the boat, and headed out to sea. As we passed the Watch Tower they signalled 'bon voyage' and we replied with a cheer. I have noticed, and every mariner will confirm this, that all frictions and discontents disappear as soon as you are properly at sea. Calm shipboard routines take over, with a general cheerfulness prevailing over the vessel.

Off Harwich we ran into the convoy. The destroyer *Atherstone* hailed us, 'Take station on the seaward side of the convoy. Speed eight knots.'

This suited the Chief. He always became moody when we had to travel at slow ahead for any length of time. He said it sooted up the injectors. His relief was short-lived. At dusk we ran into thick fog, and the order came for all ships to reduce to four knots. To keep him happy I cut one engine, and slightly increased the revs on the other. I took over from Basil at midnight, by which time the fog was so thick that I could barely see the jackstaff on the bows. One HDML was ahead of me, as he was senior, and the other astern, but I saw neither of them. No merchant ship could be seen, although I could hear them faintly.

At 1.00am there was a loud bang. The vessel shuddered, and a piece of our cross-tree fell onto the deck. We had hit the side of a large ship, but thankfully only lightly. The Cox'n had had the foresight to rig fenders on the port side as soon as the fog descended. I eased us back to seaward until the sound of ships underway decreased to a minimum and I could judge that we were once more on the seaward side of the convoy.

By dawn the fog had thinned, and morning found us ahead of the rest of the group. The destroyer hailed us and, indicating a vessel far ahead, told us to get him back in line behind the Commodore. It took us two hours to reach the ship. There appeared to be no one on the bridge. I shouted, but no answer came and no one appeared. It was now time to get out the loudhailer that had never been used.

'From the destroyer *Atherstone* get back in line behind the Commodore!' I shouted. There was no answer, and still no sign of life. I repeated the order, followed by a long pause, and finally an unshaven face appeared over the side of the bridge. 'Wadder yer want?' it said. I gave the message once more and, after another long pause, the answer came back. 'We're nothing to do with your convoy. We're the last ship of yesterday's!'

This piece of information defeated me, and I could think of no reply or suggestion. I decided that this was a matter for the Commodore to settle, and hastened back to pass this message on.

The ship in question was a rust-bucket with an unshaven appearance, rather like its skipper. Sometimes it's a relief to hand over such problems to a higher authority. After hearing the ship's reply, constrained laughter could be heard from the destroyer's bridge, and I waited for further orders, but none were forthcoming. The *Atherstone* set off at speed, collected the rust-bucket, and shepherded it into line with the others. It appeared that the straggler had been bound for the Humber, like the rest of *Atherstone's* charges. At the mouth of the Humber the convoy and its escort left us, and the three HDMLs continued north alone.

During the passage from Sheerness Simon behaved like a true member of the crew, which in fact he was. When watches changed he would greet the new arrivals on the bridge, and then disappear into the wheelhouse where he slept when at sea. However, it was some time since he had had a run ashore, and I was becoming concerned about his need for exercise. Once again, fate provided an answer. Twenty miles east of Buckie we came to a stop. A considerable shudder, followed by a grinding noise, announced that something was tangled around a screw and perhaps around both. We had, in fact, picked up a parachute on the starboard propeller. With the help of a boat hook, a rating was able, by leaning far over the side, to drag the billowing material to one side and lash it to the guardrail. With only one screw now working, and steering a very steady course, we reached Buckie Harbour where I hoped to find a diver. This proved possible, but he would not be available until the following afternoon.

It was late afternoon as we entered Buckie, which meant a twenty-four hour stay at the very least. This delay solved a serious problem, but we were able to give a few hours' shore leave to all personnel. The other two boats had followed us in, and as they had both been through some wreckage, they decided to take advantage of our diver and have their underwater gear inspected as well.

All went well and at 6.00pm the following evening we set course for Inverness where, on arrival, we were ordered to report to the Naval Officer In Charge (NOIC). While at Inverness we took on fuel and collected the latest 'Notice to Mariners' concerning the Caledonian Canal and the Western Approaches. The First Lieutenant and the cook were seen to be heading for the town at one stage, and I wondered why they were together. The reason became apparent later. No shore leave was granted, as the other two COs and I were anxious to make up for lost time. The fog, and the inspections at Buckie, had added two days to our ETA. We also knew that passage through the canal would only be safe during daylight hours. There would be shoals, obstructions and navigation marks that could only be seen properly in daylight.

Now began what was in every sense a holiday. There are forty-nine locks on the canal, at least there were that number then, and the long delays, and the nights spent moored to the bank, lulled us all into a state of tranquillity. Which was to prove dangerous for one of us later. The weather was fine, the inland water clear and calm, and the country on either side magnificent: stretches of farmland, backed by hills and mountain ranges, on all sides. It was hard to believe that we were a small warship bound on His Majesty's Service. The deep water was mainly on the south side of the canal, and I quickly realised that it was best to keep well to port, unless navigation marks indicated otherwise. At night we moored to the bank by driving stakes into the ground, fore and aft, and throwing a bowline over them.

At times I allowed Simon to run ahead for a spell of exercise, and I'd pick him up when he looked tired. At dusk the crew would go ashore if the land was reasonably flat and kick a ball about. Watches were unnecessary, so all enjoyed this luxury when the country permitted. One morning, when we were about halfway along the canal, I rounded a bend to see the leader aground fifty yards ahead. He was to starboard of the middle and on a gravelly shoal. I immediately signalled the boat astern, and pulled into the bank and moored. I walked until I was level with the leader and we talked.

'I dare not use the helm and swing the bows to port, it will only swing the stern further on, and vice versa, if I go astern. Can you haul us off?' he asked. 'No, I can't. It will only drag us on to the shoal as well. It needs a tractor, and a line to your midship section. He could then pull you off sideways,' was my reply.

I looked around, but there was not a living thing or a building in sight. If someone set off in any direction at all, it could be the wrong one. It was then that I noticed a large oak tree exactly level with the grounded boat, and on the port bank. I had an idea that might not work, but it was worth trying.

By using both main hawsers from the two boats joined together, we had enough rope to go around the tree and then around the stranded ship's wheelhouse. The line was pulled taut by the weight of the entire crew, then secured. The Cox'n rigged a fender around our bow, and all was ready for an attempt. I eased the boat away from the bank and as near to the centre of the line as I dared. Then slowly I steamed into the line, pulling it into a V-shape, and pulling at the grounded boat from its middle. She came off easily, being only lightly aground. A cheer went up from all three boats and the leader, moored ahead of us. He invited me aboard. I accepted, but insisted that he first thank my crew for all their hard work. He did this most graciously.

The next day I noticed a delicious smell of cooking was present over the whole boat. In the evening we moored as usual and all hands went to dinner, and what a dinner it was. Roast pork, crackling, peas, roast potatoes and stewed apple, all followed by plum duff.

The cook had excelled himself. I then realised the reason why he and the First Lieutenant had been seen heading for the shops at Inverness. With a permit from NOIC, they 'raided' the three butchers in the town and came away with three large legs of pork. This was sufficient for the whole ship's company. I asked Basil the reason for this feast, and he said that the pork was originally intended for a celebratory meal on arrival at Dunoon. However, he thought the rescue of the leader from the grounding had a prior claim to be celebrated. Wise man.

Further along the canal one of the lockkeepers regaled us with a story of how a 'puffer' had rammed a lock gate, releasing thousands of tons of water, and flooding the surrounding farmland. A number of lock gates had been smashed in the process. A 'puffer' is a small iron vessel of about forty-five feet in length, driven by steam and carrying one large funnel. They were mainly used for carrying coal and supplies to outlying farms and townships.

Passing from the canal into Loch Ness, we took out the binoculars and scanned the water in search of the monster, but saw nothing, though we did see numbers of fish from time to time. I thought it strange that no one attempted to fish during the nights when moored, but I have since learned that sailors rarely eat fish and that few of them like to swim, even if they can, which is not often.

At the westerned of the canal, we passed Fort William (of happy memories) and emerged among the islands of the Western Approaches. Up until then relations between the crew and myself had been good, helped no doubt by the presence of Simon who was our mascot. Now this was to about change in a subtle way and it was partly my fault. We entered the Crinan Canal on our way south, and I noticed that the country was well wooded on both sides. I had a twelve-bore shotgun aboard, which I had not used since Sheerness, where I occasionally went after duck on my days off. The canal is short, so I took the opportunity as soon as we entered. I moored to the bank and went to look for game, returning with a rabbit that I thought the cook could add to a stew.

Some of the crew were on deck and when they saw the rabbit, they froze. Nobody said anything, but silently they went below, leaving the oldest seaman behind. He approached me and, using some colourful language, accused me of bringing 'bad luck' to the ship by bringing a rabbit aboard. I was not aware of this superstition, although I should have been, for it is well known. Being superstitious myself I sympathised with their feelings and immediately flung the animal into the undergrowth.

But the damage had been done. The rating, who was almost twice my age, and a peace time regular, was known by the crew as 'Pensh', which was short for 'Pensioner', made some remark about my age. This was a serious insubordination, which is close to mutiny, and I told him so. I said that being a small ship I had no means of punishment, but, if anything else occurred from him, a full report would go into the base at Dunoon. That silenced him, as I knew it would, because his time was nearly up and his pension could have been in danger.

After this affair nothing was ever quite the same. There was nothing you could put your finger on. Ship routines were carried on as usual, and tasks were carried out to the best of everyone's ability. It was simply a question of an atmosphere that seemed to me to be slightly tainted, but my imagination, no doubt, played some part in this. Small ships with no means of enforcing discipline have to rely upon mutual respect between officers and crew. If that is missing, life can be difficult.

The remainder of our passage to Dunoon was without incident. Before leaving the Crinan Canal I was invited once more to visit the leader. We moored, and I climbed aboard. It appeared that he wanted to discuss the grounding, and what should be said at Dunoon. He told me that his Asdic dome had been down at the time and that it would have been completely damaged by now. I refused to discuss the matter and said that he must deal with the base in whatever way he thought best at the time. I left feeling thankful that I had separated us from any involvement, and glad that Basil had the sense to raise our dome before entering the Caledonian Canal.

The new base at Dunoon proved to be like the old one at Sheerness, as far as we were concerned. Work allocated to us was similar in every way. There was one exception: there were no anchor watches, thank God. We patrolled the Western Approaches among the islands, and sometimes spent a night away from our base at places such as Rothesay and Lamlash. Occasionally we would be required to ferry high-ranking personnel from place to place in the archipelago. After a week of this, I was beginning to feel irritated, and longed for some real part in this war, or at least something that was more interesting.

In a small way that something happened before the second week ended. I was called to the NOIC's office in Dunoon and given a packet addressed to NOIC, Gourock, which was marked 'By Hand Of Officer'. It was sealed with wax and I was told that it was Top Secret and Urgent. NOIC, Gourock, was the big chief himself, responsible for the defence of the Clyde, and the control of all shipping, coming and going. Much of his authority was concerned with the organisation of convoys bringing vital supplies from America. His office was situated on a point of land known as 'Clock Point' which jutted out into the Clyde, immediately opposite Dunoon.

From this position he could command a view of much of the estuary. It was high ground, crowned with a tower in which his headquarters was established. About a hundred yards off the point, a large flat-topped buoy was in place and clearly meant for messenger boats bringing urgent dispatches that could not be sent by wireless. The wind was northerly and blowing straight onto the rock-bound shore. The obvious practice would have been to moor to the buoy and, using the slight lee made by the hull, launch the dingy and row the eighty-odd yards to the beach. I looked at the chart and saw that there was at least three fathoms right up to the beach which shelved suddenly. So far, so good. We reached the point in twenty minutes, only to find a derelict, dirty and damaged drifter moored to the buoy. A shack on the deck with one side missing did duty as a wheelhouse. The vessel was about fifty feet in length, and swinging wildly in the wind. There was no way I was going to put the HDML alongside this piece of garbage. But it was impossible to jump the buoy to secure a mooring-line to the shackle in the centre of the flat top with the drifter in the way.

I looked again at the chart and confirmed that there was very deep water for a long way in all directions. I made a decision and hoped for 'sailor's luck'. The drifter would have to be cut adrift and sunk. Basil called for a volunteer to jump the buoy, and I was grateful to note that all hands went up. He chose the strongest-looking man. I manoeuvred the vessel for an approach to the buoy, keeping well clear of the drifter. This was difficult in the wind, and I had to make three attempts. At the third go I managed to place the cheek of the bow against the rope fender around the rim of the buoy, and the crewman jumped. The Cox'n threw him a sharp cleaver from the galley, which landed on the flat top. I had approached from a position uptide of the drifter, but was likely to collide with it at any moment. Full astern both, and we were clear. Meanwhile the buoy jumper was sawing through the drifter's mooring rope, which fortunately was old, like its charge. The last strands parted and the vessel drifted astern.

The next part of the operation was enjoyed by all. The bow of 1070 was shod in steel to form a ramming shoe. This was standard in all HDMLs. I hit the drifter amidships and backed away smartly. The timber was almost rotten, and no further action was needed. The drifter quickly filled and sank. I had gambled on her having an engine and iron below, such as an anchor and cable, which would take her down. Had the drifter not gone down, she would have become a danger to shipping. I fixed the position of the sinking and noted it on the chart. This would have to be reported to base.

We then moored to the buoy, a simple operation with a man already on the flat top who took our line and secured it to the centre shackle. Then it only remained to launch the dingy and row ashore. I took one seaman who kept the dingy on course with the oars. It was hardly necessary to row, as the wind was onshore. A line was paid out astern and back to 1070. We could then be pulled back against the crisp wind without having to row in the broken water. I leapt into a foot of water, and waded ashore.

The crewman hauled on the line and kept the dingy clear of rocks. It was a steep climb to the tower, and another one to the top where the office was situated, but I hardly noticed it in the relief of having carried out an operation that could have ended in disaster. The big 'noise' himself was not present, but I passed the package to his personal aide who was himself a Lieutenant Commander RN. I reported the sinking of the drifter and gave the coordinates. He made no comment, which was a little disappointing as I expected some kind of compliment.

The next two days passed in the usual way with patrols and more patrols. At dusk on the second day, I received a signal to report to the NOIC's office at Gourock at precisely 11.30am the following morning.

I had never seen the word 'precisely' used in a signal before and wondered what this summons was all about. The answer came all too quickly. I arrived with ten minutes to spare, having used the flat topped buoy off the point, and was told to wait in an anteroom. The minutes passed by until a door opened at exactly 11.30. I was beckoned into the adjoining room.

The sight that greeted me was a replica of the board I had faced, so long ago, in the Finchley Drill Hall. Behind a long table were seated five RN officers, the senior one being a four-ringed RN Captain. I never discovered if he was the big chief himself, but he was certainly important enough to frighten me. There was one difference from the board at Finchley, a difference I shall never forget. In the centre of the table, in front of the Captain, there was a sword lying horizontally in line with the length of the table. I knew at once I was facing a Court Martial.

I stood before the senior officer and saluted as smartly as I could with a shaking hand.

'Do you know why you are here?' he said.

'No, sir,' I replied.

'You are here for having destroyed intentionally a vessel belonging to His Majesty's Navy.'

Inwardly I gasped. Could such a wreck be owned by the navy? It seemed impossible.

'Have you anything to say?' he asked.

'I did not know it was a Naval Vessel, sir. I thought it was a civilian craft using the navy buoy, possibly without permission.'

It was then that I remembered that the drifter had once been painted in navy grey, and that some faded, barely visible letters on the bow were probably the letters 'RN'.

'Why did you think it necessary to sink the vessel?' asked the officer.

I then gave a full account of the proceedings off Clock Point, and of my effort to deliver the important dispatch quickly, and into the right hands. I described the weather conditions, the state of the tide and all my reasons for sinking the drifter.

'Why did you not take your HDML to Gourock and go overland to Clock Point Tower?' he asked.

I replied, 'It is approximately fourteen miles from Dunoon, sir. It would have taken us an hour and a half by the time I had found a berth, after which I would still have to travel twelve miles overland. I do not know Gourock, or the terrain ashore.'

'If, as you say, you felt it necessary to sink a piece of naval property, why did you not flash the tower and ask for permission?' he asked.

'I repeat, sir, I did not know it was naval property, and I admit that I did not think of asking permission anyway, as I was intent on delivering the package quickly.'

'Have you anything else to say?'

'Only this, sir: Dunoon impressed upon me the urgency concerning the package, and that it was top secret. This informed all my actions.'

I was then told to leave the room. About five minutes later I was recalled and stood before the board awaiting the verdict. By this time I had ceased to care. An overpowering anger gripped me. What was all this fuss about? The loss of a bit of garbage was neither here nor there when so many ships were being lost every day, with their crews and cargoes. A short silence ensued in which the Captain grasped the sword and turned it through three hundred and sixty degrees, ending in its original position. Had it ended pointing at me it would have meant that I had been found guilty.

'For your action in sinking the vessel you are exonerated from blame. For failing to signal your intention to the authority at the tower, you are reprimanded. Dismiss!'

I saluted once more, suppressing a desire to shout, 'Get stuffed!'

In my short time in the navy I had developed a deep love and admiration for the Service, which was reinforced during the years to come, but this pantomime was, it seemed to me, an unworthy exception. But later I did think that I had done several things that had deserved such treatment, but had got away with it, so perhaps it was justice delayed.

I decided not to tell anyone about the Court Martial. The word can stick to your name whether you are guilty or not. On returning to the 1070 another signal awaited me. It was an order to report to NOIC, Dunoon, the following day. No time was mentioned so I knew it must be benign, and unimportant. It was certainly benign, but to me it was important.

When I was ushered into the NOIC's inner office I was asked to sit down. The NOIC then gave me a rundown of what was to happen to myself and 1070 during the next few days. My ship was to be decommissioned in five days' time, and all hands, including the First Lieutenant, would be sent on leave, after which the crew would be drafted to other ships or shore establishments. The First Lieutenant would return and join me in commissioning a new boat that was nearing completion at McGruer's Yard at Clynder on Gareloch. Meanwhile, I was to remain in Dunoon and stand by the new vessel as she was being completed. This was standard practice for COs when a new ship was being built.

The idea was for the CO to see what was going on, note anything that he thought defective, and to familiarise himself generally with the new vessel. I would be billeted ashore, just outside Dunoon, with a family who had received Naval Officers before and knew their requirements. All communications would be by telephone, with a daily report to be made to NOIC concerning progress with the building of the new ship. All patrols and duties were cancelled with immediate effect. The next few days were to be spent thoroughly cleaning and overhauling armaments, engines and the hull of 1070. All code books and charts were to be taken to the base as soon as possible. An engineer would be sent aboard to assist our Chief in the engine overhaul.

It was midday as I left the NOIC, which meant it was time to muster the ship's company and inform them of what was to happen before leave started for the watch ashore. Everyone was delighted at the prospect of shore leave and set to with a will. The news of the decommissioning was so sudden and unexpected that I forgot to ask the NOIC for the destination intended for the new vessel and some of the euphoria I had felt when I heard the news began to evaporate. If the new vessel were to stay on the Clyde and repeat the work we had been doing then I would lose interest. In fact I decided to try again for a transfer to a destroyer or an MTB.

With these thoughts in mind I went back to the base in the afternoon and asked to see the NOIC again. He was helpful in every way but could not give me a destination as he did not know it himself. He did say, however, that she was bound for foreign service, as certain modifications in the construction had been ordered. This was enough to satisfy me. In fact, I rejoiced in the prospect, and walked back to the landing stage where 1070 was moored in high good humour.

Simon was on deck and greeted me with his usual enthusiasm, every inch of him expressing pleasure. My enthusiasm seen vanished. Simon, of course! Simon! I had completely forgotten him. Foreign Service must mean the Med at least, if not the Far East. I could not possibly take him. Hot weather, long periods without exercise, apart from the passage to wherever. No, it was out of the question. Somehow I would have to get him home to the care of my Mother. He would be happy there as it was his first home and Mother was devoted to him. I had better act now while I had the chance. A real depression settled upon me at the thought of losing him with the very real possibility of never seeing him again. It's strange, but the thought of not seeing my family again did not cross my mind. They are so much a part of you that you sort of take them with you.

Having disposed of the charts and code books I was free of all duties, apart from keeping an eye on the work aboard. First of all, I went to see the stationmaster at Dunoon. Like the NOIC, he was helpful and kindness itself. I placed the whole problem before him expecting difficulties, but he made light of everything.

'It will be no trouble, sir, and there's nae danger of him being lost. I will speak to the Stationmaster at King's Cross and arrange matters. The dog will be labelled, 'Care of Stationmaster, King's Cross' on one side, with your home address and telephone number on the other. I will give you the personal phone number of my opposite number at King's Cross, so that your Mother can speak to him and arrange to collect. There is a train leaving each day for London at 5.30pm arriving approximately at 11.30am the next day. I suggest you bring him yourself so that you can have a word with the guard who will have been informed.'

Amazing! This good man swept aside all my worries and I returned to 1070 feeling reassured. As I passed the base I thought, why not tomorrow? It's got to be done. So I borrowed one of their telephones, and rang my Mother. She was delighted to have Simon back and agreed at once to phone King's Cross and arrange collection. She would go with my Father in the morning and return with him in the late afternoon when he left his office.

I'm sure all animals are sensitive to atmosphere to some degree, but Simon was exceptional in my opinion. He was very quiet during our evening walk, and stayed close by my side. At 4.30 the next day we left for the station. I was carrying two tins of meat and a bag of biscuits, all of which was unnecessary as I learned later. Simon would eat nothing until he saw my Mother and only drank a little water on the journey. The guard had been informed and assured me that he would look after Simon in every way. My watch hands crept on to the awful moment. I patted him, and gave him a tickle behind the ear, which he loved. He whimpered a little and as I turned away he barked twice as if to say goodbye.

The van door closed, there was an escape of steam from the engine, the train jolted and moved forward. I watched it leave. In those days men seldom cried, but I confess I was near to tears. He had been such a great companion and the thought that I might never see him again was painful. I had nothing to do and Basil had kindly offered to remain on board during my watch as he was going on home leave in a few days' time. So I went to the best hotel in Dunoon and ordered a meal that I ate without noticing its taste or composition. Drink was the thing! I would get a little drunk. I had not been drunk since club nights after rugby at home. Against all we are told about the ineffectiveness of drink in overcoming sadness, that evening spree was a real help. I walked back to 1070 dizzy but in charge.

A few hours after the arrival of Simon's train I phoned home and learned that he had arrived safely. My Mother guessed that we were going abroad but I did not confirm this. I said I did not know where we were bound, which was true. Sending him back was merely a precaution.

The decommissioning passed without ceremony. The Cox'n hauled down the ensign and that was all. The crew filed ashore carrying their gear and I shook hands with each one and wished him luck, while I was answered with a 'Thank you, sir,' and a salute. The base had provided a bus to take them to the station as every man had more than a loaded kit bag to carry. Basil left an hour later and I commenced getting my own stuff together. The last to go into my bag were two souvenirs. One was a piece of parachute silk that had nearly done for us, because if both screws had been stopped we could have drifted off the swept channel. The other was the ribbon tied around Simon's neck in the Wren's common room.

The address I had been given was only a short walk from the edge of Dunoon, but I found a taxi to carry my luggage and the shotgun, which should have been sent home with Simon. One forgets so much at emotional moments. The billet was a large villa standing in an acre of garden where a small boy was playing. Besides the little boy outside, the family consisted of a mother and father and two girls. The eldest girl was about ten and her younger sister was eight, as she informed me later. They were delightful in every way, and made me very welcome from the start. Mrs Anderson asked me if I would like to have meals in my room or if I would prefer to eat with the family. Of course, I chose to eat with them.

To be once more at the centre of a family was a pleasure after the strictures of service life. The time spent with them all was a real joy and helped me to forget the loss of Simon. The sixth member of the family was a tame duck that used to nudge your leg during meal times, and open its beak to receive titbits. Rations were scarce, as they were down south, but as the Andersons kept chickens eggs were not a problem. Mrs Anderson was a magician in the kitchen who could turn corned beef, and that horrible stuff called Spam, into far nicer food with the use of herbs and spices, of which she had a vast store. After a day or two I remembered my shotgun and was able to supplement the rations with an occasional rabbit. The fields around abounded with them and

I wondered why rabbit was not on the menu more often. The days quickly formed into a routine. Breakfast, a walk into town to the ferry that took me to Clynder on the Gareloch, followed by a few hours at the yard, then home by six. The evenings were spent playing board games, especially Monopoly, although we never finished one of these games. I taught the children one or two games that we used to play at home, including charades, of which they had never heard. All together it was a happy time and a welcome change from the war. I saw little evidence of war in Scotland. No enemy planes were in the sky, and no sound of bombs, or sirens warning of air raids, filled the air. The only reminder was the news, and sometimes the sight of wounded convoys coming home from America.

CHAPTER 3

❋

From Dunoon to the Med

1941–42

My new vessel was numbered 1297 and a considerable improvement on 1070. She had mountings for heavy-calibre weapons, fans in all compartments, a larger fridge and, above all, the 'Rolls-Royce' of diesel engines were to be fitted with the help of base engineers. They were to be 'Gardners', much esteemed by marine engineers and preferred by engine chiefs of small craft. They were known for their legendary reliability and performance.

Mr McGruer, the owner of the yard, was a skilled craftsman and designer who had invented many improvements in yacht design, including the famous McGruer 'hollow spar'. I felt sure at the outset that 1297 would be first class in every way, and events later on proved this to be the case. During the weeks that I stood by waiting for the completion of the work, we had just one disagreement and that was about the small matter of a wardroom carpet. At first he refused to fit one, saying that it was not on the Admiralty list. I argued that I had been used to one and if he would not supply the article I would purchase the material and fit it myself. The next day the wardroom was resplendent with a new good-quality fitted blue carpet. I thanked him profusely.

Towards the end of the work on the slipway, I was able to borrow a sixteen-foot yawl from the yard and sailed about Gareloch, looking at the wildlife and enjoying the feel of wind in the sails as she heeled to a fresh breeze. The day came soon enough for the launch and Mr McGruer asked me if I had a family member, or a girlfriend who would like to perform the launching ceremony. I had no one available so he asked, did I mind if he asked one of the young women in the office to do it. Of course, I agreed. It was a fine morning on the day of the launch and 1297 looked a picture with fresh paint and gleaming decks, which were scrubbed clean.

From her bow hung a bottle of Teacher's whisky on a ribbon. The girl, who could not have been more than seventeen, grasped the bottle by the neck, threw it at the prow and, as the bottle shattered, she said, 'God, bless this ship and all who sail in her.' I could not be sure of these words, but I think that was what she said because the thick Scottish accent defeated me!

1297 slid gracefully down the slip and into the lock, where she was controlled by ropes and pulled alongside the jetty. The rest of the work was to be completed afloat, including the installation of the two eight-cylinder Gardner engines. As 1297 settled alongside, I thanked Mr McGruer for all the good work and for sacrificing a bottle of precious whisky.

'Ach, noo!' he replied. 'It was cold tea. Look after the pence, and the poonds'll take care of themselves.'

The following day the engines arrived on a huge lorry and were lowered into place, through the coach roof which had been left open. An engineer followed with an electrician, and the specialised work began. Two generators arrived and the whole vessel had to be wired for lights and power to all the equipment. This would require a shipwright in attendance as the furniture had to be drilled, and sometimes adapted, to take the cables. I had not realised that even when the boat hit the water there was still so much to be done.

All the work was completed in three days and we were ready for trials. All equipment was tested, circuits checked and engines run while still alongside. In the late afternoon of the fourth day we slipped our moorings and headed out into the loch. The boat was still in the care and responsibility of the yard. I was simply there to observe. We ran up and down the loch at different speeds, while the shafts and steering gear were closely examined. When the base staff were satisfied, the yard people took us to Dunoon where the vessel was handed over to the navy, but not yet to me. Until the boat was formerly commissioned she would be the responsibility of the base.

On the following day the crew began to arrive. They came aboard in a trickle that went on until 3.00pm when the last men, which happened to be the Chief and Basil, came up the gangway together. All the crew were new people and fortunately there were no beginners. They had all served in other ships and two of them in Fairmile MLs. The Cox'n proved to be a very experienced man who had served in armed trawlers. I counted myself very lucky indeed.

Basil spent two hours showing everyone the ropes, and how they should accommodate themselves to the confines of a small ship. The water tanks were filled and then something of a revelation occurred. Food sufficient for fourteen men for a month began to arrive in boxes. The base was responsible for this, and the next day I discovered how it was achieved. In Dunoon town there was a large grocer's shop that specialised in victualling ships. They knew exactly what was required for any number of men, and for every kind of ship according to size. For instance, a destroyer would have extensive refrigeration equipment and stowage space, so the nature of the supplies would reflect this. Small craft such as us would have more tinned and preserved food.

The cook seemed content with his galley, which he tested as soon as he had claimed his bunk. Under Basil's directions the rations were stowed by two seamen, and the cook filled his ready-use locker in the galley. By 7.00pm the initial work was finished and the crew were free to go ashore as the base, in effect, still owned the boat. However, a handful of men stayed aboard and the cook dished up a scratch meal of soup and corned beef for them. Basil and I went ashore and ate fish and chips in a local pub. I then went to collect my gear from Mrs Anderson, and said goodbye to the family, promising to write. They had been very good to me and I was much in their debt.

By noon the next day everyone knew their place and their jobs. The Chief was 'over the moon' with his beautiful eight-cylinder Gardner engines, and it was difficult to entice him out of the engine room. For hours he was down there with the base engineer, going over every detail concerning the trials and all the equipment in his charge. One of the seamen was rated 'Stoker', and it was his job to assist the Chief, and be able to run the machinery in his absence. Stokers had a formal training in engineering but a short and limited one. Fuel was taken on board and the tanks filled to capacity.

Shortly after midday Basil assembled the entire ship's company, including the Chief who had to be dug out the engine room, and who appeared on deck clutching a manual as I addressed them. I did not waste time with emotional speeches; I merely gave them an account of what was to happen to 1297 in the next three weeks. I ended by wishing everyone success, and I hoped everyone would be proud of their ship and of each other. The Cox'n then went to the foot of our short mast and hauled up the ensign, which fluttered in the breeze. 1297 was now in commission, and in my care.

I went ashore to collect charts and code books, and was given orders to proceed to Tobermory as soon as I considered that 1297 was in 'all respects ready for sea'. I had some latitude in this, and I reckoned that I would need three days to reach this state. Meanwhile, the armaments arrived and were mounted. They consisted of twin Oerlikons on the foredeck; twin point-fives each side of the bridge; twin Oerlikons on the coach roof, and twin point-fives on each quarter. Eight depth charges were lowered aboard and anchored, four on each side of the quarter deck, as in 1070. An experienced gunner from the base then instructed all hands, except the Chief and his mate, on the care and operation of the guns. Basil and I attended this course that lasted two hours during which blank rounds were fired, and everyone took a turn at firing and loading. Basil took charge of the manuals and appointed one of the seamen as his assistant. This man was chosen because he had been a gunner on a minesweeper.

At 6.00pm hands were split into two watches, port and starboard. Port was given four hours' leave to go ashore. The cook had been busy all day baking bread and the smell that arose from the galley skylight was delicious. He served up an excellent meal of stew, made from some of the fresh meat that had come aboard in the morning. While at Dunoon we could draw fresh food each day from the base. I questioned the cook about using our precious flour when in harbour, as we could draw fresh bread from the base each day. He said he had to practise and get used to the oven, an explanation that I was bound to accept. He asked me to taste a piece, and it was as good as the bread from ashore, in my opinion, and I told him so. 'Thank you, sir, but I hope it will be a lot better before I'm finished.' He kept his word. Our bread would become famous in days to come.

In the wardroom I went over the day's activities, and decided that two more days would be needed before I could signal 'in all respects ready for sea'. Shore leave was given from 6.00pm each day, and on the last day the leave was split between watches so that each got two hours. It was vitally important to make sure that all the men got the maximum time ashore in line with service requirements. The cramped conditions in small craft made it particularly essential. On the morning of the third day after commissioning, we left Dunoon and headed out into open water to start our passage to Tobermory, a destination that was feared by many, and talked about by those who had been there. It was a 'working up base' and presided over by a dreaded character known as 'Monkey' Stevens. Newly commissioned ships were sent there to sharpen up discipline and practise their response to emergencies.

The passage through the islands was visually inspiring. Mountains rose on all sides, and rocky headlands jutted into the sea like sentinels guarding the land behind. Sheep grazed close to the shoreline in many places and fir trees crowded the uplands. Once, a pair of golden eagles circled above us, identified by the Cox'n who was a Scot. The crew settled to their tasks and a general feeling of contentment spread through the vessel as usually happened when at sea after a long spell in harbour or ashore. This was not to last. 'Monkey' Stevens made sure of that. I was never to meet this 'supreme being', but I believe he was a four-ring RN Captain. On arrival at Tobermory we anchored.

As I returned to the bridge, after having tested the tautness of the chain with my foot, frantic flashing from the port buildings greeted us. 'Weigh anchor immediately and proceed to position Y marked on your chart No 126.' We had signalled our ETA in code by wireless when at sea, so they could have directed us before we had anchored. This was a foretaste of things to come.

A meal was served to all hands, and watches arranged for the engine room, the wireless cabin, and a guard on the bridge. Basil and I went into four-hour watches for the night. All other hands were allowed to turn in. It was bliss to turn in after the worries of commissioning a new ship and the anxieties of the first passage. Basil took over from me at midnight, and I snuggled down under a blanket and mentally said a prayer of thanksgiving for a satisfactory end to the first chapter in the life of 1297. I felt something under the blanket – what was it? Simon? No, of course, he was ashore. How long had I slept? What the hell was holding my arm? Ugh! I was awake now. It was Basil shaking me.

'Sir, from the base,' he said. 'Go to action stations and proceed to position X!' I had been asleep for exactly one hour. Action stations was sounded, and all hands turned out of their bunks and appeared on deck in various stages of undress. Some had slept in their clothes, but most were in their pants.

The days that followed were a bit of a nightmare. In essence, no one was ever off watch. Signals for action of some sort could arrive at any moment. We practised 'man overboard', scrambling-net drill, anti-submarine drill and manoeuvres of every kind. No sooner had one task been performed than another was ordered. After three days of this, everyone felt tired and irritable, but, strangely enough, this feeling faded after the fourth day and we all felt more energetic and quicker in our wits. 'Monkey' Stevens obviously knew a lot more about human behaviour than we did.

At the end of the week we were signalled to go alongside and take on fuel, water and fresh food. Shore leave could be given and there was general rejoicing all round. I went to the Ops Room (Operations Room) and received orders to proceed to Milford Haven as soon as the boat was ready for sea. We remained at the base long enough to give all hands four hours' leave for each watch.

I drew charts for as far south as Land's End, up-to-date code books, as well as a pilot book for Milford Haven and its approaches. The tides at that port were known for being fierce and dangerous. At high springs the ebb sometimes ran at eleven knots. Fortunately, it was now neaps and so Basil and I worked out a time for arriving one hour before low water.

The passage was uneventful. When passing the Isle of Man a considerable sea got up before a force five south-westerly, but the wind died in the evening, and the rest of the passage was made in light winds and calm water. Our ETA was only wrong by twenty minutes, and I congratulated Basil who had done most of the sums. The engines performed beautifully, particularly as we had to adjust our speed many times to keep in step with our ETA, which had been signalled to NOIC, Milford Haven.

A launch was ready to meet us at the harbour entrance and they led us to a berth alongside the base. A mile outside the harbour I estimated the ebb against us to be running at two knots, which coincided with Basil's forecast. During the hours on the bridge I reflected on the amount I had learned since leaving Sheerness. The affair of the rabbit, and the insubordinate rating, had taught me to think carefully before I spoke or did anything. A wrong move always had repercussions. The trouble at Clock Point and the sinking of the drifter had increased my confidence in my ability to make a judgement when faced with an alternative, and the commissioning of 1297 helped to confirm this. However, I knew I had a long way to go before I could be called an efficient and reliable CO.

While the hands were busy rigging mooring lines and fenders, I received a signal to report to the XDO's office. There, a complete surprise awaited me. All hands, including myself, were to go on two weeks' leave from the following morning. During that time 1297 would be in the sole care of the base. I knew what this meant.

Modifications were going to be made to the boat, especially the provision of extra fuel storage. This might mean the Far East, or it might not. Parts of the Mediterranean were equally distant, as far as an HDML is concerned. All hands went ashore at 9.00am and all of us, except Sparks who was Welsh, caught the same London train. I did not phone in case the order was countermanded. The navy had a way of reaching you wherever you were.

I arrived home in mid-afternoon and knocked at the front door. We had no bell, but the knocker was a large brass lion's head and I liked using it. My youngest brother Donald came to the door. He was in his last term at St Albans School and was presently enjoying a half-day holiday. He astonished me by being completely unsurprised at seeing me.

'Hallo, I knew you were coming,' he said.

'How did you know?' I replied, amazed.

'I was asleep, and dreamed I saw your hand and arm on the table in front of me.'

On several occasions since then I have had reason to think that Don was psychic to some degree. My parents were of course overjoyed at seeing me. My Mother had convinced herself that I would be abroad by this time. Simon and I were reunited, and he demonstrated his lasting affection by following me everywhere. We had many walks together, and he was trained to retrieve by the time the fortnight was over. Despite its weight, I had managed to bring my twelve-bore shotgun home with me as well as my luggage. Each morning we went out early after rabbits, or anything else that could supplement the meagre rations that could be bought by then. Good food seemed to be scarcer than in Scotland, but my Mother, who was a trained cook, did wonders with any extras that came along.

She had several different ways of cooking the rabbits, and even dealt with pigeons, when I was unable to bring a rabbit home. Eggs were almost non-existent and were replaced by a dreadful yellow powder called 'reconstituted egg'. This could be used for cooking. It could be mixed with milk, then fried to make something laughably called 'scrambled egg'. We had plenty of fruit and vegetables as these were grown in our garden. Apples, gooseberries, blackcurrants, loganberries and mulberries were plentiful, as well as various vegetables.

The first week home was marred by a tragic event. My close friend Robert Owen was killed. He had been at school with me, although two years my senior. He piloted Handley Page Bombers and had risen to the rank of squadron leader. It was said of him that you could always tell his plane as it took off from its base at Radlett, because it was steadier than the rest as they rose with their load of bombs and fuel sufficient to take them to Berlin and back. My Mother was devoted to Robert and would lend him her car whenever he was on leave. The air raids were continuing over Britain and in some way helped us to avoid dwelling upon Robert's death because so many others were suffering a similar fate.

Those who have not experienced war often imagine that the whole country was being laid to waste. It was not like that at all. Trains still ran, and were surprisingly on time for the most part. People still drove their cars to and from work, but the petrol ration was small and you had to hoard your coupons if you wanted to take a long journey. As Robert's base was near to us at Radlett, he would visit my parents sometimes between spells of duty. One day my Father offered him a horse to ride, but Robert shook his head saying, 'Good Heavens! No, Mr Beale! Thank you, but it's much too dangerous for my liking!' This from a man who led his squadron night after night through anti-aircraft fire and fighter plane attacks to carry out their missions. Such is the nature of heroes.

One afternoon I played tennis with a neighbour's daughter in their garden. She was about sixteen and I had known her since she was an infant. At one point in the game she fell over, revealing the fact that she wore no knickers. Whether this was meant for my eyes or not, I never knew, but I do remember that girls in general were becoming more provocative, especially among the middle classes. Most of the boys and girls of my generation and class were brought up under strict moral principles that lasted until marriage, or at least engagement. Now the ground was being tested and perhaps this was part of the process. War changes many things, particularly human behaviour and ways of thinking.

That same evening my Father came home from the firm looking moody. He was very quiet all through the evening meal and when pressed he reluctantly told us the reason for his silence. An official from the War Office had called at the works with a box of photos. They were pictures of atrocities allegedly committed by the Germans. Some were so horrible he refused to describe them. The firm was ordered to make printing plates (blocks) of them for use as propaganda when printed on leaflets. My Father refused. The official left, to be followed an hour later by two army trucks that drew up outside the building and disgorged a number of soldiers in battle dress. An officer then approached my Father with a paper ordering him to process the photographs. If he refused the works would be taken over by the army. The staff were as shocked by the material as Father, but there was no choice. I knew that my parent would not be happy until these dreadful images were clear of the works and on their way to the printers, who might possibly react as he did. During this leave I made a point of keeping close to our house and spending most of the time with my family. Tony, my middle brother, had left school and was presently in training at Greenwich Naval establishment, but we were able to talk by phone on most nights.

'Dick, could I ask a favour of you? I know your leave is precious so don't be afraid of saying no. If you do say no I shall understand, and it can wait until Tony gets his first leave.' It was my Mother asking me if I would mind driving her down to Bournemouth to see her sister. She had been saving her petrol for months and wished to see her sibling before war made it impossible. Of course I agreed. It was not a favour but a pleasure. I liked driving the little Austin Ten, and I knew Mother would find it tiring to drive so far by herself. We set off before 9.00am expecting to find less traffic at that time, but it was not until we had left London that the roads became clear. I smoked my pipe, which for some reason pleased my Mother. Whether it was the sight or the smell I can't say. On this occasion I was smoking 'Bondman', a strong scented tobacco. The other brands that I favoured were Capstan, Player's Flake and Gold Leaf. Later, when I had more money, I bought the expensive Balkan Sobranie. We stopped at Swindon, and ate a sandwich and drank a glass of cider in a pub called The Spur.

It was a happy journey except for the sight of three Spitfires battling with a squadron of Heinkels heading for London. It always produced a feeling of guilt to witness such a scene when one is enjoying a comfortable time on the ground. I had several friends who were fighter pilots and I always wondered, when seeing a dogfight, if one of them was up there. My aunt met us at the door with the news that she had booked three seats at the local Hippodrome which was staging a performance of La Bohème. There was time for a quick meal and we were off.

I remember little of the opera until the end. The artiste playing Mimi had a fine voice, and a very substantial figure that looked particularly large when standing next to her lover Rudolfo, who was rather small. The end was really dramatic in a way unthought of by Puccini. Mimi, singing her last dying notes, collapses and

65

dies on the bed. Unfortunately, the bed collapsed as well, and all ended in a heap on the floor. I took a long time reaching for a non-existent programme on the floor, and out of the corner of my eye I saw the shoulders of my Mother and aunt shaking, but no sound came from them.

The last three days of my leave passed quietly. Having spent the night of the opera at my aunt's house, that leave was singularly poignant, as I knew, and they knew, that it would be a long time before we were together again. When coming to the end of a very happy time it's like descending to the foot of a beautiful mountain. You look back up and appreciate the heights, then you look down at the flat land below. The sight and the feel is comfortable, but not exciting. On the evening of the last day my Mother produced a magnificent meal of boiled mutton and caper sauce, followed by apple pie. The meal was the result of coupons saved by many meals of rabbit and pigeon.

At 8.00am the next morning Father drove me to the station. Goodbyes were said. I shook hands with Father and Don, hugged my Mother, cuddled Simon and left. The train was irritatingly fast and seemed to want to widen the separation as quickly as possible. I walked from the station to Milford Haven docks unencumbered by a heavy shotgun in its case and rounded the corner of the engineering ship to see 1297 directly ahead. The sight appalled me. Huge tanks had been bolted to each side of the fo'c'sle.

I measured the tanks with my eye, and then went straight to the engineer's office to complain. I was concerned that the stability of the boat would be seriously affected by this huge amount of top weight. The engineer commander himself assured me that the calculations had been carefully worked out and that the tanks, when full, were compensated for by the addition of extra ballast, which had been fixed in the bilges. I had my doubts, but had no choice but to accept. I then learned that our destination was to be Malta.

'The tanks will be removed soon after you arrive, to increase the field of fire from your guns,' he said.

'But, sir,' I replied. 'Why could not the fuel be stored in the bilges in especially designed tanks made to fit the space?'

'Because some part of your fuel supply must be gravity fed to the engines,' came the response.

I gave up arguing and went gloomily back to 1297. The tanks looked huge as I stepped aboard, and I went below quickly in order not to have to look at them. Basil and the crew were not due back until the next day. I found a pub in which to drown my worries with a bottle of house wine to help soak up a steak pie. On returning to the docks by a different route, I noticed two other HDMLs with the deck tanks. I began to feel that I was not alone with what might be, or might not be, a problem.

The next few days passed in storing ship, taking on fuel and water, and with generally preparing the ship for sea. The crew was supplied with tropical gear and mosquito nets. Basil and I were fitted out with 'whites' from the naval store. I met the COs of the other two HDMLs and it appeared that we would sail in company with an armed escort. On the afternoon of the day before sailing, I gave permission for visitors to come on board so that the men could say goodbye to their girlfriends and loved ones. All visitors were to be ashore by 10.00pm and gangway sentries were arranged through the night, otherwise all hands turned in. Departure time was fixed for 7.00am and all hands went into four-hour watches. I was not sorry to leave Milford Haven, a dismal place with wicked tides. Everybody's spirits, which had risen as we headed out into open water, were to be dashed before we were a mile on our way. The Cox'n came on to the bridge.

'Excuse me, sir, but there is a Wren asleep in one of the bunks forward,' he said. I couldn't believe it. For the second time in this war I would have to turn my ship around against orders. 'Starboard twenty, midships, full ahead both,' I ordered.

I got the business done as quickly as possible. She was dumped ashore by the Cox'n and one other crew member. Once again I expected to be flashed by the XDO, but nothing happened. I sometimes wondered whether an angel sat on my shoulder. The other two boats and the trawler were far ahead by the time I was again clear of the harbour, and we never really caught up. I kept the trawler in sight for the rest of the day, but by evening I lost sight of her, and the other two boats had long since disappeared. I only hoped that we would not be attacked by enemy aircraft for the trawler had anti-aircraft guns which were the reason for her presence. As we passed Land's End I noticed the barometer falling rather quickly, and it continued to fall until we were thirty miles off Ushant, and then it halted at a point lower than I had ever seen before. I called the Cox'n and warned him of bad weather to come.

As yet the wind remained at about force three, but a heavy swell from the south-west began rolling towards us. The troughs were deep, and getting deeper every minute. Quite suddenly the wind increased, and within the space of five minutes it was blowing at force eight, and rising. I thought anxiously of the deck tanks. The Cox'n, wonderful man, had seen to the battening down of all hatches, and the securing of all movable objects. He put three five-gallon water breakers into the wheelhouse locker and, just before the full fury of the gale hit us, he managed to bring up an armful of bread and tinned food, all of which he stored in the wheelhouse. The cook, who passed out, was carried into the wheelhouse and laid out on the only bunk. The wind rose to force nine and beyond. All hands were on deck, or in the wheelhouse, owing to the stench of diesel throughout the boat. We were pitching and rolling so violently that fuel from the breather pipes, on top of the tanks, was spilling out and flowing down the scuppers and finding its way into the bilges. The chief and his stoker sat at the top of the engine room hatch.

Throughout the night and the next day the gale maintained its force, with no lulls or lessening of the deep troughs that lifted us into the white tops of the waves before swallowing us once more. My constant task was to keep our bows into the wind and sea. If we ever came broadside to the waves the ship would roll until she was forced under, and likely not come up again but continue the roll and sink. I cursed those deck tanks, and all the engineers at Milford Haven. I reduced our speed to four knots, which was just enough to keep her bows on to the weather. Once or twice a freak wave hit us more on the beam and it was then that the stability was tested. With sickening slowness the boat rolled until the forward deck was awash. I held my breath and gradually she came upright. Perhaps Milford Haven had got their sums right after all. In mid-morning a Dornier circled us, and I thought, 'That's all we need.'

It was impossible to fire the Oerlikons as all guns were saturated with salt water, and the trawler was out of sight. The bomber circled several times then flew away, obviously considering us too small to waste their bombs on.

During the second day the gale continued with undiminished force. All of us who could still eat opened tins and consumed the contents, throwing the empties over the side. The Cox'n again came to the rescue when this small supply was finished. He managed to prise open the galley skylight and, with the aid of a gadget he had made out of a boat hook and some netting, was able to bring up more tins. The weather improved a little in the course of the second night. The wind decreased to force seven, but the sea remained a menace to our small vessel. Deep troughs buried us before throwing us up and forward on to the crests. Gradually it became easier to keep the bows into the waves, and by mid-morning of the third day, I was able to increase speed to six knots and hand over to the First Lieutenant. I had been on the bridge for thirty-six hours, but the blanket of tiredness had yet to overtake me. I lay down in the wheelhouse and closed my eyes, but could not sleep. After a while I became aware that there was no one in sight. The wheelhouse was empty. I got up and looked out at a transformed scene. The sea had gone down to a moderate swell and the sun shone brightly. Each minute that passed brought an improvement. It was then that a long delayed exhaustion overcame me, and I lay down again and slept soundly for five hours. Basil generously donated one hour of his watch to me.

The days that followed were roses all the way, with a calm sea, bright sun and gentle winds. It's remarkable how quickly one can recover from sickness and lethargy to optimism and cheerful activity. All hands set to clean ship. The bilges were washed out with seawater and detergent. The cook returned to his galley and I returned to the bridge. At 4.00pm we reverted to four-hour watches for all hands. Nothing remarkable happened before we reached Gibraltar. Basil's courses took us within sight of headlands so that our position could be fixed from time to time. In most situations there is a silver lining if you look for it. Coasting southward in the warm sun, I reflected upon the gale and what it had meant to us all. I realised that we had been very lucky. Had the occasional beam sea been stronger, and as deep as the troughs ahead, we could have been forced under.

Furthermore, it was fortunate that the bad weather had come from a point directly ahead and in line with our course. Had it been on either beam, we should have had to turn into it and lose our position. Counting blessings helps to make the watch pass quickly. Mugs of cocoa help too, especially when accompanied by a chunk of cook's excellent bread and a piece of cheese.

We entered Gibraltar Harbour at about 5.00pm. It was very hot, and a smell of spice and strange fruits pervaded the atmosphere and seemed to be coming across the straits from the African coast. Few of us had been this far abroad before, and so found this new and exotic location exciting. No launch came out to meet us, although we had signalled our ETA, but a man on the jetty waved us to a berth alongside a minesweeper. I left instructions for the crew to take leave ashore in two-hour spells for each watch, and made my way to base to report.

Bernard Shaw once said that he was a pessimist and therefore life was filled with pleasant surprises. I too am, I believe, a pessimist, and am constantly being surprised, often pleasantly. Here was another one coming round the corner. I climbed some steps, turned a right angle and collided with an RAF officer.

'I'm so sorry. Good Heavens, it's 'Quack'!' I exclaimed. There in front of me stood a school friend named Maurice Drake. We inevitably used to call him 'Quack'. After school we often met at the Players' Theatre under the arches at Charing Cross. Quack studied law and was known for his wit. He grinned and banged me on the shoulder saying, 'Good God! Dickie Beale, no less!' We ducked into a wine bar to down a quick glass of vino and exchange news. We arranged to meet again for a meal the following evening and parted.

I made my report and returned aboard to allow Basil to have his two hours. The cook produced a stew that consisted mainly of corned beef, but was heavily disguised with other, hard to identify flavourings. That night I slept the sleep of the unjust and woke next morning feeling refreshed and ready for anything that the base was going to throw at us. I quickly learned that we were to remain in Gibraltar (Gib) for at least two weeks while some special gear was fitted. I enquired the nature of our future operations, but was told that the information was top secret and that all would be revealed when we arrived in Malta.

For our first week in Gib, life was as much as it had been at Dunoon and Sheerness. Patrols, and more patrols, but the rota was kind to us. Every third day we patrolled the straits between Algiers and Gibraltar keeping a strict anti-submarine watch, followed by two days in harbour. An armed trawler and another HDML shared the rota with us.

Quack Drake and I met as arranged and during the meal he invited me to take a trip in his fighter plane. He was flying Beaufighters, which were night interceptor attack planes. They were heavily armed and were powered by a huge rotary engine. Beaufighters were not as manoeuvrable, or as fast as a Spitfire, but they carried a powerful punch. Quack's squadron was responsible for the protection of Gibraltar and Algiers, which had just fallen to the Allies. It had been the base for the Vichy-French fleet which had either been sunk or taken over by the British fleet.

The Eighth Army, known as the 'Desert Rats', were beginning to make progress along the North African coast, and I guessed that our role in the Med would be in support of their supply lanes at sea. Malta was the centre for these operations, and the main base for all ships in that part of the world. Of course, our contribution would be minute, but every little helps, even at sea. It was late August and very hot in Gib. The Rock seemed to act as a giant radiator, collecting heat during the day and giving it out at night: nature's night storage in reverse.

After our meal we walked to the aerodrome. Quack fitted me out with a parachute and earmuffs, but without intercom connection, so it would be impossible to talk to him once we were airborne. It was still broad daylight as I climbed into the cockpit and I squeezed down in front of him. By stretching my neck I could just see out over the side of the fuselage. The mighty engine roared and we bounded down the runway gathering speed with every yard, and then the nose rose sharply in front of me, I fell backwards as the monster left the ground and climbed into space. For a few minutes we flew towards the African coast, heading inland as we crossed the shoreline. Algiers and the docks were passed within seconds, and open country spread before us, but not for long. The plane began to lose height and the sound of the engine changed to a less harsh note. I realised that we were circling and going to land.

Quack landed in a field that was more scrub than grass. He helped me out, and then he disappeared into a low building that seemed to be neither house nor barn. He reappeared with an Arab man. Each was carrying a large cardboard box, both of which were stowed in the nose of the plane between my legs. 'What are these boxes for?' I asked before noise drowned all speech. 'Eggs for the mess!' he shouted as he pulled, or pushed, the starter switch. Once more we bounded over the surface, but this time the uneven ground caused us to shake badly and I wondered about the strength of the undercarriage.

About halfway back, over the straits, he dived the machine at 400mph as I learned later and, I must admit, that I was scared stiff. My stomach rose to my gullet before settling back to its rightful place. We landed exactly forty minutes after taking off and I remarked to Quack that if he had pranged the plane at 400mph, I would have been mixed with the eggs and become an omelette. He did not find this very funny or witty, and, on reflection, neither did I.

'Prang' was RAF slang for 'crash' and, being as young as I was, I thought it clever to use it. I know better now. Each service has its own slang and it should not be 'stolen' by the others, much the same as kilts should not be worn by lowlanders!

In return for the flight I invited Quack to come aboard for a night's patrol. He was delighted and managed to swap his duty night with another pilot. On my next patrol night he joined us for dinner aboard at 6.00pm. The cook did us proud. Fresh food from the base resulted in a joint of pork, and all the trimmings.

'You do all right, Dickie. I think that I joined the wrong service,' said Quack. He was clearly in his element with a glass of wine in one hand and a cigar in the other. Quack loved a glass of wine, a habit he followed through into peacetime, and right up until his death in 2014.

As we were finishing our dinner I noticed a slight swell bumping us up against our fenders on the dock wall. I also heard wind in the mast rigging of the ships around us. I glanced at my friend and wondered if I should warn him, but thought better of it. After all, a man who could dive a plane at 400mph would not worry about a bit of a sea chop. He watched carefully as we let go, and threaded our way through the moorings into open water. He learned the terms used to instruct the helmsman and the rating on the wheel, and I then I handed the helm over to him.

He managed the helm for about ten minutes and responded to my orders with reasonable accuracy, but his efforts faded as we drew away from the harbour. An easterly meant a beam sea, and so we wallowed in the trough, rolling steadily but in no way dangerously. It was the motion we were used to in similar conditions, but to Quack it was too much. He retired to the wardroom and I did not see him again until the end of my watch at 12.00pm. He seemed to be asleep, and in the light of the torch he looked very pale. On the way back to harbour in the morning he came on to the bridge.

'Dickie, nothing would ever induce me to go to sea again, now or later. Ugh, I feel dreadful,' he said.

'You look pretty dreadful I must say.' I replied. 'The colour from your cheeks has drained into the whites of your eyes!'

'I've heard that expression before. Shame on you for using it,' he said grumpily. 'I'd rather fly a damaged Beaufighter than risk that trip again!'

After the war Quack rose to become a High Court judge and we would meet up occasionally. I once attended a case he was hearing at the Royal Courts of Justice in the Strand. For two hours I endured the waffle of opposing councils until Quack rose to give his summary. In the ten minutes that he spoke, he summarised all that they had said, and reduced their words to an understandable form. His obituary appeared in the *Daily Telegraph* in 2014, and was headed, 'Sir Maurice Drake,' accompanied by a photograph and a full page of his professional life.

It was the last day of our patrols, and for the next week we would be in the hands of the dockyard and their shipwrights. Quack tottered off to his base, while I reported to the XDO. I was told that a smoke-generator would be fitted to the stern, a repeater of the Asdic recorder would be fitted in the wardroom, plus certain other modifications. I asked if the wretched deck tanks could be removed, having worked out that we carried enough fuel to take us to Malta, but was told that was a matter for Malta to decide. We were now able to give full shore leave each day, retaining a sentry on the gangway and one officer aboard.

Quack and I met once more before we left, and spent a happy few hours at a bistro eating, drinking and talking. Strangely, he preferred reminiscing about school days as was still his preference in peacetime.

One afternoon I lay on my bunk, it being too hot to do anything else and fell asleep to be wakened later by a loud snoring noise! When I realised that it was not me snoring, I opened one eye to see a thin saw blade moving back and forth, an inch from my nose.

'What the hell! What for God's sake is going on?' These words were shouted as I sat upright.

'Sorry, sir, I did not want to wake you.'

'But you did wake me. Who could sleep through that? That doesn't matter. You could have blinded me with that blade if I had moved my head by even an inch.'

That angel was back on my shoulder again. The shipwright apologised profusely. He was cutting out a rectangle in the bulkhead behind my bunk, in which would be fitted the recorder-repeater mentioned by the XDO. In the end I did not report him to the base engineer but I did think about it.

When next on deck I noticed that one of the other HDMLs had left, and so perhaps now is the time to relate the extraordinary tales that later circulated about that boat. It was rumoured that the CO had damaged the ship's screws on some wreckage, having just left Gibraltar on his way to Malta. He managed to beach the vessel and signal for help. He was told that no ship was available to tow him off until a boom defence vessel could be spared, which might take several weeks. So the whole ship's company became part of the landscape. They moved the galley ashore and erected a thatched roof over it. They also cultivated vegetables on a strip of soil above the shingle. The navy called this 'going native'. Eventually help did arrive and the HDML was towed back to Algiers, where the dockyard had been taken over by the British. This yard took in work from Gibraltar when the Rock was hard-pressed.

The yard in Algiers was mainly staffed by Arab workmen, who were in many respects highly skilled, but they needed supervision when dealing with certain problems. The HDML was hauled up the slip, stern first. The damaged screws were removed and replaced by new ones sent over from Gib. The work was quickly completed, and the ship launched with engines running, but not engaged. She hit the water. The CO called, 'Half ahead both!' and the vessel shot straight back into the slipway smashing both screws and the rudders. The screws had been put on the wrong way round, reversing their drive and causing this calamity.

The last I heard about this boat was some months later in Malta. Apparently they mistook the island of Pantelleria for Malta while approaching it at night. The island had been heavily bombed by the Allies, and was ready to give up. The HDML tied up for the night at a harbour wall and then, realising that they had made a mistake, intended to leave in the morning. As they were letting go, the mayor of the island came down to meet them and, presenting his sword on a cushion, he surrendered the island. The CO at once embraced the situation and formally accepted the surrender, making the gesture of breaking the sword across his knee before leaving.

I later saw this boat in Malta. This was after it had been hauled off the beach and repaired for the second time and then had got underway for Malta, calling at Pantelleria en route. I happened to be in the XDO's office when the notorious vessel entered Valletta Harbour. I was looking through the window overlooking the entrance and the large number of new arrivals. It was clear that preparations were taking place for something big. I had never seen so many destroyers and transports in one place before. In one corner a number of HDMLs were berthed, with another one approaching. The fo'c'sle of this vessel was covered in wire netting and chickens were hopping about in a pile of cabbage leaves and bits of straw. The 'master of Pantelleria' was apparently not to be parted from his farmyard, which had been carefully assembled during his six weeks on the beach.

After this digression I must return to Gibraltar. Work continued slowly owing to the great pressure that the dockyard was working under and, as a result, the crew enjoyed more shore time than they were used to.

The boat's smoke-generator was made of steel, was a little taller than a dustbin and about the same circumference. The First Lieutenant, his assistant and myself were all instructed in its operation. A manual supplied with the generator had illustrations of its various valves and dials. I hated the look of the wretched thing and, when viewed in conjunction with the deck tanks, I thought 1297 looked like part of a scrap-metal yard. I was appeased to some extent when the base armourer arrived in a van with all our guns, which had now been cleaned and were free of salt, oiled and tested. He also brought canvas covers for the mountings, which had been unobtainable at Milford Haven.

With time to spare while the dockyard tore apart 1297, I took the opportunity one day, in spite of the heat, to climb the Rock and saw some of the famous Barbary apes that are said to hold the fate of Gibraltar in their simian hands.

One afternoon I walked over the border into La Linea with a fellow HDML flotilla CO. The town was *en fete*, with posters everywhere advertising a bullfight that was to take place that day. In fact, it was due to start an hour after our arrival in town. My companion and I decided we would attend the fight. We only had British currency, but knew that would it be good enough for anywhere in Europe. With the directions obtained from local people we met in the streets, we hurried toward the stadium. We were passed by a number of open carriages, each filled with gaily dressed ladies with skirts billowing over the sides of the carriages in a variety of patterns and colours. These same ladies sat around the edge of the bullring and arranged their skirts over the barrier in a chain of bright material that stretched right around the ring. We managed to get two seats in the shade, which cost twice as much as those in the sun, but they were worth the extra money as it was a stiflingly hot afternoon.

There was a parade of sorts to begin, then the bull was let into the ring. The animal was chased around by various people who were 'minor' matadors – well, at least that's what it seemed to me. From the outset I felt an overpowering dislike of the whole business, but I felt that one should see the whole spectacle right to the end before preaching against it. It was a sickening two hours that I would never repeat. Next came the picadors, men mounted on broken-down, hollow-backed horses, with ribs showing and seemingly near to death. These poor creatures were ridden into the bull so that its horns could reach under the horse's belly and speed its demise. The riders, or picadors, had lances with which they stabbed at the bull, making it bleed and turn savage with rage, very unlike the docile beast that had entered the ring.

The bandilleros were the most skillful in my opinion. They stood facing the bull, then threw darts that pierced the bull's withers. The darts hung there so that the bull could see them, making it become even more agitated and angry. When this cruelty had lasted for perhaps half an hour, the matador appeared. He performed his movements with a sword and red cloak, which every reader of Hemingway knows about, before finally dispatching the bull with a thrust of his sword to the heart. I understand that if the matador had missed his target he would have had to pay a fine, because he was under contract to 'kill', I repeat 'kill', a certain number of bulls in the course of the corrida de toros.

By this time my friend and I had both been shouting 'Viva, El Toro!' for several minutes, and when the poor beast had finally sunk to the ground, we saw, on looking around, a man with a long-bladed knife approaching us. This was no time to sit and wait for a final thrust like the bull, so we leapt from our seats, exited the place in double-quick time and kept going until we had put several streets between ourselves and the bullring.

We found ourselves in an unfamiliar part of town. A pair of tall iron gates came into view ahead of us. In the garden behind were tables and chairs, which suggested a cafe or perhaps a restaurant. Coffee would be a good idea, we thought, as well as a place to hide from the knife-man who may have been still on our tail. A woman came out and beckoned us inside the building, where there were more tables and chairs. We ordered coffee and cakes, and waited.

The place was completely empty of people. A silence brooded over the scene and no sounds could be heard coming from the depths. Thus it was a small shock to hear, as if on cue, doors opening above us. I looked up and saw a gallery with stairs that wound down from the roof area to the ground floor where we were sitting. It was a tall building and there were at least a dozen doors that opened out on to the gallery. Girls appeared, and filed down the stairs. As they came level with us, each one in turn raised her shift, which was her only garment, and then sat briefly on our laps. Apart from a flimsy shift, the young women were naked, and they all seemed very young to me.

Meanwhile, the woman had locked the iron gates with a key from the huge bunch that dangled from her waist. Being still a virgin, and mindful of the posters in Finchley Drill Hall, I was shocked, and afraid in a way that I did not understand. I rushed into the garden and demanded to be let out. The woman was most unpleasant. She refused to open the gates at first, but when I pushed between her and the house and threatened her with physical violence unless she did, she obliged.

My friend stayed the course. When I asked him for a report the next day, he said that he'd only remained for an hour. The girl was only twelve, and so he just talked to her for that hour, gave her some money and left. Thinking about the events of that afternoon, I later also wondered about the livelihoods of the ladies in the carriages and around the barrier at the 'corrida'.

The day eventually dawned when we received our sailing orders. Food, water and fuel were taken aboard, watches were set and we left harbour at dusk the same day. Basil's courses once more proved a pleasure to follow and the passage was remarkable for its lack of incident. I had a thought, as we passed Gib and headed east, that at last we were joining the war and not sitting on the edge of it. However, it was impossible to sustain this idea for long. We saw no enemy aircraft and heard no gunfire the whole way.

The island of Malta loomed out of a heat haze one morning, then disappeared, and I wondered if I had experienced a mirage. It was a full hour before I saw it again, this time large, unmistakable and close. We had signalled our ETA some time before and entered Valletta as the sun reached its zenith. The harbour was crammed with warships and transports of all sizes. I could see no place where a small vessel could tie up. A light started flashing from one of the buildings and we were directed to go round to Sliema Creek. This was more like it. There were Fairmile MLs, HDMLs, MTBs and trawlers moored in various places.

Most vessels were moored 'stern to', with an anchor out forward and a line to the shore that was provided with bollards. The reason for this way of tying up was two-fold. First, there was only a small section of harbour wall vacant and, second, it was much safer to keep the hulls of the boats clear of land if possible, because rats were rife in Malta. They lived in holes in the soft sandstone rock that surrounded the water on all sides, and they carried bubonic plague. At that time, plague was present in Rabat and in North Africa, and vessels often arrived from there, bringing dates and vegetables.

We berthed amid the other HDMLs and, for the first time, did so 'stern to'. I had no experience of this method, which is very rarely used back in the UK. Having dropped anchor, well out from the shore, I went slowly astern until the cable was taut. Fortunately, there was someone on land to take our lines, which were hauled until rigid. We had to launch the dinghy, as a gangplank was not yet in place. I noticed that the boats around us had baffles on the shorelines to stop rats from coming aboard. These were mostly made from the lids of biscuit tins and cut around to give a sharp edge to the circumference.

I went ashore to make my report to the XDO and to take in the geography of the harbour and surrounding buildings. The base was on the other side of the water which was crossed by hailing a 'dgħajsa'. This was an open craft, sixteen feet long and similar in appearance to a gondola. It was rowed forward by a man standing upright. These constituted one half of the Maltese taxi service. The other half served the land in the form of open carts, bearing a sunshade and drawn by a pony. They held four people and were known as 'garrys'.

Malta had been heavily bombed by the Luftwaffe during the first eighteen months of the war, and showed signs of much damage. Fourteen thousand tons of bombs were dropped during this period. At one time, when the air raids were at their height, many people left their homes and lived in caves that abound the island. There is very little soil covering the rock and at one time all ships over a certain size had to bring a quantity of earth as part of their harbour dues. As a result, much of the island's vegetable produce was grown at St Paul's Bay, where the soil was thickest. Malta's many churches were beautiful, built from the local sandstone that is easy to quarry and work.

At the time of our arrival the raids had largely subsided, owing to the brave efforts of a fighter squadron that had been established on the island, and the huge firepower of the great number of ships assembled in the harbours of Valletta and Sliema. Malta had been kept alive by a constant passage of convoys carrying food, which were protected by the Royal Navy and the RAF. The RN lost many ships in the process, and more than 500 fighter planes were lost over Malta alone. By the time we joined it, the task force being assembled on the island was fully operational. A very busy and well-equipped dockyard and a naval base with every facility were present on the island.

The XDO informed me that a major operation was being prepared. This was obvious from the traffic in the harbour, but he would give no further details. Meanwhile, we would be employed in various ways and were to keep our vessels, in all respects, ready for sea at all times. A packet of sealed orders would be issued to each boat. These were not to be opened until a signal was received from the operations room at NOIC's headquarters.

I returned on board and assembled the crew to inform them of most of what I had been told. I let the men know that maximum leave would be granted, but that every man must remain within sight and sound of the ship as we were all on constant stand-by. Shops and bars could all be seen plainly from the waterfront so there was no problem with these instructions. Basil and I dined on board. Cook provided a meal that was edible, but only just, as provisions from shore were not yet in stock. I did not know that this would be the last meal the two of us would enjoy together.

The next day I went to the base to investigate amenities, if any, of the civil side of the naval establishment. There was a comfortable common room in the Officers' Club and a well-appointed dining room. Stewards in white coats waited at the tables. The food looked and smelled delicious, though it was clearly a problem to protect the dishes from the swarms of flies that hovered above each covered receptacle.

This was the first time I had been in a Royal Naval Officers' Club. Hitherto I had confined my visits to the operations side of the bases I had visited. Here was an example of the peacetime, pre-war navy. The club had large, carpeted rooms furnished with wicker chairs, oriental-style sofas, magazine racks and side tables carefully arranged in between. White-coated stewards flitted about the rooms ready to respond to the slightest need of the officers and their wives. I ordered a drink and sat at one of the small tables listening to the talk around me. On this day only women were present and the conversations were, I suppose, typical of the time.

'My dear, it's a scandal, a positive scandal,' said one woman. 'My husband's two years his senior, and the man's got his command before John!'

'Really, are you sure?' said the other.

'Of course, I'm sure, I looked it up in the Navy List.'

There was always a copy of this valuable work on display in one or other of the rooms, and it was much consulted by the ladies. I made many visits to the club and heard this sort of talk quite often.

On returning on board there was a surprise waiting for me. Basil was busy packing his gear. He had been appointed CO of one of the other HDMLs moored near us. The appointment was to take immediate effect. I was delighted for Basil's sake, but sad to lose him, he had been a loyal friend and a first-rate No 1.

There was also a signal for me on the wardroom table, informing me that another officer would be joining 1297 as First Lieutenant the following day. I shook hands with my No 1 and thanked him for all his good work on board, especially for his chart work. We opened the only bottle of gin on board and shared a quick drink to mark the occasion. I drank a toast to his success and watched him go ashore with real regret.

The following morning my new First Lieutenant arrived and was introduced to the crew. Later that day the Cox'n asked me if I would pass on to Basil the crew's best wishes and regrets that he had left us. I was pleased about this and, of course, I did so. It is often a difficult time in a small ship when an important member of the ship's company leaves. A lot of readjustment has to be made, and inwardly I was a worried man, although I tried hard not to show it. It is a sign of my regard for Basil that I could never remember the new officer's name, and cannot even recall it to this day. I shall therefore refer to him as 'John'.

For several days we had no duties to perform, and the time was spent overhauling the equipment from stem to stern. John settled in quickly. He had been No 1 on another HDML, which was fortunate, but he didn't have that ready turn of phrase that had enabled Basil to communicate so easily with the crew.

A period of waiting now began, a period with minor jobs to fill the time before the 'big event'. On one of these days I was ordered to move from my mooring, take the boat round to Valletta Harbour and berth alongside the dockyard. For me it was a great day. The authorities were finally going to remove those wretched deck tanks, and what a difference their absence made. At last we looked like a ship again and, in spite of what Milford Haven had said, I knew the boat would handle better.

One or two anti-submarine patrols were ordered, usually in company with other HDMLs, because during our four days in the dockyard the very latest anti-sub detection was fitted and echo-sounding equipment was installed. These instruments could only properly be tested at sea. The officers and men of the HDMLs quickly got to know one another, and ship visits took place often. On one such occasion the COs assembled in one of the wardrooms and held a water party. The water in Malta was practically undrinkable unless heavily disguised with alcohol. There was no natural spring water on the island, so it had to be distilled from seawater. It really was ghastly stuff. One day a tanker arrived from the UK bearing tanks of delicious Cornish spring water. The word spread quickly and the little ships were the first to get alongside and fill up with this liquid from heaven. The senior CO then invited the others to a water party. Glass after glass of cold Cornish water was gulped down, until we actually became drunk. I do believe it is possible to get drunk on water, especially if you have been deprived of it for long enough.

Soon after the water party, I received a signal to berth alongside the base where I would receive further instructions. As we were tying up, a group of officials arrived with a very important-looking person, who I later was told was Lord Gort, the Governor and Commander-in-Chief of Malta. I was instructed to take him to a frigate that was patrolling some thirty miles south-east of the island. I was given a rendezvous while my No 1 took the great man into our small wardroom.

The weather was calm and the passage uneventful. However, we nearly lost Lord Gort during the transfer to the warship, because he refused to be given a 'bosun's chair'. This could have been lowered to our deck, and hauled up again with the person in it. Instead he tried to manage without it. As he reached out to grasp the frigate's gunwale, the vessels parted in the swell. He slipped partway down between the two hulls, but the crew members of the warship managed to grab his arms, just in time, before the vessels came together. Had we lost this important figure, the course of the war in the Mediterranean might have changed. We said a few prayers of thanksgiving for the life of the great man, Viscount Lord Gort, VC, and then returned to our berth at Sliema Creek.

I had not as yet had time to get to know John, our new First Lieutenant, so we decided to eat on board and spend the evening in conversation. It appeared that he had had six months' experience as First Lieutenant in one of the other HDMLs in Malta, having been sent straight from the UK as a passenger on the light cruiser *Calypso*, a sister ship to the *Arethusa*, my first ship. He was a serious young man, a year or so younger than me, and seemed very keen to do his best. His chart work was efficient, but he lacked the polish that Basil gave to his work. We discussed many things, with particular reference to discipline. I told him that he would have a well-trained crew to deal with and one of the best Coxswains in the flotilla. We were always referred to as a 'flotilla', even though the six HDMLs rarely worked together.

We finished talking, and the bottle of Cyprus wine, and went to bed. We were woken at two in the morning by an uproar that seemed to be coming from around the corner where the main fleet was assembled, in Valletta Harbour. The noise was hard to categorise: shouts, ship's sirens, drumbeats, all mingled in a cacophony of sound. It did not die down for at least an hour, after which sporadic bursts of noise continued, gradually fading until it finally stopped and peace reigned. By then it was 4.00am.

In the morning I discovered the cause of the commotion. To put it simply, the cause of the disturbance was the 'Barber's Pole', no less. This was a most important totem, or symbol, of daring. Any ship that held it was open to a sudden attack by another ship, and at any time. It found its way around the fleet in this way, and by some sort of bush telegraph, its whereabouts were always known. When conditions were right, such as a long stay in harbour, you could be sure that the ship holding the totem would be raided. At such a time the authorities, in the person of officers, would be strangely absent.

In spite of the firm discipline that governed naval life, the powers that ruled were strangely tolerant of occasional outbursts like the 'Barber's Pole' episode. Any opportunity to lighten the existence of the personnel, living in often cramped conditions for many days, would be encouraged, or at least tolerated. The officers, by whom I mean the COs, often sent each other amusing, and sometimes rude, signals via flashes from an Aldis lamp. Here are a couple of examples probably well known to naval and ex-naval people.

Admiral Somerville, CO of the Mediterranean fleet at the time, received two decorations on the same day, which was very unusual. Somerville was flying his flag in a battle cruiser making for Malta to join the task force assembling there, when another capital ship, also heading for Malta, flashed him a signal, 'What, twice in a day at your age?' Somerville's reply was to order all guns to maximum elevation!

There was also a story circulating in the base concerning a mistake in the wording of a signal. It was customary for senior officers, four-ring officers and above, to employ a woman from ashore to look after their laundry, so that whenever they were in harbour a signal would be flashed to the watchtower, requesting the woman to be sent. The lady in question would be ferried out to the ship where she would inspect the officer's wardrobe and take ashore anything to be washed or dry cleaned. On this occasion the signal read, 'From CO HMS **** send Admiral's woman.' Followed immediately by another signal, 'Correction, insert "washer" between Admiral and woman.' I have no idea whether this was true or not, but it was supposed to have some basis in fact.

I must have received several signals of a frivolous nature, but I only remember one. We had recently repainted the hull of 1297 using a camouflage pattern, as we were likely to operate close to shore sometimes. A passing destroyer flashed us saying, 'Who knitted that?' I forget our reply. It was common practice to use biblical quotations to disguise the real meaning. That's enough about signals.

The evening following the 'Barber's Pole' event, I dined at the Officers' Club, and it was a luxury to have a drink brought to one on a tray, and to be waited upon by stewards at table. I ate a splendid curry, with rice and mango chutney, followed by apple pie and coffee. I remember that evening meal well because it was the last one before I went down with a bad bout of 'sandfly fever'. This is an unpleasant complaint with flu-like symptoms that last about a week. I had a high temperature and could not stop my limbs from shaking. Somehow I managed to get ashore and report to the base sick bay. I was put in the Naval Hospital, where I stayed for five days, wondering if 'the balloon' had gone up in my absence.

When I came out I was reassured to find everything as it had been before. The ships that I remembered were still at their moorings, and the earlier feeling of expectancy seemed to have dissipated to some extent. It seems that it is at such times 'Action Stations' are sounded. After a day or two I felt well enough to take an interest in life ashore as well as life aboard.

During this prolonged period of waiting, I took the opportunity to explore the island and to swim off the eastern shore, away from buildings and people. It was during one such swim that I met a Wren who was also in the habit of swimming there. We got to know one another a little, and I invited her to a meal in one of the cafes, followed by a visit to the cinema afterwards. We sat in the gallery, and although I don't remember the film, I do remember that she ate apples during the evening, and spat the pips over the barrier and on to the audience below.

I did not meet her again, but I tried my luck with a Maltese young lady whom I met in a church that we were both admiring. She was the daughter of one of the five great families who owned and controlled the civil side of Malta. Apart from owning most of the land that was not in the hands of the Navy or Air Force, they owned huge business interests that reached into many countries that bordered the Mediterranean.

The young lady I came to know belonged to the Scicluna family. She invited me to the Scicluna mansion to meet her mother, the Marquise. This lady exhibited every sign of ancient nobility. She walked with a slight stoop and carried an ebony, silver-mounted stick. The house surrounded a courtyard on four sides, which was shaded with palms and cooled by a fountain in the centre. Her husband, a man of enormous girth, sat beneath one of these palms and gazed into space without moving a muscle or twitching an eyelid. He seemed to be made of stone. His hands were spread on a silk square that covered his knees, and his fingers were extended to reveal nails that grew at least six inches beyond their roots. They had curled into tubes. It must, I thought, be part of some religious observance.

The Marquise was probably of French extraction and conversed with her family only in that language. The daughter took me to her room where she played gramophone records and offered me iced tea. It was a colourful experience, but the sight of those nails unnerved me. I did not repeat the visit and used the exigencies of the service to excuse my hasty exit from an affair that had never really begun.

Shortly after the Scicluna visit I was lucky enough to hear the great pianist Solomon, who was visiting Malta. Born Solomon

Cutner in the East End of London in 1902, he was universally known only by his first name. I heard him play by accident. I was returning from a walk and passing down a street through a residential area of large well-appointed houses, which mercifully had not been bombed. Towards the middle of one row there was a house, larger than the rest, from which came the most beautiful piano music I had ever heard. It was Solomon practising for that evening's performance.

For nearly an hour I stood by a corner of the building and listened. The wonderful succession of notes lifted me out of the street on a bubble of sound. I forgot my ship, I forgot Malta, I forgot the war. When the last notes died away, I saw him get up and leave the room. Through the window I saw that there were no music sheets at the piano; I did not know until then that these great artists stored everything in their heads. It was Solomon who on that one afternoon taught me to love and try to understand classical music. In the days that followed I was to think often of that afternoon. It was a prelude to what was to come. The same evening I received a signal to open the sealed orders.

There were two signals waiting for me in the wardroom when I returned aboard. One instructed me to 'ensure, I repeat, ensure' that HDML 1297 was 'in all respects ready for sea'. The other was a short command. It simply said that I was to open the sealed orders at noon the following day.

I assembled the ship's company and informed them that the operation for which we had been sent from the UK was about to start. The First Lieutenant and myself then inspected the entire ship from stem to stern, especially the guns. Everyone had been given an action station earlier in the UK, and they were all tested, several times, before leaving Gibraltar. They were tested again during our rounds. The Chief reported all well in the engine room with no mechanical problems. It was then only a question of waiting the next few hours and attending to personal things, like a letter home etc. The cook produced a sumptuous curry with rice and chutney, which was every bit as good as the one I had had in the Naval Club. It also had the advantage of being free from flies. He followed the curry with a plum duff, which was always a favourite in the navy. John and I studied the charts of southern Italy and Sicily, as I was convinced that the operation would take place in that area. The Eighth Army had made great progress in North Africa and part of their strength was likely to be employed in Italy, rather than the Balkans.

Precisely at noon I opened the sealed orders in John's presence, and we pored over the contents. A copy of a chart of southern Italy and Sicily was enclosed, with a star marking one of the beaches on the southern side of the island. This was to be our objective. We were instructed to sail in our own time and to reach 'position X' by midnight of that day. At ten knots, which was our usual cruising speed, I reckoned on leaving almost at once, certainly not later that 2.00pm. All hands were mustered, and at 1.30pm we passed out of Sliema Creek and set course for Sicily. The orders stated that we were to remain in 'position X' until directed by C-in-C Operations, who was Admiral Vian.

CHAPTER 4

❋

Italian operations

1942

It was approximately 100 miles to our beach, and there was time to check everything once more, and to feed the ship's company in daylight hours. There was no knowing how long it would be before we would be able to eat again once the action had started. The weather was unusually calm for the time of year. There was no wind, and the sea was glazed and rigid. A feather could have disturbed the surface.

The afternoon dwindled into dusk, and suddenly it was dark. There was no moon and clouds hid the stars. The conditions had been chosen with care, for it was impossible to see very far in any direction. I now understood the reason for the sealed orders that were not to be opened until the day of departure. Then, an hour before midnight, I witnessed a scene that I can still see in my mind's eye to this day.

It was almost 11.00pm when the clouds cleared before a light breeze and the surface of the water became bathed in bright starlight. I looked astern to see what looked like thousands of ships, each in its own pool of sparkling sea. A vast armada was moving quietly towards the beaches of Sicily. Then suddenly there was a hissing sound, one that grew louder every second, and announced another sort of armada, nature's own armada. A few yards from us the surface was suddenly broken, as if glass was being shattered, and huge black shapes leapt from the surface, dived and then leapt again. There must have been more than fifty of them, because I gave up counting after thirty. They were swordfish and they kept diving and leaping until they had passed out of sight. I tried to forget this wonderful sight, although I felt privileged to have seen such a spectacle, and concentrate on the business at hand. It was only later that I realised how lucky we had been to see at close quarters something so dramatic and probably so rare.

There was certainly a huge force coming up astern. Every part of the visible ocean was occupied, and I felt a twinge of sadness for the Sicilians who were to receive this mighty onslaught. We arrived at our position and waited for orders. So far there had been no action ashore. We were less than two hundred yards from the beach with no sight or sound apparent. I remember being surprised by the quietness of this great force approaching the shore.

At 1.00am a destroyer flying the Admiral's pennant came alongside, and the C-in-C himself stood in the waist and addressed us through a loudhailer. We were instructed to lead the landing craft into the beach as they were disgorged from the mother ships. The landing craft were roughly thirty feet long and held about thirty men and their equipment. At the same time as these carriers were heading for the beach, Landing Craft, Tank (LCTs) were arriving with the heavy armour. Each LCT carried eight tanks and other wheeled transport. We were told not to make smoke unless ordered. A number of infantry transports had got ashore before any sign of resistance became apparent. There was a small amount of rifle fire and the occasional sound of something heavier.

Daylight saw the remainder of the army in our sector disembark safely, land, then disappear into the interior. The almost silent approach seemed to have worked. Round the corner of a headland, nearer to Syracuse, the majority of the invading party were deployed and it was impossible to know how they were faring, or what resistance was being offered. We remained on station for two days, and in the late afternoon of the second day the destroyer returned and ordered us to proceed to Syracuse at first light the next morning.

We entered Syracuse in the late afternoon and I looked for a place to tie up. There was a vacant piece of harbour wall with some fishing boats at one end. As the landings had been a surprise, it was unlikely it had been mined. Fishing boats proved to be a useful guide in this respect, in many places later on. I believe we were the first ship to enter, but I cannot be sure of this. Some of the other HDMLs might have been hidden in other parts of the port. Fighting was still going on in the outskirts of the town. Columns of smoke could be seen rising from the buildings, and the sound of bursting shells and machine-gun fire was audible, though distant.

I wanted to give the crew leave but could not be sure of the safety of the place. Unarmed sailors could be an easy target for snipers. So I decided on a bit of reconnaissance and, having armed myself with one of the two revolvers on board, I strolled ashore. The street bordering the waterfront was deserted but, on turning into the town itself, I was astonished to see shops still open with a few customers entering and leaving. A figure in battledress tapped me on the shoulder from behind, making me wheel round, gun at the ready.

'Amazing, isn't it, how quickly they get going? You can engage the enemy at one of the street and they will open for business at the other end!'

It was a relief to hear the voice of an English soldier. He was part of the garrison left behind to administer the town until the arrival of the navy, who would then take over the port and establish full control. He said the initial landings had been as easy as 'Kiss your Aunt Fanny', but resistance had stiffened inland. Most of the army facing them was Italian, but he said it seemed that German officers were directing them. It was a pleasure to talk to this soldier, who wore the stripes of a sergeant and spoke with real authority. He assured me that the town itself had been thoroughly searched for snipers and the population showed every sign of relief that the British were taking over. He explained that the resistance, on the outskirts of town, was caused by a detachment of German infantry occupying a ruined church. They had several machine guns, and seemed well supplied with ammunition.

'They won't last long,' he said. 'Once we start using the heavy stuff.' The sergeant assured me that my men would be in no danger if they kept to the shopping areas. He then saluted smartly and marched off. I reflected that we were lucky to have such men to protect us on land, however much we might pride ourselves for our competence at sea. The crew had been confined aboard for most of three days and nights, and I was glad to be able to let them get some exercise. As the son of my Father, I believed implicitly in the value of exercise and was determined always to use every opportunity to give leave for a 'run ashore'.

No 1 assembled the hands on the fo'c'sle and I warned them to be vigilant at all times and not give away any information, no matter how innocent, of operations or our presence in Syracuse. The most serious warning related to looting. Anyone caught looting would immediately be reported to the Garrison Commander and the offender arrested. Everyone was to keep within sound and, wherever possible, within sight of the ship. For the rest of the day two hours for each watch would be allowed, this would give everyone time to see the town in daylight. In future we would revert to the normal four hours for each watch, duty permitting.

John then went ashore, promising to look for a way to get fresh water, of which we were badly in need. We had about two days' supply left, after which it would be severely rationed. I then went below and, knowing that a sentry was on watch on the bridge, I crept into my bunk and fell instantly asleep.

John was kind enough not to wake me, and it was midnight before I awoke to the sound of a ship's screws turning. The vibrations carry long distances through water and penetrate the hull if your ear happens to be against the ship's side. I went on deck to see a destroyer manoeuvring alongside ahead of us, and I was glad that we were well tucked in by fishing boats at the other end. In the morning I saw that it was the same warship from which Admiral Vian had addressed us, but his pennant was no longer flying. No doubt he had transferred his flag to another vessel, as other landings were taking place further up the coast towards Catania.

John told me that he had had no luck in finding water, although there were hydrant points on the quay. If all else failed, I reckoned that I could get water from the destroyer. Usually larger warships were willing to help smaller vessels like us in these matters. I need not have worried, because even as I registered this thought, a number of naval vessels entered the harbour. Two armed trawlers, a frigate and a tanker all anchored in the middle of the dock. Apart from fuel, tankers nearly always carried fresh water. It was a large tanker and I felt sure that it was here to supply everyone until an onshore water supply could be organised.

Without wasting a moment I ordered hands to let go and, with engines at half speed, headed for the tanker. It was essential to get there before the rush started. I already saw two trawlers and an HDML, which had appeared from nowhere, making their way in the same direction as us. Luckily we arrived first and hailed the tanker, who assured us that they could supply water and fuel. We made fast and enjoyed the sound of water flowing into our tanks. We took on fuel and returned to our berth.

The buildings fronting the harbour wall were quickly requisitioned, and an armed guard placed around them. Men from the two warships then carried equipment and boxes into these premises. By evening the process of setting up a naval base had been completed. The frigate and destroyer left before dark. Two cargo vessels took their places at the dock wall and immediately began landing transport in the form of Jeeps and pick-up trucks. Other vessels arrived every day for the rest of the week, bringing food, clothing and chandlery.

Two days passed before an authority in the base was established. During this time maximum leave was given, watch by watch. I happened to be on the bridge when the port watch was going ashore and noticed that Sparks, who normally wore a beard, was clean-shaven. I asked what had happened to his beard, and he said that he had been to a barber for a shave. I was appalled. I told him that I considered that he had taken a very great risk. Fighting on the edges of town had still been going on while he was in the shop. The barber may have lost his house, even had family and friends killed or wounded by our gunfire and the chance to use a cut-throat razor for a purpose other than a shave may have been too great to resist. As soon as possible I warned the whole ship's company of this danger.

We were left in peace for all of three days and then received our first signal from the new base. 'To HDML 1297 – proceed to

north-east corner of harbour and berth ahead of trawler H75.'
There were three other HDMLs in this backwater and I decided to
visit them while hands were making fast. Two had been engaged
in the same task as we had on the beaches further north. One had
sustained minor damage from gunfire and the other, like us, had
encountered no resistance.

The CO of the third HDML was ashore when I visited,
but he came aboard as I was leaving. To my surprise and
pleasure it was Basil Knight. He had followed us out a
week later from Milford Haven and so he missed the storm
off Ushant. A few days out from Malta he had experienced
serious engine trouble and had to limp the rest of the way
on one engine at half speed. His ship had spent the entire
six weeks of their stay in Malta in the hands of engineers. He
then proceeded directly to Syracuse without taking part in the
landings. He must have entered Syracuse while I was ashore or
in the wardroom. It was a further five days before any of us
were given any duties.

The air raids, which had mysteriously halted during the
invasion of the southern beaches of Sicily, now started again
in earnest. Fighters from Malta did heroic work in protecting
Syracuse and the newly won territory. Nevertheless, many bombs
were dropped on the harbour, but luckily most of them fell in the
water. In the port, the ships put up a heavy barrage that prevented
accurate bomb aiming.

Soon enough the boring patrols began for the three HDMLs,
which meant two nights in port and one at sea, which I suppose
was a luxury. 1297 had carried out two of these patrols, which
meant keeping an anti-submarine watch in the approaches to
the entrance to Syracuse Harbour, when on our return from
the second at 8.00am and having been relieved by Basil's boat, I
received a signal to proceed to the base and report to the XDO,

who was now in operation. I was instructed to remain alongside until a high-ranking army officer arrived on board. He was to be given every facility in the way of comfort that the navy could offer, and we were to carry out his wishes consonant with the safety of the ship. This could have meant anything, I thought. Did 'safety' mean that we were to avoid action? It was a puzzle soon to be solved. The XDO left the room and returned with a large-scale chart of the Albanian coast. He pointed to a very tiny inlet with a small town behind it marked Preveza.

'That's where you are to land him,' he said, 'But if you see evidence of mines the operation is to be aborted until further instructions are signalled to you.' The word safety was now explained. The XDO gave me the chart and I left.

Our passenger arrived an hour later and was piped on board. I saluted him. He was a Major General, as I learned as we shook hands and exchanged names and titles. He wore full army uniform bearing the insignia of his rank, and bore two revolvers in holsters around his waist. In addition, he carried a map-case, binoculars and a small rucksack.

The distance to Preveza was approximately 300 miles and I reckoned we would need 30 hours to complete the passage. I explained that we would arrive in the late afternoon, at roughly 6.00pm if we left at 12.00 noon. It was then 10.00am. I took him down to the wardroom. All hands went to dinner at 10.30am as an easterly was blowing, which would make our meals difficult at sea. The cook did his best, but no fresh provisions were as yet available at the base. We ate oxtail soup, followed by corned beef fritters, tinned carrots and bread. The coffee helped disguise the taste of the fritters. The General seemed to enjoy it, though he was probably too polite to do otherwise, and ate with gusto.

At exactly 12.00 noon we slipped our mooring and made for the entrance. At sea I noted the weather with some concern.

I had calculated on a speed of ten knots in order to arrive before dark, but the easterly meant that we would be in the trough the whole way. A beam sea would not necessarily hold us back, but life would be very uncomfortable. The ship would heave and roll, like a cow in labour.

For the first watch the General stood with us on the bridge. The colour drained from his face before an hour had passed, but he stood his ground. The boat certainly rolled, and unless the wind veered or backed, it would be one long roll the whole way. At 4.00pm John came up to relieve me, and cook sent up cocoa with some bread and cheese. Noble chap! It could not have been easy down in the galley. Excluding the gale off Ushant, this was the most difficult sea we had encountered since leaving Milford Haven. I looked anxiously at the General. I offered him some cocoa and something to eat. He only shook his head, lurched to the ship's side, and was sick. He could barely stand and I helped him down to the wardroom. He collapsed onto my bunk, where he remained for the rest of the passage.

During the night the wind veered a little, which reduced the roll somewhat, but produced a bit of a headwind, which was likely to slow us down. I therefore called down to the Chief and asked him to increase the revs very slowly until we were three-quarters ahead. The boat was now pounding violently but maintained the necessary speed. It was essential to reach Preveza before dark in order to find our way in and, above all else, to be able to check for mines in the clear water. I was banking on the water being as clear as it was off Sicily.

The four-hour watches came and went with no further change in the weather, and at 4.30pm on the day after we left Syracuse, we sighted land. It looked as if my speed calculations might have been correct. The difficulty that now arose was to be able to identify the inlet for Preveza in such a broken coastline. Six in the evening found us cruising close to the shore with a mine lookout on the bow. The pilot showed several landmarks and, Heavens be praised, a water tower behind the town marked Preveza. We had only to look for a water tower, and that would be it. Fortunately, the sea was now calm and we were in the lee of a headland. A headland would be the most likely area to shelter an inlet to a small port, and that proved to be the case. We steered straight for the headland and within minutes a water tower came into sight. The sea was clear and revealed no mines as we crept slowly into the tiny harbour. There was only a broken-down timber jetty, but fortunately one end looked intact and solid enough for us to make fast.

I went below to inform our passenger. His eyes were closed and his face was stained with dry saliva. By his side was a bucket that contained the evidence of his suffering. 'Excuse me, sir,' I said. 'But we are now alongside in Preveza Harbour. It is 6.30pm and there are two hours of daylight left.'

I then went straight back to the bridge so as not to embarrass him as he recovered. I had barely reached the bridge before he appeared, his face wiped clean, his uniform straightened, his cap on and his equipment in position. I was astonished because I was expecting him to remain on board for at least an hour while his body regained strength and perhaps accepted some food. He stood rigidly upright, literally commanding his limbs to obey his mind, thanked me, saying that he would not be returning, shook my hand and marched ashore. I watched the upright figure until he was out of sight. Not for the first time I had occasion to admire the courage and discipline of our soldiers.

I decided to leave after the crew had been fed. John ordered food for all hands as soon as possible, and I climbed ashore for a quick stroll while it was being prepared. The small town was a ruin with hardly a house left standing. It consisted of one street lined on each side by ruins. I decided to walk to the end of the road and return. The place was deserted. No human being was to be seen or heard; utter silence prevailed. The place had been shelled by either the Germans, or possibly by one of the warlords operating throughout the Balkans and Greece. I was halfway back along the street when a figure came out of one of the buildings and walked towards me. I was armed with a revolver and cocked it in readiness should it be necessary. The man, dressed in tattered overalls with patches of camouflage, passed by me without turning his head or showing that he had seen me. One side of his face was moving. Maggots were doing the job of more civilised medical attention.

Dinner was yet another version of corned beef, and I wondered why no one bothered to fish. The small harbour was alive with fish. I could see them swarming around the hull and the piles of the jetty, but I rejected the idea of catching some of them for the wardroom. I did not want to give the cook more trouble after he had struggled so manfully to overcome his own seasickness to keep us fed, working in a place little bigger than a cupboard. We still had some of his excellent bread, and that made up for a lot.

At 9.00pm we cast off and headed for Sicily, speed eight knots. The beam wind was still with us but a little more on the starboard quarter so that the roll was less, but the movement was lumpy. By midnight the wind fell away to nothing, and the rest of the passage was made in an ever-decreasing sea, which became calm ten hours from home.

The war ashore had moved some miles north of Syracuse while we had been away and now raged around Catania, where very stiff resistance was being experienced. John and the cook spent much time during our harbour days trying to obtain some fresh food. They succeeded only in finding vegetables, which they managed to purchase using our ready-use fund.

We were back to the patrols for the next three weeks, until one morning at the end of October, when we were ordered to proceed to Catania, which was now in the hands of our forces. With the fall of that port, rapid progress was possible. Supplies could be brought nearer to the front lines and it would not be long before the whole of Sicily would be in our hands. The instruction was to carry out an anti-submarine watch the whole way, and to search the harbour for obstructions to shipping, such as cables and boom defences. The harbour was thought unlikely to have been mined, because shipping was seen to be using it immediately before its capture. But cables can be stretched across in a matter of minutes. These orders were executed and we were able to report no obstructions.

Catania was surrounded by farmland. During the three days we were there the cook and No 1 came to know some of the farmers and were able to purchase some fresh vegetables and a quantity of flour. Meat was still a problem. We were all heartily sick of corned beef and Spam. On one visit they noticed a small pig grubbing in the yard. It was less than a month old and still feeding from its mother. They bought the piglet for forty cigarettes, with the idea of fattening it up for Christmas. I saw no objection to this, provided the animal was kept on the upper deck and never allowed below. One of the crew had been apprenticed to a carpenter in peacetime and within a couple of hours, during his watch ashore, he knocked up a quite respectable hutch made from wood that he had found in a deserted barn. I did not ask too many questions about this and assumed that the Chief had lent him tools from the engine room.

The little pig quickly made himself at home in his hutch, which was secured to the gun mounting on the coach roof behind the dinghy. This was a sheltered spot out of everybody's way. He didn't seem to miss his mother's milk, and appeared quite happy living on vegetables, of which we had a plentiful supply. In calm weather he was allowed to run loose on the deck, and quickly endeared himself to the crew by allowing people to play with him. They called him 'Diesel' on account of his slippery skin.

At first light of our fourth day in Catania, we were recalled to Syracuse. I noted as we left, several large cargo vessels and a tanker, escorted by a destroyer, entering the harbour. The base flashed us as we entered Syracuse, and I was requested to report to the XDO as soon as possible. We were lucky enough to find our old berth vacant.

At the base I gave a full account of conditions in Catania so far as I could judge. I reported the abundance and availability of fresh water that could be obtained from hydrants on the harbour wall. We had filled our tanks and found the water delicious. The mountainous country surrounding Catania probably produces this spring water.

After giving my report I was instructed that I was to allow four men, heavily armed and dressed in Italian uniforms, on board. They were dirty, run down and terribly dishevelled. They were part of a special force under the directions of a brilliant soldier nick-named Popski. This force was comprised of less than fifty men at that time, and all were specialists. Each one spoke a number of languages, and each had to have a particular skill. They operated behind enemy lines, asked for no help or back-up and received none. These men were of several nationalities, including, among others, Hungarian, English, French, Romanian and Russian.

I was given a password and told that they would be having a conference on board. I was to carry out their instructions, which were to land them off the coast of Italy at night. When ashore they would destroy a strategic bridge vital to the enemy's ability to move troops and supplies south. The capture of the whole of Sicily was imminent. It was now important to hold up reinforcements from the north of Italy, so that Calabria, particularly the toe of Italy, could be invaded without facing huge resistance. Of course, there were other routes south, but this one lay in the path of a large concentration of German and Italian armour and infantry.

At 11.00am the next morning when I was on the bridge, our sentry reported that an Italian 'tramp' was asking to speak to me.

'The funny thing is, sir, he spoke good English,' he said.

'That's all right, sentry, I know about this,' I replied.

I asked the 'tramp' for the password, which was given. He, and the three other men with him, followed me to the wardroom and began their conference. They produced a map and held their discussion in Italian which, as far as I could judge, was faultless.

When they had finished, in view of their poor condition, I invited them to take some food, but they refused and only accepted a mug of tea. They were now all speaking English with only a slight accent, which sounded slightly German to me. One of the men was a specialist in unarmed combat. He showed me a piece of cheese-wire with a toggle on each end. It was said by the leader that this man could stealthily creep up on a sentry or guard without being detected, provided the man did not turn round, to within a foot, slip the looped wire over the man's head, pull the toggles tight and sever the head from the body.

Silence was the essence of all their work, and when an operation was completed, they simply 'melted' separately into the countryside. They stole their food, and sometimes transport, from the enemy or the local inhabitants. One of the other men specialised in ballistics. He was an expert in laying fuses and calculating exactly how much explosive to use on any particular job.

I now have to make a confession: I have no memory of the passage. The distance from Syracuse to their chosen landing place was approximately four hundred miles, which required forty hours in reasonable conditions. The departure was fixed for the last day of October, which was in four days' time, when there was no moon, but I do not remember leaving. However, I do have a mental picture of them leaving the boat and paddling ashore. Sometimes I think that it was in fact another HDML that Popski's men left Syracuse aboard, but it was definitely my vessel on which they held their conference, which therefore makes it most likely that it was my vessel that transported them. I shall assume that 1297 did the job.

The chosen landing place was roughly twenty miles north-west of Bari, which was later to become the second most important Allied base in the Adriatic. Although the passage is a blank in my memory, I do remember creeping in close to shore to watch these brave men set off for the beach in their rubber inflatable. The third and fourth men at the meeting were not there, and only two men went ashore. They carried an infra-red lamp and I asked them to signal me when they were ready to return. 'Thank you, sir, but we shall not be returning. The inflatable will be on the beach if it is of any use to you.' With that they paddled away.

I could just make out their figures in the gloom as they reached the beach and waded ashore. In less time than it takes me to write this, they vanished. Such people are rare, for they not only embody a remarkable set of skills; they possess the energy and willpower to employ those skills in the most difficult situations. They rise to any occasion, and seemingly nothing stops them but death or destruction. As with the passage out, I entirely forget the journey back to Syracuse.

Supplies of fresh food and commodities began to become obtainable from the base at Syracuse, and it was a great day when the cook came aboard with joints of beef and a quantity of salt pork. The joints were large and had to be butchered before they could be stored in our fridge. The Cox'n knocked on my door soon after this manna from Heaven had arrived, 'Excuse me, sir, but the crew have become fond of 'Diesel' and do not wish to slaughter him for Christmas. He is a sort of mascot. They would like to keep him until he is too large for his hutch, and then let him loose ashore. Would that be all right?' he said. 'Certainly, Cox'n, good idea,' I replied, as I too did not relish the idea of taking the little pig's life!

The whole of Sicily fell to the Eighth Army before we had completed another week of patrols, and Allied forces were gathering for the attack on the mainland. The 'toe' of Italy was the next planned operation. The great port of Taranto, a main objective, is situated in the huge Bay of Taranto, and was to become, after Malta, the No 1 naval base in the whole of the Mediterranean.

Events on land began to happen rapidly. The 'toe' of Italy surrendered very quickly, and Taranto fell into our hands. Every day the Eighth Army pushed a bit further into the mainland until meeting heavy resistance north of Taranto. Then the advance slowed to a stop, and it was some weeks before the strategic port of Bari was taken. Landings had also been made on the 'heel' of Italy, which secured the port of Brindisi. Brindisi became a useful base on the way up the Adriatic, and we sometimes patrolled that area.

An engineering department had been set up there in the Italian workshops, and facilities existed for engine overhaul. Our beautiful 'Gardners' had received no attention since leaving the UK, and Chief was of the opinion that they should be thoroughly serviced either in Malta or Brindisi. As Syracuse was still our base, I signalled the NOIC, requesting leave to put the work in the hands of either Brindisi or Malta. I heard nothing for twenty-four hours.

When the answer came it was a surprise. I cannot remember the exact wording of the message, but it instructed me to put the work in the hands of the engineers' base at Brindisi. The vessel was to be handed over to the base, and two weeks' leave given to all hands, including myself.

Now begins a period of which I am ashamed to this day. In Brindisi the crew drew pay from a temporary pay-office, and reckoned to spend it in Bari, which was a thriving town. Bari was captured a few days before our leave began. A seamen's mission was established, and an Officers' Club was opened in one of the hotels. The Chief remained on board for the first two days of leave, and most of his time was spent in the engine room with the base engineers.

Meanwhile, an Entertainments National Service Association (ENSA) concert party arrived to give a performance in Brindisi town hall. I cannot remember much about the show, but I met a female member of the cast afterwards, an event that became in every way a turning point in my life. We ate a meal in one of the cafes still open and at 12.00pm I took her on board as she was keen to see a naval ship, even one so small as our HDML. All the compartments of the ship were locked, the Chief having finally started his leave. I had a key to the wardroom and we drank a glass of wine and talked a little.

Readers of today may not believe what followed. I was twenty-three years old and had never experienced sexual intercourse, nothing beyond petting. Suddenly, in the moment after drinking the last of the wine, I became aware of death and aware that I might die before ever having known the secret of birth. I had absolutely no feelings for this girl, no attraction whatsoever. What took place on my bunk was, so far as I was concerned, purely a matter of animal instinct. I was worse than a novice, I was a complete stranger to the act, and this girl had to teach me everything. She stayed the night on board with me, and by morning the inner spring of desire had been flexed. I wanted more and decided to keep in touch with the girl if it were possible. She left me soon after 8.00am saying that the concert party would be spending the night at a place called Monopoli, before going on to Manfredonia where they had a week's engagement. Bari was well provided for with two theatres, and there was no place for a little concert party.

We had arranged to meet that night under the church clock in Monopoli at 11.00pm, and if there was no church clock then the church nearest the town centre would do instead. I had no idea how I would get there, and as I had done once before, I left it to chance. The concert party left Brindisi in their three trucks, one of which was for the props and scenery, and the other two were fitted up as sleeping quarters for the men and women. The girl vanished behind the port buildings, and I turned my attention to 'Diesel'.

He would have to be set free as there would be no one left on board to feed him after I had found accommodation for myself ashore, but his hutch was empty. Some thoughtful member of the crew had come to the same conclusion as myself. I learned later that 'Diesel' had been let loose in a field outside the town. It said much of his 'deliverer' that the pig had not been sold for meat.

That matter solved, I locked the wardroom and went ashore in search of breakfast, and to find a way to Monopoli before nightfall. I passed a general-cum-baker's shop near the docks. This would have to do. A loaf of bread, some sausage and a bottle of beer constituted breakfast, which I ate sitting in the shade of a plane tree. Although it was near to Christmas, it was still warm and most naval personnel were still in 'whites'.

I noticed a number of military vehicles heading north. I signalled one of them for a lift. The white uniform and cap-badge did the trick. The driver stopped and very politely invited me into his cab. I knew that Monopoli was almost exactly a hundred miles north of Brindisi, and realised that we would arrive well before midday. The road to Bari and beyond was alive with people and vehicles. Most of the traffic was military, but many of the figures were men and women who, like myself, were on leave and looking for a lift. Resistance in this part of Italy had quickly crumbled. The population co-operated fully with the military in an effort to return to a peacetime way of life as quickly as was possible. Men and women from all three services were able to walk the roads to visit the small towns and villages as safely as they would have in their own country.

The situation north of Manfredonia and in the rest of Italy was, however, vastly different. Mussolini's army, backed by a much larger number of German troops than had been present in Sicily and the 'toe' of Italy, were now holding up advances on all fronts. It was many months before the push up the Adriatic could gain the sort of momentum that accompanied our landings in the extreme south.

We arrived in Monopoli at 11.00am. I thanked the driver, and started off to explore the town. It was a poor place doing its best to smile. There were posters advertising the concert party. There was a fairground roundabout, on a patch of weedy grass, near the church which, I noted, did not have a clock. I wandered down to the beach but decided against having a swim as I didn't have a towel, and so I carried on exploring.

I came across the concert party trucks parked outside a dismal-looking hall. I could hear noise within, shouts, laughter and much banging of wood against wood. I thought that they must have been erecting some kind of stage. No doubt they would need the rest of the day to finish the work, eat and possibly rehearse, so I decided to leave it until our arranged time before trying to see the girl again. The fact that I cannot remember her name illustrates my utter lack of any other feeling but lust. Once more I record my shame.

At the northern end of the town I discovered a cafe that boasted two tables outside, and a bar. This was a cheering sight as I was beginning to regret the whole enterprise. It was now about 1.30pm by my watch as I entered the place. To my surprise, it was clean and the bar well stocked. I had a drink and ordered spaghetti Bolognese, which turned out to be excellent. There were some apples on the bar, and I ate two for dessert. I finished by drinking the worst cup of coffee I had as yet tasted. I think it must have been made from acorns. My spirits rose. After all, I was on two weeks' leave, what did it matter what happened later. What did it matter where I went, or what I did, as long as it did not disgrace the Service. Later, I would come close to doing that very thing.

I thanked the woman in charge as well as I could in my limited Italian. I then went in search of somewhere to sleep later. There were a number of establishments that we would call B&Bs in the town. I chose one that looked a bit better than the rest, and knocked on the door. No one came. I knocked and banged for several minutes until a woman came out from the house next door. She indicated by signs and simple phrases that the owner would not be back until later. She said that there was plenty of rooms vacant and that I could book a room with her and she would pass it on to her friend. I thanked her and went off looking for somewhere to pass the intervening hours until my rendezvous.

I passed a shop that had once sold newspapers, then turned back and went inside. There were no up-to-date papers, only yellowing copies of old ones. I asked if there was a library in Monopoli but was told that there wasn't. But I learned that the shop had at one time sold books as well as papers, and they still had some left in stock. Wonderful! Here was a real stroke of luck. In my joy at hearing this I quite forgot that we were in Italy and that it was unlikely that there would be anything in English. I was wrong. There were several in English, two in German and several dozen in French; I found a copy of *The Mill on the Floss*.

There were now six hours to wait before meeting the girl, and the battle between lust and comfort began in my head. Should I carry on waiting or hitch a lift back to Bari where there was a comfortable Officers' Club and a theatre? There was plenty of military transport going south to Bari and beyond. Lust won, a decision I later regretted, but for now it was necessary to find somewhere to wait and read my book. I tried the cafe where I had had lunch, hoping that they would remain open until at least 10.30pm. I explained the position and received a real welcome, although they normally closed at six. *The Mill on the Floss* and a bowl of soup at 8.30pm filled the time nicely.

I walked to the church half hoping that she wouldn't be there. Such is the inconsistency of man when he gives way to his senses without consulting his brain. Feelings come and go, and we are at their mercy. The girl was there in the churchyard. I had realised just before meeting her that evening that there was nowhere we could go at this hour to make love. What a silly euphemism that expression is. The ground was dry, but hard and dusty. I thought of the various B&Bs I had seen, but shrank from the task of confronting them. In England, in those days, it was almost impossible to take someone to a hostelry for sexual intercourse unless you faked marriage. I reckoned it would be more difficult in a mainly Catholic country.

We embraced briefly. I was about to ask her if it would be possible to use one of the concert party's trucks, when I caught sight of the roundabout. Romance took over at once. Here was the chance to do something unusual, something in a way romantic.

It would transmute the base metal of lust into adventure. Why not on the back of a roundabout horse? The great machine had a canvas cover all round the base with a loose flap for entry. Inside it was quite warm, and the open top allowed sufficient light in for the business in hand and, to be honest, that's just what it was, business.

The floor of the roundabout was dirty, which made it easy for me to insist that we use the back of a horse. I remember nothing of the event except the extreme discomfort of the place. I was glad when it was over. Initially the girl had taught me what I needed to know, and I tried to summon up some feelings for her beyond lust, but made little progress. On the way back to her colleagues she told me that they would be in Manfredonia at the end of the week.

We briefly embraced again, and as I made my way back to the B&B, I was thinking that I would try to see her again the next day. Once more, the body was dictating events. It was now past midnight. I began to doubt the likelihood of anyone opening the door to me, but was surprised to receive an answer to my knock almost immediately. I was taken up a narrow flight of stairs and shown into a large almost bare room. It had a double bed in the centre. A washstand with a jug of water and a bar of soap stood against one wall under the window. I could see nothing else in the room beyond a chair by the bed. A bright moon flooded the room with light through the window, and to my tired eyes it all looked reasonably clean. I paid the woman the twenty-five lira asked for and shut the door. I washed my face and neck, then dried myself with a piece of towel that was on the chair. I removed my trousers, shoes and top tunic, lay down on the bed and at once fell into a deep sleep.

Some time before dawn I shifted my position a little and stretched out one arm to help me turn on one side. My hand did not come into contact with the pillow. Instead it met a ragged substance that had no base. What on earth could it be? I scrabbled around with my fingers to determine what I was touching. Good God! It was hair! I sat up to see a woman dressed only in her shift. In the faint morning light I discerned figures squatting on the floor against the walls. I did not count how many, but in retrospect there were at least five or six. I did not wait to determine the gender, but grabbed my clothes and made for the street. Luckily, the front door could be opened from the inside, but in the dark it was difficult. I dressed in the street and decided that I had had enough of Monopoli and that making love on the back of a roundabout horse had lost its charm.

It was several hours before any traffic passed me on the road to Bari. Eventually I was picked up by an army truck that took me right to the door of the Officers' Club: here there was comfort and common sense.

During the next four days I returned on board, collected my spare uniform and underclothes and had everything laundered by two Italian ladies who worked for the Officers' Club. What a pleasure it was to sleep in a well-appointed bunk with a proper mattress, to eat food in company with other naval officers and to hear their stories. John, my No 1, was also there, as I guessed he would be.

I still had a week's leave left and I spent three days exploring the countryside. I visited some deep caves near Fasano where stalactites hung from the cathedral-like ceiling and stalagmites rose in pillars from the floor like organ pipes. It was an awesome sight. In one place two of them had grown to within an eighth of an inch of touching. The guide said that they would meet in five years' time, at which point a US soldier broke a piece off one of them saying, 'Well, I guess it'll take a bit longer now.' I found this pointless act more depressing than an act of violence to a person. I can't think why, but perhaps war lessens our regard for human life. Near to these caves were some others leading inland, and here the huge cheeses called Gorgonzola were stored. Each one was as large as an average motor car tyre and as thick.

I cannot really account for what happened next, but the day after my visit to the caves found me in an army truck heading north once more to Manfredonia and sex. The body was again dictating events. The journey took most of the day, finishing just as dusk was falling. The driver delivered me to the one hotel that was open. As in Bari, it had been requisitioned by the military, but this one served both forces. It was a poor place compared with Bari, but I was glad of anywhere decent to sleep.

The meal was adequate, the wine sour and the sleeping arrangements primitive. There were no cabins, only dormitories: two for the army and one for the navy. Each room held twenty beds, ten on each side, with a gangway down the centre. I went first to an army dormitory by mistake and was directed upstairs to the naval part of the building. Feeling tired and glad of somewhere to lie down, I followed arrows marked 'Dormitory' but stopped at an improvised bar where I hoped to get something to remove the taste of the awful wine. Sitting at the bar I made plans for the morrow. The first thing to do was to locate the concert party and the girl, and to arrange a time and place to meet later. Then some breakfast, if I could find somewhere better than this place.

My eyes began to close as I made my way to bed and sleep. How was it that one could stay awake at sea for thirty hours or more if necessary, but ashore 'the arms of Morpheus' claimed one so easily? Ah, at last, here was the dormitory and bed. I threw my small kit bag onto a bed near the centre, took off my shoes and stretched out using the kit bag as a pillow, there being nothing on the bed except a mattress. I hadn't noticed the rest of the room as I lay down, but felt sure that I heard voices talking in low tones further down the room. Something about one voice was familiar, or was I dreaming? It was a girl's voice, of that I was certain. Suddenly a man's voice said, 'Ow! That hurt!' and a girl laughed.

This time there was no mistake. I got up and walked towards the bed where the talking had come from. It was her, the girl I had come so far to see. Her head was poking out from under a sheet and a man's hand was across her neck. The rest of him was under the cover. The girl and I looked at each other for a full minute. There was nothing to be said. I slept soundly that night, having received the shock that I needed. It takes a kick on the behind to bring about a change of feeling sometimes, and this was a kick I deserved.

I set off back to Bari the next morning without breakfast, and was on foot until I was picked up by a naval transport going south. My uniform was still clean and in good order, having just been laundered at the Officers' Club by the two good ladies, whom I blessed in my thoughts. I did not want to disgrace the uniform while on the road, and it was good to see officers and men of all three Services on the highway. In a foreign country there was no other way of spending a bit of leave. We stopped somewhere and bought some bread and sausage, and drank water from the driver's gallon container. He was a peacetime leading seaman, of advanced years for a serviceman and nearing the end of his commission. I found him good company. His wise remarks came from experience and helped to make me realise how utterly stupid and selfish I had been. I was selfish for blaming the girl. She at least was honest, in that she did not pretend to be any better than she was, whereas I had. It is for this reason that I think of the affair with shame today.

There were two days left of my leave and I spent them reading The Mill on the Floss, walking the countryside outside of Bari, and on the last evening going to the theatre. A travelling Italian opera company was giving a performance of Lucia di Lammermoor. The singing, as far as I could judge, was of a high standard, especially in the role of Lucia, which is very difficult and demands a huge range from the artist. Two things prevented the evening from being a complete delight. One was the noble effort of the management to dress the cast in kilts. They wore what looked like, and could only be described as, check tablecloths. Being small men, instead of brawny Scotsmen, they looked even stranger. The other thing that cast a shadow over the proceedings was perpetrated by the British. There were large numbers of sailors of all ranks in the audience, most of whom sat in the gallery. During Lucia's most difficult aria, which requires every ounce of energy and concentration, an inflated contraceptive floated down from the 'gods' and landed in the stalls, presumably on someone's head. Fortunately, there was no laughter, but it was a sad sight and one that would not have endeared us to our hosts.

In spite of my introduction to sex and its dreary aftermath, I had enjoyed my leave. It was wonderful to have been free of responsibility for a spell, to be a single person again and beholden to no one. The walks in the countryside, the meals at the Bari Officers' Club and in the odd cafe had all been a pleasure.

The Chief, wonderful man, was the first back from leave and already in the engine room when I arrived. John and the crew trickled back during the afternoon, and by 6.00pm we were a ship's company again. We took on fuel and water, and I signalled to Syracuse that we were 'in all respects ready for sea'. Nothing happened for two days. Then I received a signal to proceed to Taranto and report to the XDO. The passage marked the change from local patrols to longer ones between ports that were far apart. I was given no arrival time so sent an ETA of forty hours ahead. The three hundred and fifty miles were completed without incident, and Taranto was a revelation. The vast bay on which it is situated was busy with ships of all types and sizes.

Many ships were Italian, going about their business as if it were peacetime. I saw three warships at anchor outside the port. There was plenty of room to moor against the long harbour wall, and to my surprise, a car was sent to take me to the naval base. As I sat in the back seat I began to feel rather important, not only because of the car, but because I had been summoned from as far away as Syracuse.

The XDO did not waste words. He had a chart ready when I entered. He pointed to an island in the Greek Peloponnese, but close to the Turkish coast. The island was called Kos and is well known to tourists today. A minesweeper had lost her screws and rudder in an explosion when a mine had got caught in the sweeping gear under the stern. She had drifted ashore and was grounded on the beach. The ship had been there for five or six weeks waiting for help, but the war had passed her by. No vessel large enough to tow her back to Taranto could be spared, and so it was a matter of great good fortune that no one had been killed or even injured. Part of the transom had been holed, and that was the extent of the damage to the hull. Watertight doors had been closed throughout the vessel, which was otherwise intact.

My assignment was to collect the personnel and deliver them to the naval base at Taranto. It was a long passage to Kos, some eight hundred miles, and I needed four days' sailing time at ten knots to do this. This information I imparted to the XDO. I asked how many crew were aboard the vessel and was told eighteen. This was a serious problem. We should have to draw rations for that number, take on sufficient water and clear spaces for them to sleep. The XDO wished me luck, and I departed to begin preparations for the task. In truth, I was pleased to be rid of patrols for a while.

For days, it seemed, we threaded our way through the Greek archipelago. 'Islands to the right of us, islands to the left of us shimmied and blundered,' but it was me who did the blundering. Three times I mistook a piece of land for Kos. Fortunately, I had a pilot volume that was very well illustrated and showed in clear detail all the landmarks. However, sometimes it is not until you are close to the shoreline that you are able to see these landmarks. If I had strictly obeyed our dead reckoning it would have saved a bit of trouble.

There was, however, no mistaking Kos when we did see it. The landmarks were easy to recognise. Sure enough, there was the sweeper hard up on a sandy beach. The water was clear and I had a mine lookout on the bows. At very slow speed we sounded our way to the minesweeper's side. Most of the hull, possibly two-thirds, was still in deep water. The first thing that struck me was that there was no one in sight. The ship appeared to be empty. John was beside me on the bridge, and he had the glasses. He started to laugh and handed them to me. Far up on the beach was a shelter with a thatched roof. A figure in naval uniform was attending a stove, and was obviously cooking something. I looked around and noticed something else. An electric cable stretched from the sweeper's engine room hatch to a small building, which was at the start of a road. Later this proved to be a shed, which housed a primitive generator and a supply system for a hamlet close by. The sweeper was clearly 'exporting' power to the locals. Here was a classic case of 'going native'.

I climbed aboard the vessel in company with our Cox'n. I searched the ship. No one! Everything was open and there were signs of recent occupation. The stove from the galley was missing together with the tank of diesel that supplied it. The Cox'n and I walked down the gangway from the bow to the beach. The planks were tied smartly together and looked permanent. It was obvious that the ship's company were planning for a long stay, if not for good. The rating at the stove told me that the CO and the Engineer

My mother, Constance Beale.

My parents on their wedding day, just a few hours after
peace was declared at the end of the First World War.

My father, Harry George Beale, left,
on his favourite horse, Paddy.

The ill-fated HMS Hood. She was sunk with great loss of life a few days
after I was aboard as relief 'washer-up' in the wardroom pantry.

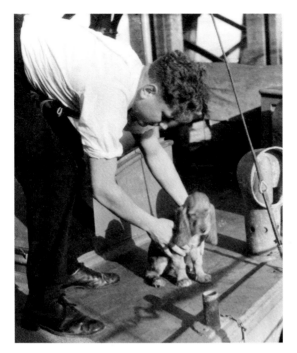

Introducing Simon to the Navy.

Me in naval uniform with Simon.

Simon, a special dog.

Me at Gibraltar Airport, about to leave in search of eggs.

My first command, HDML 1070 leaving Sheerness.

Left, Morris Drake (Quack) and centre, me, beside a Beaufighter.
Later, Quack became a High Court judge: The Hon. Sir Morris Drake DFC.

Ljerka Ebenspanger, aged seven at Fasano, Italy.

HDMLs leaving harbour.

My last command, ML 135 underway off Bari.

The bridge wheel of ML 135.

By the KING'S Order the name of
Ty. Lieutenant Richard Henry Beale,
R.N.V.R.,
was published in the London Gazette on
12 June, 1945,
as mentioned in a Despatch for distinguished service.
I am charged to record
His Majesty's high appreciation.

Brendan Bracken
First Lord of the Admiralty

Mentioned in dispatches.

would be returning later in the day. They had gone to the other side of the island to buy food. He said that the generator that served the few houses nearby had been smashed in an air raid.

'Where is the rest of the crew?' I asked.

'I don't know, sir. Scattered about the island somewhere. Most of them have friends in the village,' he replied.

'Do they come back here to eat and sleep?'

'Some do, sir. I'm cooking for them now.'

'Are you saying only some of them will return this evening?'

'Yes, sir.'

I was non-plussed. What the hell was I supposed to do? I returned on board to talk the matter over with John. We came to the conclusion that we were not equipped with the powers of arrest. No one at Taranto had suggested this. The best we could do was to search the island, as far as was possible, to try to persuade anyone we could find to return with us to Taranto. If they did so voluntarily, they would be in no danger of punishment. They might even be complimented for their resourcefulness.

John and I were looking out of the wardroom hatch when we saw the CO of the minesweeper, his Chief and two ratings return on board. They were quickly followed by the cook from the improvised galley, who was carrying two metal containers, which presumably held their dinner. An hour later I boarded the vessel and asked to see the CO. One of the two ratings was on the bridge finishing the last of his meal.

'I'll fetch him, sir,' he said.

'Thank you, but tell me where are the rest of the crew?' I asked.

'Most of them have girlfriends and I've heard that one of them has married his girl. There's a rumour that the Cox'n has been made mayor of the town on the other side of the island,' he blurted out.

The rating seemed to want to get all this staggering information off his chest, and to separate himself from any part of it. The sight of 1297 alongside clearly influenced this rush of information. He then disappeared below, while I pondered the extraordinary turn of events. How could all this have happened in so short a time as five or six weeks? The answer came soon enough. The CO appeared and invited me to his cabin. He laughed when I mentioned the matter of the length of his stay on Kos. 'Six weeks? Good God, no, we've been here for three months!' he said.

That explained a lot, but not everything. The CO was an Royal Naval Reserve (RNR) Lieutenant. The RNR were mainly ex-Merchant Navy personnel who had been given wartime commissions in the RN. This man was senior to me, which made my position difficult. 'Why have you not managed to keep your crew together, you must have known that you would be rescued someday?' was my first question.

He replied, 'For the first month it was extremely hot in this sheltered cove and the men were unable to sleep below. I allowed them to sleep under the trees above the beach, and from there they spread into other parts and got to know people. By the end of the second month I gave up trying to keep the ship's company together. I decided to do what I could to persuade these three ratings and the Chief to remain in or near the ship. I was tired of searching the island, especially as I began to think that we would be here for the duration.'

I could see the logic of all this as it emphasised the difficulty of small ships in preserving discipline without the power or means of arrest. I decided to carry out a rudimentary search of the island the next morning, and to sail the same day with whatever number of men that I could persuade to come with me. John discovered two in a wine bar and frightened them with tales of punishment.

This meant that altogether we sailed with seven, including the CO and his Chief. If there was an advantage to be gained from our failure to find the rest, it was that it proved much easier to accommodate seven passengers than eighteen for the four days of our return.

The XDO Taranto was an understanding man and accepted my explanation for failing to complete the task as ordered. A few hours before arrival I sent an ETA, which resulted in an armed escort waiting on the landing stage for the men of the sweeper. I wished the CO luck and signalled the base, asking for permission to remain alongside for the night and to be supplied with fuel and water the following day. These requests were met and, at midday the next day, we sailed for our base at Syracuse.

We arrived on the last day of November. The crew started talking about Christmas, but long patrols and periods in Catania, Brindisi and Taranto filled the weeks until then, and the months until spring. Christmas came and went with a celebration that was a credit to us all, especially the cook. He and No 1 had foraged far and wide for victuals suitable to the occasion. They had returned with four capons and two large hams, managed to purchase in exchange for a pound of coffee drawn from the base. Some fresh fruit, cheese and vegetables were also obtained from the naval store ashore.

It was a feast fit for a king. It is the custom in the navy, at least on some ships, for the officers to wait on the crew on Christmas Day, and to serve the meal to the ratings. John and I donned aprons, which we made out of a torn sheet, and did the honours. Sparks had a squeezebox (concertina) and gave us a rendering of several carols, which we partially drowned with our own singing. Each man got a generous tot of rum from the Cox'n's store, which helped make the party go with a swing. Long after John and I retired to the wardroom, to eat our own meal, singing continued.

I was very pleased about this, and felt proud of these good chaps who had come so far with us in this small ship.

Sporadic air raids had continued throughout the months we had been in the Adriatic, and the rapid progress made by the Eighth Army had slowed to a halt north of Bari. Far more German soldiers were engaged in the defence of the ports and countryside, and the war in the main part of Italy looked as if it might be a long one. From time to time odd fragments of Mussolini's forces gave themselves up, both at sea and on land.

Bari was becoming an important base for repairs and the servicing of ships engaged in the war north of that port. A fighter base had been established at Corsini for the protection of Bari and the surrounding area. It was an American squadron. They flew Mustangs, which were very hardy machines with square wing tips. They were well armed, extremely manoeuvrable, but not quite so fast as a Spitfire. They did sterling work keeping the skies above Bari clear of enemy bombers, and had many victories to their credit. Later in the war I was to have dealings with them, and got to know their Wing Commander.

The weather was now quite cold and whites were no longer the chosen gear for officers and men. By now nearly all of the crew had found facilities, in one port or another, for keeping their clothes clean, apart from their pants and shirts, which they usually washed themselves in buckets. In spite of this, something happened that frightened me more than bombs. The Cox'n reported to No 1 that bed bugs had been found in one of the bunks. He was obviously shocked. A thorough investigation of the entire fo'c'sle was carried out. The bunk in question was removed and burnt on the harbour wall. I demanded, with all the authority that I could muster, that a replacement be supplied and fitted by the Syracuse shipwright's department. Meanwhile, the owner of the bunk had to sleep on deck.

Fortunately, no other bugs were found after every man in the fo'c'sle had spent hours in the search. This was a great relief to us all, and a lesson in 'cleanliness at all costs'. It may seem strange to a peacetime reader that we should worry about such things when bombs were falling and men and women dying in the war everyday. My answer is that it is better to deal with an infestation at the outset, rather than to let it grow to a point where it might damage efficiency. Great troubles often grow from small beginnings.

A new bunk was made and fitted within two days by the base shipwright who was, interestingly, an Italian boatbuilder taken over by the navy. At the same time I received a note from NOIC's office stating that this must not happen again.

The day after the new bunk was fitted we were due to take over patrol work at Catania, but a very serious air raid took place over Syracuse the night before leaving, and the order was cancelled. The air raid was spectacular. Many vessels were hit, including an ammunition ship moored in the centre of the harbour. The resulting 'firework display' was dramatic and great damage was caused by shrapnel.

CHAPTER 5

✳

Wounded

1942–43

Now, instead of Catania, we were ordered to patrol, once again, the approaches to Syracuse. During the first hour of the patrol, an Italian submarine surfaced about two miles from the harbour entrance. It was immediately engaged by one of our armed trawlers, also on patrol like ourselves. The U-Boat surrendered and came to a stop. We were signalled by the base to proceed at once to the sub and to remove all signal books, code books, charts and any other confidential material we could find. We had to deliver everything to the NOIC's office forthwith.

The vessel lay quietly hove-to in a calm sea. It was therefore easy to come alongside; two men on the deck took our lines. I chose one of our ratings to accompany me. Each of us had a revolver in hand as we climbed aboard. The bridge was badly damaged, and three bodies crowded the small space above the main hatch. The bodies were badly mutilated and I yet remember being surprised that there was so little blood in evidence.

The two seamen kept their hands in the air until I signed to lower them. I made them go down the ladder before us, and to stay just in front until we reached the base of the conning tower. We were then quickly surrounded by the rest of the crew, all with their hands in the air. There was a lot of chatter and some shouting, which indicated that they all wanted to be taken prisoner and sent to England. I did speak and understand some basic Italian at the time, and asked for all the confidential books, charts and codes. Leaving my crew member in charge with his revolver, I followed one of the sub's crew, whom I took to be their Cox'n, to a safe. It was locked. He had to go up to the bridge to retrieve the key from one of the dead officers. When he returned with the key he was also carrying a code book and a list of recognition signals. The safe was opened and the contents placed in the kitbag I had brought with me.

When the Italians saw that we were leaving, a great cry went up, imploring us to take them with us. They produced presents of all kinds. I accepted a small Beretta pistol, which I thought might be useful when on leave, as there were now many renegade servicemen roaming the country, desperate for food and money. Also a pair of binoculars that came in for general use on board 1297. I did not see why the base should have all these things, but I was firm in refusing any personal gifts. The uproar became intense, and in the end I promised to signal Syracuse to ask for their intentions concerning the submarine.

Back on board Sparks made a radio signal, as we were out of range for the Aldis lamp. Our signal read: 'Request instructions reference submarine and crew. Confidential material secured.' The answer came back almost immediately. 'Boom defence vessel HMS Lothian now under weigh, will tow enemy into harbour. Return with all speed.'

Most of the Italian crew were by this time on deck. I assured them that a ship was on its way to tow them into Syracuse and that they would be taken prisoner. I was not sure about the whole of this promise, but the sight of Lothian in the distance reassured them.

I delivered the material to the base and was pleased to see that all the important buildings had escaped damage in the raid, but I was told that most of the local fishing fleet had been sunk. I also learned that although many of our ships had suffered only minor damage from shrapnel, two of them had been sunk.

Although I was not to know it at the time, the surrender of the submarine and the air raid marked the end of life as it had been. Everything was about to change.

The day after the submarine episode, I happened to be in the base and was happy to hear that the crew of the sub would indeed be taken prisoner and sent back to England. A promise is worth nothing if not kept.

That evening found us back on patrol again about a mile outside the entrance. It was thought that more of Mussolini's navy might be coming home, and we were there to keep watch. I was on the bridge when I heard a shout from the stern. No 1 and the Chief were examining the smoke apparatus, from which a thin column of smoke was escaping. I left the bridge to the Cox'n and went to investigate. I never quite reached the machine, and was about three feet away, when it blew up. The three of us were drenched in chlorosulphonic acid and went immediately over the side, which probably saved our lives.

I remember nothing of the next few hours. When I became conscious of my surroundings, I was in an aircraft and someone was holding my hand. I have no idea how I got back on board 1297, though I clearly remember going over the side. I could see nothing. I opened my eyes wide, but everything was black. It was only the roar of the engines and the feel of being airborne that told me where I was. It is a fact that if one sense is removed, others can become enhanced to compensate to some extent. It happened very quickly with me. As soon as I realised I was blind, my hearing became sharper and my sense of smell strengthened.

My nose and ears told me where I was. At first I wasn't afraid of not being able to see, because the relief at still being alive was so great, all other thoughts took second place, but as the flight continued, fear crept through me like a cold draught. The nurse talked to me in low tones and her close presence was more than just a comfort – it saved me from panic. I have no memory of leaving the plane. I've no idea how I got to the hospital, or where it was situated.

I have often since wondered if I had been unconscious most of the time after going over the side. Did they drag me? I don't know. I only remember being fully aware when I found myself in bed, in a tented casualty-clearing station, which was in effect a hospital.

My head and eyes were heavily bandaged, but the sounds and the strong smell of disinfectant revealed my whereabouts. A nurse sitting by the bed told me that I was in a large tented hospital, in the desert outside of Tunis. She said that there were twenty-four beds in the ward, twelve on each side, and that it was an army hospital. I do remember that it was very, very hot, and I tried to think what time of year it was, and came to the conclusion that, in English terms, it was early spring. I remember nothing of the operation on my eyes and I asked about this.

'You, and the other officer, have been very lucky. We have a famous eye specialist named Dr Logue in from Prague, and you are his first cases.' I later learned that he had rubbed his hands because, although casualties from Italy and the parts of North Africa not yet in Allied hands were arriving day and night, so far there had been no eye cases.

In the days following the operation the bandages were kept in place, and then one morning I was taken to another part of the hospital, and the bandages were removed. I could only see large grey and black patches, but no shapes or colours. The nurse had told me that if anyone could restore my sight, it would be Dr Logue, but I was depressed by this first trial. I cannot remember if any other treatment was given, but every day from then on the bandages were removed for a short spell. I could see a little more each time, until the day came when I could see shapes, colours, faces and the rows of beds. Soon after that the bandages were left off altogether. I don't remember seeing John, my First Lieutenant, but knew that he was in some part of the hospital.

I can't remember any meals during my stay. I was, however, conscious of other things, such as the staff and other patients. I marvelled at the devotion and self-sacrifice shown by the doctors and nurses. They worked day and night to care for the injured who arrived in a constant stream throughout the twenty-four hours. They got little sleep, and it was not uncommon to work for thirty-six hours non-stop. I remember a senior doctor ordering a nurse to go to a bed immediately, 'I said now, nurse, that is an order!'

The nurses themselves carried a lot of authority as they all had two 'pips', and sometimes more, on their shoulders. These were equivalent to a Lieutenant or a Captain in the army. This authority was exhibited close to me one morning. The patient next to me had been seriously wounded by a mine that had exploded in his face, causing fourteen fractures in the facial bones. He was heavily bandaged and was fed through a slit in the dressing. A ward assistant known as a 'sick-bay artificer' was feeding him with something that looked like custard. He kept dribbling some of the stuff on to the bed and on to the patient's chest. This was seen by one of the QARANC (Queen Alexandra Royal Army Nursing Corps) nurses. The atmosphere became electric.

'You come here! I heard you laugh at the mess you've made. You will now change all the bed linen and the patient's shirt.

You will then sweep out this entire ward. You will then wash the floor, after which you will report to the Medical Officer, who will have been informed of your behavior.' She stopped speaking, and there followed a silence of catharsis. I doubt if this nurse was much older than twenty-one, but her authority was without question.

Opposite me in the ward were two soldiers suffering from what was then called 'anxiety neurosis'. This is usually caused by 'shell shock'. These two talked quickly to one another all day and night. Eventually they were removed, presumably to another hospital in the UK.

Once my sight was restored I began to take an interest in life again. I had dictated a letter home a day or two after arriving at the casualty-clearing depot to a nurse who, after writing it for me, posted it. It was now time to write a proper letter, assuring my family that I was not blind, but could see normally. I learned after the war that they had received the standard telegram stating that I had been seriously wounded. This must have caused them much unnecessary worry.

On my last Sunday in the hospital, an event occurred that I can see in my mind's eye to this day. It was straight out of a story by Somerset Maugham. The temperature was hotter than ever, but a slight breeze was blowing into the ward through the open flap of the tent at my end, and a certain amount of sand was coming in with it. Outside, in the blazing sun, a Salvation Army band was entertaining us with hymn tunes. I could see the sun reflected from their instruments, which somehow seemed to increase the heat and the feeling of being roasted in an oven. A lady in a flowing cotton dress and a parasol appeared in the entrance. She was the wife of the British Resident, I was told, and she was doing her rounds. She literally flounced from bed, to bed, saying a few words at each. When she came to the man next to me, the one with a fractured face, who was smothered in bandages, she stopped and said, 'How are we? A bit uncomfortable for a day or so?' With that she put a hard-boiled egg on the bed and passed on! The hymns continued.

The next day I was discharged and told that I was to have a month's leave at a rest house in Tunis. An army truck took me to a large house that enclosed a courtyard on four sides. Although in an area of some devastation, it was untouched. The courtyard gave welcome shade, with the aid of a palm tree and a fountain fed by a spring. At least I thought that it must be supplied that way as I saw no machinery.

The family living there were French Arab and I cannot imagine a happier or friendlier household. They did their best to make me feel at home by including me in their way of life. There were two young daughters of about fifteen or so. One was called Florianne, but I forget the name of the other. The family spoke French most of the time, but sometimes a little English for my sake. The girls wore ordinary European clothes and had no special restrictions placed upon them. I used to go to the beach quite often to swim, and sit by the water's edge, and they were allowed to come with me if they wished. It was a peaceful and happy time.

One day there was a big commotion in the house. From early morning there was much chatter and laughter, which I tried to understand, but it was an accent that I could not penetrate. I knew it to be French, but the Arab overtones disguised it. The master of the house was a tall, handsome man who always wore traditional dress, although his wife did not, which was strange. He disappeared on the day of the excitement and returned in the afternoon with a whole sheep. A feast of huge proportions was about to be prepared. Many hours later, I had lost all sense of time, guests started arriving. All were Arab, and like my hosts, they all spoke French. I went to the beach and was told that one of the girls would fetch me when it was time for the meal.

When I arrived back at the house I was led into a large, bare room that I had not seen before. The centre of the floor was of polished stone, surrounded by elaborately woven carpets. The guests, about ten in number, sat cross-legged on these mats, and I was shown to a place between them and the family. A loud gong sounded once from somewhere in the building. This was followed by a number of servants entering the room carrying an immense copper tray bearing a mountain of rice and semolina. Protruding from this were legs, joints and portions of mutton. The scent of herbs filled the air and the feast began.

Normally in the house meals were served and eaten in the Western style, using plates and knives and forks. But this was a traditional occasion and I did not want to make a mistake. I watched the others carefully for a minute or two before eating. I quickly learned how to take rice and pieces of meat from the mound without spillage. I also noticed that it was their custom to pass a particularly choice morsel to a neighbour. This happened often enough to make me realise that it was a question of etiquette, rather than kindness. I tried to follow their example.

When nothing was left but a few grains of rice and some bones, servants appeared as if by magic. They bore bowls of scented water, in which we all washed our hands, drying them on the spotless white towels hanging from the waist of every servant. Dishes of fresh fruit then arrived, followed by small porcelain cups of very strong, very sweet black coffee. During the coffee three men entered with musical instruments which they began to play. The strange cadences of Arabian music played upon my senses like a drug conjuring wild scenes in my mind's eye, which gave place to drowsiness and finally sleep – or was I unconscious? I never knew, for I was led from the room by my host, who had wakened me by gently stroking my cheek. In the morning I apologised to him for having the bad manners to fall asleep at his banquet, but he only laughed saying that even Arabs sometimes fell asleep when such music is played.

I still had another week of leave left after the feast, which I spent exploring the town and being on the beach with the two daughters. It was an idyllic interlude, especially for a young man who had had responsibility thrust on him before he was properly ready for it.

The house had a fine library of mainly French titles, but a few were in English. I found a copy of Galsworthy's Man of Property and Jane Austen's Pride and Prejudice. I finished the Jane Austen but didn't complete Man of Property, because at the end of the week I received a signal from NOIC, Syracuse, which was passed to me from the naval base at Tunis. This was only a small affair, but they managed to send a messenger with a note transcribed on to a sheet of notepaper. It simply said that I was to report back to NOIC, Syracuse, in three days' time.

I set about getting my few clothes washed and ironed. I had very little. The few things I had consisted of a crumpled white uniform, two shirts, some pants, shoes and my cap. These are the things I had found in a bag beside my bed at the hospital. I have no idea in what, or how, I was clothed in the plane. I was about to leave the house to search for a laundry, when my hostess stopped me at the door. She held a shirt, a pair of cotton trousers and a pair of sandals. She took from me my bag of dirty clothes and indicated that I was to take everything off and to put on the clothes she was carrying. At the end of the day, I came back in time for the evening meal to find laid out on my bed all my things, washed and ironed to perfection.

I do not recall how I travelled back to Syracuse. I have no recollection of a plane flight or a sea passage. I think that it must have been by sea as vessels of all kinds were travelling between all the captured ports in the Mediterranean. However, I do remember saying goodbye to this generous family, and thanking them from the bottom of my heart for all their care and kindness. A month is enough to make strong bonds, especially if there is goodwill on both sides, and tears were not absent, especially from the girls.

CHAPTER 6

❋

A new command

1944

I arrived in Syracuse as dusk was falling and immediately began a search for all my gear, which included two expensive blue uniforms, apart from everything else. There was no sign of 1297 anywhere in the dock, and with a sinking heart, I climbed the steps to the NOIC's office, little suspecting what was in store for me when I got there. NOIC, Syracuse, was a three-ring RN Commander who had earned the respect of those who worked for him and those who had to respond to his orders.

'Sit down, Beale,' he said. 'I have some news for you. But before I give it to you, I would like to know how you are feeling. Are you ready in mind and body for active service again?'

'Oh yes, sir, of course, I am,' I replied. 'I never expected anything else. I feel fine, and have been very lucky, I know. The trouble is my ship is no longer here, and she can't be on patrol unless you have appointed new officers, and besides all my gear is on board!' All this came out in a rush and was quenched by the Commander raising his hand, a half-smile on his lips.

'I'm glad to hear you are well and anxious to resume service. We will talk about your clothes and possessions later. I had to be certain of your attitude before giving you the news I spoke of. You have been promoted to the rank of Lieutenant RNVR and appointed CO of ML 135, relieving Lieutenant Peel, who is to return to the UK. The official citation will be given to you in Bari, where ML 135 is based. As for your possessions and clothes, they are here in my office.'

If I had been outside in the open, I would have looked up to the stars, expecting them to fall on my head! I was astounded, and for moments I couldn't think of anything to say. The news was almost more than I could bear. Eventually, and in a broken voice, I said, 'Thank you, sir. I am dumbfounded, it's all I ever hoped for, but never expected. I will do my best, and hope that my best will be good enough.'

We then talked about 1297. She had been sent to Catania with a new officer and the same crew. I learned that the Cox'n had brought the ship in and put her alongside after the explosion. He had also organised the removal of the three of us from the water, and kept us warm with blankets. For this work he had been awarded a special commendation from the Admiralty. I guessed that NOIC, Syracuse, was responsible for this.

'Now, Beale, here is your stuff,' he pointed to two kitbags by the wall, 'and you will sleep tonight aboard 1302, whose First Lieutenant is on leave. She is at the northern end of the dock. I have transport leaving my office at 8.00am tomorrow: Make sure that you're on it.' With that, he shook my hand and wished me luck. I put on my cap, saluted, collected my bags and left.

It is difficult in peacetime to understand, or appreciate, the elation that the news afforded me. To have one's hopes and dreams satisfied in the space of five minutes was hard to grasp, and as I descended to the ground floor it all began to feel unreal. I was still walking on air, but the stars had gone out. Near the entrance I passed the Engineer's office which was in the process of being dismantled and transferred to Brindisi and Bari. The sight reminded me that to my shame, I had not enquired about the Chief or tried to find out what had happened to John, my First Lieutenant! I retraced my steps and knocked on the NOIC's door.

'Come in. Well, Beale, what is it now?' he asked. I made my request for information and was told that John had been sent to an army rest camp attached to the hospital in North Africa. 'Don't worry, Beale, it's not in the desert but in green country around an oasis. Fig trees, date palms, that kind of thing.' The Commander saw my frown at the mention of an 'army rest camp' and continued, 'Your No 1 returned here yesterday and is, at present, aboard HDML 1304 moored at the northern end of the harbour.'

'And the Chief, sir? What happened to him?' I asked.

'He has been flown back to the UK, and will probably be invalided out of the Service. He was badly burned on his chest and front,' he replied.

'What about his sight, sir?' I said.

'Our Medical Officer (MO) gave him some temporary treatment which was designed to last until he got to an English eye hospital. That is why he was flown back immediately. The MO thinks his sight will be saved,' came the reassuring answer.

'Thank you, sir!' I saluted, made my way downstairs again and headed for HDML 1302.

The news about the Chief shocked me. For a time at least, it prevented any further euphoria. He was such a splendid man, who did his job with more than expert enthusiasm; he did it with love. I tried to think if there had been any way in which I could have forestalled the situation.

I discussed it with John, with whom I met up before boarding 1302. 'You could not have made any difference, because you arrived after the leak, and it exploded before you reached us,' he said. I had to be content with that. I asked him about his rest camp sojourn. 'Wonderful!' he said, 'A Jeep at my disposal, and a WAAF (Women's Auxiliary Air Force member) to look after me! What more could you want?'

He told me that he was to join an HDML based in Malta, and was only waiting in Syracuse for transport. I said how sorry I was at being unable to say goodbye to the crew, especially the Cox'n. 'I should've liked to thank them all and to have wished them luck.' We drank a glass of wine with his CO; I wished them both luck, then left and headed for 1302 and a night's rest.

The next morning the transport and I were both on time, and we left the dock buildings at 8.00am sharp. The vehicle was a pick-up truck loaded with part of the contents of the Engineer's office. The driver was an Italian motor mechanic who had been put on our payroll, and was proud of the fact that he now wore overalls that bore an anchor on the sleeve. He proved his value in more ways than being just a driver. We stopped twice for food, and his confident manner always secured good service for us and the best food that the house could offer.

The distance to Bari was not far short of 400 miles, and it was late at night before we arrived. The base at Syracuse had telephoned the Officers' Club booking me a bed, but I wondered where the driver would sleep as it was past midnight when we pulled up outside the club. 'I sleep here,' he said in broken English, pointing to the cab seat.

I thanked him, giving him a twenty-five lira note, and humped my bags to the entrance. A guard was on duty and, taking one kitbag, he led me to a cabin. Excellent! I did not expect to have a room to myself. The space had obviously been part of a large bedroom which had been divided into four. I slept little, thinking of my new appointment and of being able to call myself 'Lieutenant', which sounded so much better than 'Sub-Lieutenant'.

As the distance from Syracuse had increased, the shock and sadness over the Chief had diminished, and now the full realisation of my new position took root. At around 4.00am I fell asleep and did not wake until almost 10.00am. I leapt off the bunk and started dressing before I remembered that my time of reporting to Commander Ward at the base was not until 2.30pm. How thoughtful! They had given me time to get things together. The navy has always impressed me by its humanity and tolerance as long as Service requirements are put first.

I got undressed again, had a shower and a shave in the bathroom next door and then thought about breakfast. The navy, at the time, had a saying about going ashore: 'You go ashore for a shit, shave and shampoo.' The first of those had not yet taken place, but doubtless the sight of my new command would do the trick.

In the mess I ordered what is now called a full English breakfast. Eggs, bacon, sausage and, wonder of wonders, mushrooms, toast, marmalade and coffee, which I ate while reading a copy of The Times that was only two days old. Here was luxury. It all seemed too good to be true. I then sorted out my clothes.

The two blue uniforms were in a bad state after their time in the kitbag, and the other white one also needed urgent attention. At the reception desk a member of staff answered my enquiry as to a laundry with another piece of good news. 'Leave everything on the bed, sir. We have facilities here for dealing with all that.'

I was surprised at his perfect English. I had expected an Italian at the desk, until I noticed the scars on his face and hands. He had clearly been badly wounded at one time. It happened occasionally that a wounded serviceman would opt to stay with his friends in the Service, rather than return to the UK. People with no family or relations often would have nothing to go back to.

With time left over before my 2.30pm appointment, I could not decide whether to go to the docks to try to get a sight of ML 135 or to leave it until I had reported to Commander Ward. I decided to leave it until later and that I would explore Bari instead, as I had seen little of it during my last visit.

The naval base at Bari overlooked two anchorages. The main one was Bari harbour, which had mooring space for many ships. A long dock and harbour wall gave space for a large number of vessels to tie up alongside. There were facilities in the dock area to haul out and repair ships, and there were two divers permanently in residence.

On the southern side of the main harbour there was a smaller second anchorage known as Porto Vecchio, closed on three sides and with a very narrow entrance. Enough water for one ML or a trawler to anchor in lay between the curved harbour wall and the rock-bound shore. It was principally used by the Third ML Flotilla, which I was soon to join. The whole flotilla, a matter of six vessels, could anchor in Porto Vecchio, provided they moored stern to wall, with an anchor out ahead. After the walk around town, I went there to assess the situation. A friendly officer at the Club had told me that the Third Flotilla was moored there and he thought that it was now denied to all other ships.

He was right, the harbour was empty of boats, and I was glad to be able to study the place for an hour or so to work out tactics for dealing with high winds in that narrow space. The flotilla was obviously at sea and ML 135 was with them. It transpired that I was not to see my new command for another two days as they were operating among the Dalmatian Islands, on the eastern side of the Adriatic.

Commander Ward was a three-ring RN officer in charge of minesweeping operations in the Adriatic, and a legend among the vessels he commanded. He made me welcome. Sharky Ward, for that was his pet name in the Adriatic, gave me a brief history of the Third Flotilla ML, praising their exploits and their value to him as an inshore force. This group of Fairmile MLs were the first small ships to come out to the Mediterranean as ancillary convoy escorts. They went through heavy air attacks over a long period in the process.

When the fall of Sicily was imminent, they were fitted with minesweeping gear, and given the task of clearing the approaches to the ports in step with the Eighth Army as it fought its way up the leg of Italy. The main shipping lanes were swept by large ships known as 'Fleet Sweepers', and one of the tasks of the MLs was to sweep in front of the big ships so that they were in safe water while they dealt with the majority of mines which were laid in deep water to catch merchant vessels and warships.

I learned that Johnny Peel, the present CO of 135, was going home for some long overdue leave and that I was to take over from him as soon as his ship returned. This presented me with a problem. I did not want to rely on the First Lieutenant and the crew for details about the running of the ship. I would have liked a couple of days with Peel so that he could show me the ropes. However, Peel was a law unto himself. 'What rubbish!' he said, 'Of course, you must come out with me for an hour or two so you can see how she handles. We'll sink a gin or two in the evening, and go over anything you want to know.'

This resolve of Peel could not have been guessed at while I was in Sharky's office. I came away feeling worried. Sharky Ward had given me a chit with his signature on it, he instructed me to go to the base clothing store and obtain braid and epaulettes for my uniforms. These marks of rank must be in place before going aboard 135. This order gave me great satisfaction and, with the help of the Navy Club, I found a seamstress in the town who did the job for a few liras. My clothes had been expertly laundered, cleaned and pressed and I picked them off the bed in astonishment that so much could have been done in so short a time.

I spent the evening, after a dinner of soup and locally caught fish, reading a typed extract taken from a recent book on mine sweeping. It was essential that I should understand the basic principles of 'Double L minesweeping', which consisted of towing a high-tensile steel wire some feet below the surface of the water. When it made contact with the mooring wire of the mine, it would sever the wire with an explosive cutter fixed to the sea end of the tow. It was a real concern to me that I knew nothing about minesweeping, which meant that I would have to rely on the experience of No 1 and the crew in more ways than I should have liked. However, my job as CO would be to 'con' the ship, and keep it on a steady course exactly behind the float of the sweep wire of the ship ahead, leaving no 'holidays' or areas of unswept water. All this was obvious and I turned in feeling a little more optimistic.

Two days later I was in Sharky's office looking out to sea through his window, which commanded a view of the water north, south and east. I had been warned by him of the ETA of the Flotilla. He invited me to wait in his office and have a cup of tea, which was brought in by a Wren rating. We talked of the war, and he asked about my injury and my peacetime life at home. During our second cup of tea he described fully the extent of the sweeping operations and their ultimate objective.

'The SO (Senior Officer) of the Third Flotilla, Beale, is Lieutenant Phillip Fellows, a splendid young man, on whom I rely very much. He will lead the sweeps as usual, unless put out of action, in which case ML 405 will lead. As he said the word 'lead', I happened to look up.' 'There they are, sir!'

Far out on the horizon, a group of six MLs sailing in perfect line ahead could be seen, lit by the late afternoon sun. At that distance they looked like destroyers, and I've always believed that idea dictated their design. Of course, in the near distance their smaller size became apparent.

I thanked Sharky for the tea, made my excuses and left. I rushed down to Porto Vecchio in order to watch them moor, and hopefully to learn something. There was a sentry box on the jetty and I watched from it, unseen.

The flotilla came to a stop about three cables from the narrow entrance. This was to allow the SO to come in and moor in the restricted space at the inner end of the small harbour. It was beautifully done. The stern of his boat was almost under my nose and, from where I stood, the bow appeared to be among the rocks. The next in was 405, followed by 135. She was really a picture to make the spirits rise and the heart beat faster. Johnny Peel brought her round in perfect time to avoid the two already moored and the one behind. When all were in, secured and a gangplank made fast, I boarded 135 and asked to see the CO, who had gone below. I gave him a salute, half in jest and half in earnest.

'Lieutenant Peel?' I asked.

'Yes, that's me. What can I do for you?'

'I'm your relief, Lieutenant Beale. I watched you come in to see how it's done in this narrow place.'

'Beale! Am I glad to see you,' he said. 'I've been waiting three months for you. Come below.'

The wardroom was a palace after the cramped quarters in an HDML. Johnny Peel poured a generous tot of gin for us both, and added tonic and ice. All very civilised and 'big ship stuff'. There was obviously a fridge somewhere in the wardroom, but I tried not to look surprised, knowing that all would be revealed later.

'Cheers and welcome aboard,' Johnny said. 'I say again, am I glad to see you! I got the signal for my return almost three months ago. Not Sharky's fault, by the way, Sharky Ward, that's our boss at the base, splendid chap, no, it's that bloody lot in Malta or the Admiralty or somewhere! They knew they were going to be short of inshore sweepers, so they hung on to me while they made up their minds.'

'I was told at Syracuse that I would be required to take over immediately,' I replied. 'Well, they would say that, wouldn't they, after all the delay which is their bloody fault. What rubbish, I'll take my time and hand over properly. No good starting off at half-cock. Tomorrow, we'll go out for an hour to see how she handles, and after that we'll go through the boat, from stem to stern, then we'll have a bit of lunch and I'll answer any questions that you might have. We are in harbour for at least another week, while we store up and take on fuel. You never know what Sharky has in his pocket for us, so don't bank on anything I say,' said Johnny.

At this point Johnny's No 1 came down the hatch and entered. He had been supervising work on deck. 'This is Sub Lieutenant Peter Butcher; Lieutenant Beale, your new CO.' I glanced at Butcher's face and thought I saw a slight frown, but it may have been my imagination. Peter Butcher was later to prove a most valuable man in many ways, and above all he was an expert in the management of the sweeping gear.

The three of us stopped talking shop and exchanged gossip. Johnny Peel was laughter all the way, in complete contrast to Butcher, who seemed a serious young man without much of a sense of humour. As darkness fell, saying that I would return the next morning at 10.00pm, I made my excuses and left to return to the Club.

The hand-over was a real success, I believe, and a relief to us all, including some of the crew. For an hour we manoeuvred the ship in every way I could think of. I checked the turning circle at various speeds; tested the time it took for the vessel to answer to the helm at slow, half and full speeds; and finally, her capacity for carrying way after her engines were stopped at a range of speeds. ML 135 handled like a dream and was much more responsive than anything I had served on before. Johnny Peel then took over the bridge, while I went aft with Peter Butcher, who gave me a complete run-down of the sweeping gear.

The gear consists of two winches. One houses the long mine-cutting wire with a float at the sea end, and is held at the required depth by a paravane, called the 'otter'. The other winch controls a short wire attached to another paravane immediately under the stern, this one is called the 'kite' and keeps the ship end of the wire at the required depth.

We then streamed the port sweep, and I took over the bridge for ten minutes feeling the effect of the weight on the boat. The process was repeated with a starboard sweep, and then with both out together. We had been out for three hours when Johnny Peel said that he needed his gin and tonic as it was lunchtime. We headed back towards Porto Vecchio after Peter Butcher and his assistant Leading Seaman Grayham had hauled in the sweeps.

'Difficult place, our harbour. It takes a bit of getting used to. Rocks and not much room, as you saw. If you have to pass any boats on the way to your own slot, as we'll have to do today, it's best to give them a 'toot' on your foghorn, as we are about to do now. That warns them to slack their anchor chains so that we can pass ahead.' With that he gave an almighty blast that was entirely consistent with the man himself.

At this point I surprised everyone within hearing by saying, 'If you don't mind, Johnny, I would like to be alone on the bridge and take her in myself.' Peter Butcher looked shocked, and Johnny said, 'But don't you want to see how it's done first?' 'No, trust me' I replied.

I had many gaps in my knowledge and experience, but I knew that I was good at ship handling. I had observed the process for Porto Vecchio from the sentry box, but didn't tell them that. I wanted, above all else, to give my new First Lieutenant and the crew of 135, confidence in the new CO. From our operations during the morning I had a pretty good idea as to the temper of the boat, and I have always been sensitive to the manner of the vessel under me. Johnny shrugged and left the bridge, followed by Peter Butcher.

'Slow starb'd twenty, midships, steady as you go. Stand by to anchor,' I called. But all was ready on the fo'c'sle anyhow. 'Stop both. Hard aport. Slow astern starb'd. Let go anchor. Stop starb'd. Take up slack as we go astern. Slow astern both. Stop both. Haul taut and secure.' We fetched up seven feet from the wall. Our lines were made fast by a man on the jetty, and our gangplank was removed from its place at the guardrails and the shore end made fast.

Johnny came up to the bridge and took off his 'minesweeping hat' and shook my hand. 'I think that calls for a gin!' His hat was a straw boater whose crown had come away from the brim in the front, so that there was a slit through which he could see ahead. The crown shielded his head and eyes from the sun and the slit enabled him to see. We entered the wardroom where we drank two G&Ts while the steward laid for lunch. 'Beale, what do they call you? Surely not Beale all the time?' he said. 'In my last job I was called Dickie by other officers in the flotilla. My Christian name is Richard,' I told him. 'What flotilla was that?' Johnny asked. 'Oh, very small fry. HDMLs, we came out for the Sicily landings.' 'Well, until tomorrow when I leave, it's Dickie.

Peter Butcher and the steward arrived together. Peter was carrying an octopus big enough to be worth cooking. 'It was caught in the 'kite'. If cook won't deal with it, I'll give it to someone ashore.' The steward was bringing lunch, which consisted of corned beef sandwiches, pickled onions, with cheese and slices of stale bread. Johnny looked critically at the spread. 'Not a feast fit for a king, unless he happens to be starving!' he said.

But to me it was indeed a banquet because it took place in a beautiful wardroom, in a beautiful ship, and I had just brought off a difficult manoeuvre, which could so easily have failed. As a result, I noticed a marked difference in Peter Butcher's manner. He no longer looked so serious and had become more relaxed, and chattered away like everyone else. 'Sorry about the food,' he said. 'We've been away a week and got low in everything. Tomorrow we take on stores, water and fuel, and the cook and me will have a hunt around onshore for some fresh stuff.'

After lunch Johnny led me through the ship from stem to stern. A Fairmile ML is thirty-seven feet longer than a HDML and everything, above and below decks, is more spacious. The arrangement of some compartments differed considerably. In the fo'c'sle there was a compartment for the anchor cable and some spare mooring lines.

The fo'c'sle was huge compared with an HDML's and housed sixteen men. Next came two cabins, one on each side of a central gangway. One was the wireless room, and the other had two bunks, for the Cox'n and the Chief. Abaft of these was a compartment holding fuel tanks that contained three thousand gallons of 100 octane aviation spirit.

The galley was the next in line moving aft. This was also much larger than I was used to and contained refrigeration equipment. The engine room contained two Hall-Scott 12-cylinder, 650 horsepower engines, which gave the vessel a top speed of twenty-one knots in reasonably smooth water. The wardroom took up the full width of the ship. It held two bunks, which were really upholstered seats, with backs that would lift up to provide two more bunks if needed. There was a full-length wardrobe for each officer, and a table. The steps leading down to the wardroom ended in a spacious area that contained a pantry on one side, with a small washroom and heads on the other. There was a fridge behind the ladder. The pantry had facilities for preparing and storing food. It also had means for heating food and a water supply – an undreamed of luxury, in my opinion. The last compartment of all was the tiller flat which held the steering gear: a large assortment of ropes, for all occasions, a spare anchor, fenders and bolts of canvas. Boxes of ammunition and shells for the Bofors gun were in a steel container next to the fridge.

Towards evening I returned to the Officers' Club, ate some dinner and assembled my gear for removal to 135. The next morning at breakfast, while savouring a good cup of coffee, I went over the events of the day before. Peter Butcher was obviously a very capable officer, conscientious and thoroughly reliable as a minesweeping supervisor. The Engine Chief had responded quickly to my orders down the voice-pipe and on the telegraph, which made the operation of mooring in Porto Vecchio so much easier. The crew were quick about their work on the upperdeck, and showed every sign of long experience. In fact, I reckoned I was joining a going concern in tip-top form, and all I had to do was carry on the good work. However, one thing bothered me.

The man I was replacing was undoubtedly a character. Johnny Peel was older than most of us. It seemed that he exercised an effortless authority over those who served under him. Coming as he did from a well-known family in UK, and having longer experience in the Service than the rest of the officers in the Flotilla, it was natural that he should occupy a rather special place in the minds of those around him. He had, in answer to a question of mine, told me that his family owned the famous firm John Peel & Sons, boot and shoemakers to the Royal Family and other crowned heads of Europe. I knew their premises well. It was at the top of Oxford Street, near Marble Arch. I had often admired the beautiful footwear in their windows. They were particularly well known for their bespoke riding boots, which would have no doubt cost a fortune. There is a deal of difference between the confidence that is gained by experience and the confidence that is natural and does not need to grow. For all these reasons, Johnny Peel would be a hard act to follow.

Somehow, I had to hump two heavy kitbags down to 135, but was fortunate enough to get a lift in a navy truck going that way. My kitbags and I were dropped on the harbour wall and Peel, who was on the bridge of 135, saw me. At once a seaman was sent to collect my gear and bring it down to the wardroom. That's what I mean by effortless authority.

Chaos reigned down below. The entire floor space of the wardroom was covered with Johnny's belongings. Several years of Service was reflected there. Together with all his clothes, the stuff filled four kitbags and I wondered how he would manage ashore. But, true to style, Peel sent for one of the crew and gave him a message, addressed to Commander Ward's secretary, requesting transport to the Club. In a remarkably short time a navy Jeep arrived. The driver removed all the bags and departed.

Johnny then sent another message, this time to ML 402, inviting the CO aboard for a farewell drink. 402 was commanded by Lieutenant Phillip Fellows, the SO. 'He may be ashore, Dickie, but if not, I thought that it would be a good opportunity for you to meet the young bugger. He's a brilliant sweeper and we are all very fond of him.' Much later Fellows was to meet my Father, but that's another story for another time.

It was by then only mid-morning, far too early to start drinking, but Johnny was already behind the bar, so to speak. I don't really like gin, but so far I had felt it best to go along with the general mood and pretend that I did. This would have to change though. I was already learning from the one-time CO of 135.

'Any questions, Dickie?' he asked.

'Yes, there is one. We've never talked about the crew. Is there anyone you would like to replace?' I said.

'No! They are all good chaps in the main, as far as I know. You would have to ask Peter for any inside information on this subject.'

Another lesson learned. This was 'big ship stuff'! One must not encroach on the First Lieutenant's territory but keep a distance.

The family atmosphere in HDML 1297 had no place here, and I made a quick resolve to be more reserved without being unpleasant. That would be difficult because I'd always wanted people to like me. To some extent I must now substitute 'like' for 'respect', and I hoped that perhaps the mooring in Porto Vecchio had helped in this regard.

We talked of events ashore and at sea. Johnny made to pour me a second G&T but, quite firmly, I refused (I thought I might as well start now; if I could face out Lieutenant Johnny Peel, I could do it with anybody). He pressed me once more, then gave up, smiled and poured the gin into his own glass. It takes one strong will to recognise another!

A Bosun's pipe sounded, signalling the SO's arrival. It was the custom in the Third Flotilla ML to pipe the SO aboard as recognition of his status as SO. The other officers visited each other's boats without ceremony. Fellowes was a good-looking, slightly built man of about twenty-five. His features had something feminine about them, and a lock of hair fell over his forehead when he laughed. Much later I was to meet a man with similar characteristics, whose exploits became known throughout the Service, at home and abroad.

'Phil, this is Lieutenant Dickie Beale, my long lost relief,' said Johnny. 'He takes over today. Dickie, this is Phillip Fellows, SO of the Third, and a pretty good egg when he's not reading *The Mine-Sweeping News.*'

We shook hands, more gin was poured, and I raised a hand saying, 'Not for me.'

'You must have something, Dickie, to speed me on my way!' said Johnny.

'Have you any wine, you know, just ordinary plonk?' I asked.

'Of course' said Johnny, 'Peter, excavate the wine locker, would you?'

Then ensued one of the most enjoyable hours I'd spent for years. The four of us talked, laughed and drank until Johnny, looked at his watch and said, 'Right, this is it! I must start the long passage home. Can't face any more corned beef! Are you listening, Peter?'

We all wished him luck and a long leave. As a last goodwill gesture, he presented me with his 'minesweeping hat'. Of course, I never wore it. The hat was Johnny's signature, but I kept it on board, as a souvenir. I went with him and watched as his determined figure disappeared round the curve of the wall. Would I be able to take his place? I wondered. Somehow I had to fill that space.

The SO and I sat together in the wardroom while he gave me a thorough summary of minesweeping as it applied to us. Different kinds of mines required different methods of clearance. We in the Third ML Flotilla were only concerned with moored mines, which constituted the vast majority of the devices laid.

Phil Fellows left me at dusk, and I set about stowing my gear. It occurred to me that a chat with the Chief would be useful. I rang for the steward and asked him to knock on the Chief's door, and request him to come and see me. 'Chief, is there any problem that we ought to deal with before the next operations?' I said. It appeared that there was nothing outstanding. Fuelling had taken place while the SO and I were talking, and had been supervised by No 1 and himself. Like most Chiefs, he was proud of his engines, and his account of their capabilities and their foibles added to my feeling that this was a well-run ship.

Peter Butcher then returned from the town where he and cook had been hunting for extra rations to complement the official stuff from the base. 'Not much luck, plenty of veg but no meat or poultry,' he said. 'I reckon the Officers' Club gets it all.'

Dinner that night was unfortunately a taste of things to come. Corned beef fritters, potatoes and tinned peas. Peter and I talked for a while after the meal, then he produced a pleasant surprise. From the bottom of his wardrobe he brought out a wind-up gramophone and some records. 'Do you like music?' he said. 'Johnny never let me play it when he was aboard. He disliked classical stuff and just about tolerated anything else.'

The strains of a Mozart concerto graced the handsome wardroom. I just leaned back, shut my eyes and absorbed the sound and the atmosphere. This was something unexpected. Although I was completely ignorant as far as classical music was concerned, I had always enjoyed listening to it and was willing to learn. Peter taught me a lot in the course of the year ahead.

Two or three days passed at rest in Porto Vecchio. Then a signal arrived from Sharky Ward's office requesting my presence in his conference room at 11am the same day. When I arrived the other COs were already there. We sat around a long table, with the Commander at one end and our SO at the other. Sharky then commenced an outline of our next operation, which was to take place the following day. At a point north of Monopoli we were to sweep a channel leading to the harbour and clear the approaches to it. We were then required to repeat the operation south of Monopoli. Nights were to be spent in Brindisi. Sharky's secretary brought in a briefcase and emptied the contents on to the table. Six envelopes littered the green baize, each one with the name of a CO on it.

The letters were all the same. They were typed versions of the Commander's lecture. Each envelope contained a photo of the relevant Admiralty chart, with the area to be swept clearly marked.

The duplication was to enable any boat to take over the lead in case of damage to the SO. We then adjourned to the bar next door where Sharky gave his time to each one of us in turn. I was told by a member of his staff that he referred to us as 'His Boys'.

First light on the following morning found us in line ahead, on passage for the sweep area. As newcomer to the force, I was placed last, which in fact was the easiest position to occupy. It was only necessary to keep inside the after-float of the sweep wire ahead, without having to worry about anyone astern.

Far behind a trawler laid marker buoys every mile, to mark the boundary of the swept area. At the end of the designated sweep the whole force would turn around 180 degrees, and sweep along the line of markers, which were then picked up as the last boat passed. They were then relaid on the next leg. It was a lengthy and tiring business, requiring care and concentration from all concerned. On completion the Flotilla 'took in sweeps' and headed for the southern area to be swept. With both operations completed, the Flotilla entered Brindisi Harbour as darkness was falling. As I was eating the usual dinner of disguised corned beef, I remember feeling more tired than a thirty-six hour spell on the bridge had caused in the past. Peter organised a sentry watch, otherwise all hands were permitted to turn in.

We remained in Brindisi for two days awaiting further instructions. When they came, they were for the already cleared area to be widened on the shore side.

It was several weeks before we cut our first mine, but it seemed that the boats ahead did pretty well, as the sound of rifle and cannon fire indicated. When a mine was cut it came to the surface and was exploded by gunfire. The sudden pull on the sweep wire could be felt through the hull, and even on the bridge, when a mine was engaged. The whole crew would gather on deck to watch the explosion. Great fun! At such moments I felt that our lives at sea were justified when compared with the army, which, in my opinion, faced greater dangers and more hardships than we did.

For five or six weeks we continued these operations which were always prefaced by meetings in Commander Ward's conference room. On one such occasion a diversion took place. The Commander's secretary was a Sub-Lieutenant RNVR and it was he who typed the orders and put them in the envelopes that he later tipped out of his briefcase on to the table. This time the Commander pressed the bell for his secretary and lit his pipe. The Sub-Lieutenant entered bearing the famous briefcase. He opened it and out poured a shower of contraceptives on to the green baize cloth. The small packets scattered far and wide – enough for everybody! When the laughter died down Sharky removed his pipe and said, 'I see, gentlemen, that you are more concerned with matters ashore than afloat. When your priorities are revised we will adjourn to the bar as usual.' I was never to discover which one of us had intercepted the secretary's briefcase, which was always on a side table in the anteroom before a meeting.

This long spell of work came to an end one evening in Barletta Harbour. We had just finished a sweep to the north of that port and were gradually moving up the Adriatic, keeping pace with the Eighth Army. I was looking forward to a quiet drink and dinner for once. The cook and Peter had, at last, found success ashore the previous night. In exchange for some coffee and twenty-five lira, they had purchased half a pig and some green vegetables. Although our cook was not in the same class as our brilliant one on the HDML, the meal was a real treat after weeks of Spam, corned beef and tinned carrots. Peter and I soaked up the last of the gravy with stale bread, and then turned to some tinned prunes, of which we seemed to have an unlimited supply.

Then there was a knock on the wardroom door, and a sentry entered with a note from the SO. It read, 'From NOIC, Mine Clearance Adriatic. Return Bari for leave and engine service.' The evening was lit by the stars and the strains of Beethoven's Fifth Symphony floated up the wardroom steps and joined them. The prospect before us felt like the promise of Christmas when I was a child. Peter and I spent a truly wonderful evening listening to music, moistened with a little wine, and dreaming of leave. I pushed aside a thought that perhaps I should be conferring with the Chief and going over any possible defects that should be listed for the base engineers. What the hell, I could do that in Bari. I looked about the wardroom and decided that it needed something. What was it? Yes, of course, it needed a picture. That was also something to attend to in Bari.

Unfortunately, the return to Bari was never completed. A signal was received cancelling the last instructions, instructing all COs to report to NOIC, Barletta, at 11.00am. A conference was held at which it was decided that the Third ML Flotilla was to be used to bring off refugees from the Adriatic coast at night. We were each given a copy of a piece of chart showing the section of beach allocated to each ML. Apparently, there had been a massacre in Biograd and people were fleeing from the area. As far as I can remember this was the last time that the Flotilla was together as one force. From then on I was given individual assignments, some quite dramatic, such as those in the Gulf of Patras later on.

One night, a few days after the conference in Barletta, ML 135 was at anchor off the Dalmatian coast, near the island of Pelješac. We lay about two cables off the beach awaiting a flash signal from among the trees ashore. It was 2.00am, there was no moon and the clouds were low, obscuring the stars. Gunfire was heard inland, with an occasional bright light from a star shell. Our dinghy was launched, ready to leave for the beach. The timing was perfect, at exactly 2.00am flashes from the trees spelled out 'SOS'. A group of people and a child emerged from the shadows. We brought back fourteen adults and one little girl, aged about seven. She had been separated from her parents who were in another ML further up the coast. But for this one mistake, the rescue operations were faultlessly planned and executed by the Special Services who were operating covertly among the inhabitants, in spite of the German invading force.

We landed the refugees at Bari, as instructed. I was ordered to moor at Porto Vecchio. The child was to remain on board until her parents could be found. We made up a bed for her in the wheelhouse. I learned that her name was Ljerka, which is Serbo-Croat for Lilian. She was a brave child and seemed to accept our assurances that her parents were on another boat and that they would all be together soon. Two days later the parents were found and a Red Cross nurse came to collect Ljerka. The whole crew, and myself, were sorry to see her go; she had become a sort of mascot. Little did I guess that I would see her again, in more than one country, and that we were to exchange letters long after the war had ended.

A whole week passed in Porto Vecchio. Every day I expected to be sent on another mission to the Dalmatian coast, but no order came. Instead we were told to move to Bari's main harbour and hand the ship over to the base engineers for a general engine service. Two weeks' leave was granted to the ship's company, which was later extended by another week. Now began an enchanting time, if such a description can be used while a war is in progress. At any rate, the next few weeks were a wonderful respite from the strain of minesweeping and the discipline of life aboard. For the first few days Peter Butcher and I lived at the Officers' Club.

During this time I met the army Sergeant who was in charge of the spare parts supply for army vehicles. He had a number of trucks that were not considered reliable enough for active service, and were cannibalised for spares. He gave me one, and I found it adequate for a bit of local jaunting. It was a five-ton pick-up truck and with it I was able to explore the countryside. Soon after gaining possession of the vehicle, I read a signal on the reception desk at the Officers' Club, inviting men to spend their leave at a rest camp for officers which had been opened at a place called Fasano, some twenty miles distant from Bari. I remembered being near there a year before, and decided to investigate.

The rest camp proved to be an entire village of houses up in the hills. They were called trulli. These buildings are notable for their conically shaped roofs that resemble a dunce's hat. These remarkable structures are tiled with stone pieces, laid in such a way that from the inside you could see daylight between them. But rain did not and could not leak in, although wind certainly could blow through, which kept the house cool in the very hot climate of that part of Italy. There were about ten of these houses in the settlement and I've never understood to this day why they were all vacant.

I had a slip of paper from the club assigning me one these dwellings, and I walked into the yard. The war so far had held many surprises, but none so unexpected, or so pleasant, as this one: Ljerka ran out to meet me. A number of refugees that the MLs had rescued had been given temporary employment as caretakers at the rest camp. It was sheer luck that I was directed to that one. Her parents, Terka and Dragutin, followed close behind the little girl and general rejoicing filled the evening air. A fine meal followed, for Terka was a good cook; much wine was drunk and many songs sung, before sleep overtook us all.

I could see why the little girl had been so brave when she had been separated from her parents. Even before that episode they had been through so much, and been near to death at times. On my first morning Ljerka, her parents and I sat on a stone bench in the yard and ate a simple breakfast of cheese, bread, toast and jam. Over the meal they told me of their escape from the Nazis and its horrifying aftermath. Dragutin Ebenspanger (or Charles, for that was his name in English) had been a shoemaker in Biograd, which was under German occupation. One morning, announcements from loudspeakers in the streets and posters on the walls ordered all builders, carpenters, electricians, tailors, shoemakers and manual workers to assemble in the stadium. Everyone thought that they would be found work, but instead, like sheep, they went to their doom. Machine-guns opened up on the assembled crowd and a terrible massacre took place.

Charles, and one or two others, had some premonition that all was not well and did not go to the stadium. Instead they fled into the dense forest that covered much of the countryside. He had put all their important belongings, some food and containers of water on to a handcart, and led his wife and daughter into the woods, where they existed for two months. Ljerka caught a fever during this time, but by some miracle she recovered. When I heard this story I knew that the rumours of atrocities had a real foundation and that the huge effort being made by the Allies was totally justified. There was no other way.

The hardships these people had suffered, and my own part in defending them, drew us together as a sort of family. Happy days were spent in the mountain air or making trips in my pick-up truck. On one such trip Ljerka and I went to Fasano to look again at the huge Gorgonzola cheese store in the caves. On the way back I had to slow down almost to a halt to let an army vehicle pass, and on pulling away again, the vehicle suddenly felt heavy and sluggish. Ten miles further on I was stopped at a roadblock, and six Italians, who must have jumped in the back when I had slowed down, leaped out and headed for the woods!

Some days I drove into Bari with Ljerka and we would go to the Officers' Club for lunch. Her mother took special care on such days to dress her in her best clothes, all of which Terka had made herself. The little girl always sat bolt upright at table and was ready to answer any officer who spoke to her. No one seemed to think it odd that I should have such a guest for lunch. I think this was because Bari was awash with refugees, and children were often separated from parents and in the care of others for a short time.

On days when it became very hot Ljerka and I would go the beach, which was five miles from the hills, and swim all day, collect shells and make sand castles. Terka would give me a spare pair of knickers for her daughter and a towel, instructing me to dry her and change her wet pants, which had done duty as a swimming costume. Also included in the small sack would be some sandwiches and a bottle of water for our lunch. What a different world it was back then. Who today would trust their seven-year-old daughter to a man they hardly knew?

Whenever I was free I would visit the three of them, and Ljerka became like a daughter to me. I always looked forward to the evenings when the last of the meal was finished, and the singing and storytelling would begin. Ljerka would climb on my knee and add her little voice to the harmony. The whole family spoke English, as well as Serbo-Croat and Italian. They appreciated any contribution I was able to make. Those days and nights were as precious to me as anything that has happened since, outside of my own family life.

Like all good things, the idyll had to end and I am reminded in retrospect of Shakespeare's lines, from *Cymbeline*, 'Golden lads, and girls all must as chimney sweepers come to dust.' However, the next operation was not really the end but only an interruption. The breakdown of the truck coincided with the end of my leave. I was just able to get Ljerka back to her parents before the shaky vehicle gave up the ghost. It made a dreadful noise as I crept into the dump from which I had taken it some three weeks before.

When I arrived on board 135 there was a signal waiting for me to report at once to Sharky Ward. Over the next two hours the crew and Peter Butcher also came back aboard. I was directed to sail to a small fishing port named Corsini, to the south of Bari, and to sweep the approaches before entering. The instruction stated that a narrow channel between high walls led into the harbour itself. The order gave me two days to store ship, take on water and fuel, and then to depart as soon as we were in all respects ready for sea.

The instruction included a warning to take every possible precaution when entering the narrow channel, as mines fixed to iron tripods might be encountered. If any of these were found we were to withdraw at once and report to base. The Chief and I then had a long talk with the base engineer, who had been responsible for the servicing of the Hall-Scotts. He assured us that the engines were in excellent condition and that very few parts had needed renewal. The base had also exchanged one of our two generators for a new one and had overhauled the other. I was amazed that completely new units as expensive as generators could be produced at Bari. Malta was the only place I knew in the Mediterranean to have such things, and I left the two engineers feeling confident about my ship and its future. As usual, Peter and the cook had little luck in their search for extra rations in the town, apart from a good supply of vegetables.

The passage to Corsini was uneventful, and we commenced sweeping the approaches at roughly 5.00pm on a calm afternoon.

No mines were found, but I dared not enter the narrow channel as the visibility was not good enough to be able to see any tripods beneath the surface. This was always the job of a mine lookout on the bow. As it was a calm night I was able to anchor about two cables from the beach. Peter arranged watches for the two lookouts throughout the night. The next day I waited for the maximum amount of overhead light before entering the channel. I reckoned that this occurred near midday, but I hated waiting and was impatient to get on. Very, very slowly we entered and, thankfully, the water was clear. We inched our way into the harbour, and nothing was seen. I looked for fishing boats in the belief that mines would be less likely to be in an area where they were anchored.

The fishing boats were all crowded up into one corner of the small harbour and moored to the wall. The rest of the wall was vacant, which suggested that mines might be alongside. I stopped at the end of the narrow channel and pondered this. The water in the basin was opaque, which might mean that it had recently been stirred up by the passage of a vessel. At that moment the problem was solved. One of the fishing boats moved away from the wall, headed across the centre of the harbour and passed into the channel, narrowly missing us as she went by. They were clearly outward bound for a night's fishing and this restored my confidence in the place. A busy port is a safe port.

When alongside I reported to the commander's office and asked for instructions. The signal that came back puzzled me. It was worded in an unusual way. It simply read: 'Remain Corsini until further notice.' This implied that we might be here for days, or possibly weeks. I was reading this signal on the bridge when a Jeep drew up on the jetty above, an American WAAF jumped out and passed a piece of paper to me on the end of stick. It read: 'To CO ML 135 from Officer Commanding Fighter Squadron US Air base Corsini. Request your company for dinner this evening at approximately 8.00pm. Please reply.'

I called to the WAAF driver and asked her to wait for a few minutes while I consulted my First Lieutenant. Peter was enthusiastic to say the least. 'Oh good' he said. 'We might touch them for some decent food. The Yanks live like kings.' Peter, like so many No 1s, always had an eye for the main chance. Their duties and responsibilities required a practical attitude to nearly all situations. The WAAF confirmed that the building on the hill, behind the harbour office, was the US fighter base headquarters and that they would send transport. 'Peter, if I'm needed, fire two rounds from the Bofors,' I said. I would hear that noise if I was a mile away, and this is only a matter of yards. I then scribbled a note of acceptance and thanks, and told the driver that I needed the exercise and would walk.

The US Commander held the equivalent rank of Group Captain in the RAF, and was a man who impressed me by his modesty, in spite of the fact that he was in charge of the most important defence force in an area stretching from southern Sicily to Ancona. Above all else, he guarded the air space over Bari that had become the biggest supply base and repair centre in the Mediterranean after Malta. He was short, muscular and scarred about the face and arms. A black patch over one eye emphasised the intense blue of the other eye, and enhanced his general piratical appearance. I asked him about the patch and he confirmed what I had already guessed. 'Shot down over France, Captain. Never saw the lucky guy, but it must have been an ME (Messerschmitt BF 109) on my tail.'

I warmed to this man, so generous to his enemies and careless of his injuries. The meal was superb. I made a point of remembering it so that I could tell Peter, because I knew he would ask. We ate roast turkey, followed by American apple pie and waffles and maple syrup. Excellent coffee rounded off the meal. The local wine was drinkable, but the Commander hankered after a drop of Scotch, which was unthinkable in the US forces. I promised to do something about this. I asked him about operations and the well-being of his squadron. Here, this brave man hesitated before answering. I saw his scarred face crumble slightly as he began to relate events of the past month.

'Well, Captain,' he said. 'I've just lost two of my best pilots. They were both tall men, and their heads came above the seat which is armour plated. I need a bit of armour plate to put above the back of the seat so that their heads and necks are protected. Both of these guys were shot up from astern. The average pilot is OK in a Mustang, but if a guy is really tall there is no protection.'

'Cannot the mighty US change the seats?' I asked.

'Captain, I've sent signals all over the Mediterranean, and one to the White House, but the bastards don't answer,' he replied. 'There is a small tanker sunk in the harbour. It has an armour-plated bridge. I sent a swimmer down to confirm this. I've got the cutting gear and a workshop, but I need a diver to go down and do the cutting. Would Bari lend me a diver? I guess they must have one.'

'They've got two, but they work non-stop servicing ships of all sizes from MLs to frigates and merchant vessels. They literally never stop, except to sleep,' I told him. I knew this as a fact because one of our Flotilla had damaged a rudder and had to wait a week before being investigated.

The word frigate led me to think of another navy warship, a light cruiser, one that was anchored among the islands on the other side of the Adriatic. It was our new base when operating on that side of the water. I knew that they had a diver who only had the MLs and a few trawlers to deal with. It was unlikely that he would be constantly working. Now comes a point in this narrative when my memory fails me: I know I planned the next event but cannot remember carrying it out.

The plan was for me to cross over to the islands at night, to borrow a diver from the cruiser and then return with him to Corsini and the US airbase. The American commander said there would be no problem about getting him back to where he belonged. He would be flown back in a helicopter. 'I'll have my chopper standing by ready to fly him back the moment he finished, Captain,' he said. 'If he does the job, he won't regret it. I'll see to that.'

Well, that was the plan and, of course, everything depended on the CO of the cruiser *Calypso* being willing to release the diver for thirty-six hours or so. Much later I was thanked in kind by the squadron CO, which seems to confirm that the clandestine passage, against all orders, actually took place but, as I say, I've absolutely no memory of it. I'm therefore going to assume that it happened and record what I think may have taken place.

I've wondered since then whether I may have subconsciously excluded the affair from my mind because of the risk it posed to my career, and to whatever job Sharky Ward had in store for me. Here is what I think happened, and I hope the reader will forgive me if I'm wrong. On returning aboard after the dinner at the US base, I called for the Chief and consulted him about spares.

'Chief, is there anything we need urgently in the way of spares,' I told him in confidence of my plan, and the reason for it. 'You see, Chief, the squadron is vital to the defence of Bari and this part of Italy. They are losing pilots for want of a bit of armour plating.'

'Well, sir,' he said. 'I could use a spare slave cylinder for the Lockheed steering. The present one is old and not performing too well.'

'What? Are you serious?' I said in response. 'You mean you have let me sweep with 'double L' gear knowing that the steering was faulty? That could have been a disaster.'

The Chief made a faint noise that might have been a chuckle. 'I've got a mate in Malta, sir. Slave cylinders are hard to get, but he makes sure I've always got a private supply. I've got two, sir, but they are off the record.'

'Thank you, Chief. We will be underway in thirty minutes.'

I then spent a few minutes reflecting on two signs that hopefully pointed to a successful outcome. One was the strong wording of the instruction from Sharky's office, which was to remain in Corsini until further notice. That certainly suggested a stay longer than twenty-four hours. The other was the ability of the US Air Force to supply us with 100 octane fuel, which was what they used in their planes. I had seen the tanker and been promised as much as I wanted.

Midnight found us thirty-five miles outward bound from Corsini, speed 16 knots, distance to cover 130 miles. At 9.30am we were alongside the *Calypso*, and I was in the CO's office. 'You are asking a lot, Beale,' he said. 'Does Commander Ward approve?' In my mind I was taken back to that far distant day when I faced a recruitment board in that awful drill hall in Finchley. Should I tell the truth or lie? I decided not to lie. The Lieutenant Commander, RN, listened while I gave him the whole story finishing with, 'You see, sir, those Mustangs are vital to the defence of Bari and the whole area, and they are losing pilots for the want of a bit of armour plating.'

'Surely, Beale, the US Air Force will take care of this matter?' he said. 'The CO has sent signals all over the Med but without any response,' I replied. 'He told me that he had even sent one to the White House. I suppose something will be done in time, but he needs the material now and it's there in the harbour. He has a workshop and cutting gear, now he only needs a diver for an hour or two. I know that the divers at Bari are working round the clock. It's no good asking them. I know too that I'm risking my career, but I'm banking on getting back before any signal arrives from Commander Ward.'

'You may have already been called and given no reply,' he said. 'We have arranged a constant radio watch, using members of the crew so that Sparks can get a few hours' sleep, nothing so far,' I replied. The Lieutenant Commander, RN, CO of HMS *Calypso*, was silent for about ten seconds. He then scribbled something on a slip of paper and handed it to me. 'Give that to my Supply Officer, and make sure he knows that the man will be returned by helicopter. I'm going ashore, Beale, and I don't expect to find you here when I get back.'

The return journey was completed in eight hours, during which I held my breath metaphorically, in case we were spotted from the air or received a signal. Nothing was heard or seen. How lucky can you be? We entered Corsini Harbour at 6.30pm. The fuel tanker was waiting for us together with a Jeep to take the diver to the US base. I have forgotten the diver's name in the same way as I've failed to picture in my mind's eye the passage to *Calypso* and our short time there. I just hope that it all took place and was not a dream!

CHAPTER 7

✳

Clearing mines in the Greek islands

1944

We stayed for a week in Corsini Harbour without a signal from Bari. Peter and the cook had moderate success ashore, and were able to purchase a number of chickens, and a goose, in exchange for coffee, a little sugar and fifty lira. Peter arranged shore leave for the whole crew, leaving only a sentry and a radio watch on board, but while ashore they had always to be within sight and sound of the ship. I had two more dinners at the US fighter base and the heartfelt gratitude of the CO. Much later he emphasised his gratitude in a different way.

After eight or nine days, we received a long signal from Bari instructing us to take on fuel, water and stores. It also said that arrangements had been made with the US base to replenish our victuals, where possible, and to supply us with aviation spirit. It also stated that water was available from the jetty. On completion we were to report when our vessel was in all respects ready for sea. It is not often that one can pre-empt an order from the 'controlling power' ashore. I had already taken fuel from the US base, and Peter had discovered the source of the fresh water supply within an hour of us being in Corsini. However, it had never occurred to me to ask for rations from the Americans and, even if I had, I would have hesitated. The thought of asking them for food made me uneasy. Any doubts I had were soon allayed with the arrival of a Jeep-load of iron rations for twenty-one men for three weeks. Peter and I looked at the boxes and wondered just what our next assignment would be. Three weeks is a long time to be away from base in a small ship.

After making my report we didn't have long to wait. Within the hour we received instructions to proceed to position X, for which the co-ordinates were given, and to rendezvous with the Mediterranean Fleet sweeper squadron, under the command of Captain Jefferson, RN. Until further notice we were to operate under his direction only. Peter and I immediately retired to the wheelhouse where, by luck, the first chart we looked at was the right one. The co-ordinates put position X approximately five miles east of the mouth of the Gulf of Patras, in Greece. At our cruising speed of ten knots we would need twenty-six hours to make the passage, which was well within the designated arrival time.

It was 11.30am when we left the wheelhouse, Peter going below to see the cook and me to study the pilot publication for the area, which was littered with islands. The relevant pilot publication was always kept on the bridge by the voice-pipe, so I replaced it and went below. From below I called Peter, through the voice-pipe, telling him to inform the crew that we would 'slip' at 5.30pm and clear the channel entrances by 6pm. The cook fed the ship's company at 3.00pm, giving everyone time for a smoke, and perhaps a bit of shut-eye. As this could be the last meal in calm water for some time, Peter arranged for the chickens to be roasted, but saved the goose for later when, perhaps, one or two more could be added. The dinner was a great success and long remembered on days when we were back on the dreaded corned beef. The roasted birds, with green vegetables and roast potatoes, were followed by American tinned plum duff. I smoked my pipe for half an hour and enjoyed the feeling of having fed well; Peter played his gramophone.

At 6.05pm we were to be found three cables to seaward of the Corsini channel entrance, heading south-south-east at ten knots. The sea was calm, and from the crew's quarters the sound of a mouth organ floated up the hatch into the evening air. Both Peter and I reckoned that a radio watch was no longer essential. 'Sparks' was relieved of his duties until we were under the command of Captain Jefferson; from then on he might get little rest. The watch on deck was busy squaring up mooring lines, fenders and other equipment, and cleaning all guns, which were tested using blank rounds. Peter went aft with his assistant, Leading Seaman Grayham, who was a most excellent man. He and Peter had long worked together on the care and maintenance of the minesweeping gear, and were once again checking the apparatus, for it surely would be in operation before too long.

The night passed comfortably with the usual changes of watch. I handed over to Peter at midnight, and came up again at 4.00am. The calm weather held until 8.00am when the sky darkened and a nasty chop, driven by a north-easter, furrowed the surface. The day was unpleasant, but not dangerous, and I was glad to think that everyone had been well fed the day before.

By 6.00pm the wind eased and the sea flattened to some extent. Throughout the day the cook had kept us going with soup, bread and sausages. A few minutes after six he handed me a mug of cocoa and a hefty cheese sandwich. I remember thinking how lucky I was to have such a crew. They were efficient, cheerful and willing. Unfortunately, I was soon to lose one of them.

'There they are, sir,' said Peter, handing me the glasses. Sure enough, five grey shapes were faintly visible on the horizon. I drank the last of my cocoa, and studied the view ahead. I had not expected to see anything before 7.00pm, but there was no doubt about it: As the shapes were on exactly the right bearing, it must be them. As the distance between us decreased, the grey patches grew longer and assumed the profiles of ships. My heart beat a little faster as the vessels grew larger. I do not remember having seen a Fleet Sweeper before, which was odd because the coasts around the UK must have been swept by some of them. I wondered why I hadn't seen one in Malta, then I realised that the HDMLs had spent their time in Sliema Creek, while the larger vessels were in Grand Harbour.

Compared with Mine Sweeping Trawlers and British Yard Mines Sweepers (BYMS) as they were called, these ships were huge. They were almost as long as a light cruiser, but much wider in the beam and with a high superstructure. From a distance, they resembled assault ships. Up close, they took on their proper size and shape. We dipped our ensign in salute when within a cable's distance, and I used the loudhailer for permission to come alongside. This was given and ratings, high above us, stood by to take our lines. The officer of the watch leaned over the side and invited me aboard. They threw down a rope ladder and I climbed stiffly to the deck. Long hours spent on the bridge of a small vessel are not the best preparation for such 'mountaineering'. A Bosun's Pipe sounded as I touched the deck. That was such a thrill. I had never been piped aboard before, but I was the CO of a naval ship and, as such, was entitled to the courtesy.

I saluted the officer of the watch who was a Lieutenant, RN, and he returned it. The ceremonies over, he held out his hand saying, 'Welcome aboard. The C-in-C Mine-sweepers wishes to see you. I will take you to his cabin.' Captain Jefferson put me at ease at once. He held out his hand in answer to my salute, and I took of my cap. 'You did well, Lieutenant, exactly on time.' It was then 8.10pm, our rendezvous time given by Bari.

He motioned me to a chair and, to my surprise, offered me a drink. 'I don't drink spirits, sir, but if you have any wine, red or white?' I said. 'Of course, wise man, Mother's Ruin, not to mention rot-gut rum, does no one any good,' he replied. He poured each of us a generous glass of wine from his bottle rack on the sideboard, then sat back and began to outline the plan of operations in the Gulf of Patras. So that was it. Patras. It was an interesting part of the world. I knew that Lord Byron was buried there, but I mustn't let my thoughts wander.

'At 6.00am tomorrow you will proceed to this position here.' Jefferson unfolded a chart extract and pointed to a large cross at the mouth of the Gulf, 'It will be marked by a Dan buoy, with a trawler beside it. You will wait there until I signal out sweeps. On sighting the executive flag, you will stream both sweeps and steam on this course at four knots, passing through the centre of the narrows at Patras Town. A BYMS will join you at Patras and lead through the narrows. They have a 'knacker' on the bows, and it is believed that acoustic mines may lie in the shallower water there.'

Back aboard 135, cook had been busy, as evidenced by the smell of the eternal corned beef fritters that hung about the deck. Going down the wardroom hatch I looked up at the quarterdeck of the Fleet Sweeper and noticed her name for the first time. She was called *Boscastle* and I made a mental note to remember it when writing up the log after the meal. I also noticed the enormous winches on the stern, holding miles of sweep wire, and the huge size of the paravanes. It made me realise what a vast area these ships could sweep in one run once the initial cut had been made, and the leader was in safe water. That was our job, and Heaven help us to do it with credit.

At precisely 6.00am we let go our lines and headed for the trawler, which I could just see. Sparks stood beside me on the bridge because Captain Jefferson had told me that all signals would be made by Aldis lamp, except the executive flag ordering out sweeps. At 6.25am we reached the trawler and stayed as close to the buoy as possible, which was somewhat difficult as the north-east wind of the day before had returned. It was unlikely to be noticed by the big vessels now steaming towards us in perfect line ahead formation. Peter and Leading Seaman Grayham were standing by our winches ready to obey the signal. At 7.00am I heard a shout from Peter and the sound of a splash as the 'otter' went over the stern, followed by three more splashes as the second 'otter' was streamed.

By counting the splashes I knew when both port and starboard sweeps were out. I dared not look astern as it was absolutely essential to keep exactly on the course that was given to me. I was greatly assisted in this by prominent landmarks on each sides of the entrance to the Gulf. My hand-held compass gave me perfect fixes all the way in. Suddenly I felt the familiar jerk of the hull as both sweeps became fully streamed, and the tow started. With both sweeps out, I was worried that I might not be able to maintain a speed of four knots, and cursed myself for not mentioning this to the Captain.

Keeping my eyes faced forward, I sent a lookout aft to ask No 1 to stream the log, and let me know our speed. In those days there was no GPS or other means of checking your speed. There was a gadget called a Chernikeeff Log that depended on water pressure passing through a pipe in the ship's bottom, but ours had long ago ceased to work. When working with the Third Flotilla there was no problem, as we would constantly adjust our speed in accordance with our distance from the float ahead. However, this situation was different because those 'big boys' ahead of us could not keep altering their speed. It had to be a constant four knots. The answer came back from Peter: '3.5 knots.' This wouldn't do, and I called down the voice-pipe for the Chief to increase revs very slowly. When our speed eventually reached four knots I gratefully called the Chief to stay at that number of revs.

We were now entering the mouth of the Gulf that was sheltered from the north, and conditions had become calm, even pleasant, and so I risked a quick look astern. With alarm I noticed that a huge ship's bow seemed to be right under our stern, but I quickly realised that it was in its proper position, just inside our starboard 'otter'. I marvelled at the precision with which those vessels operated. Every ship was exactly the same distance from the 'otter' ahead. I quickly turned back to the business in hand and shouted to the mine lookout on the bow, just to keep him on his toes.

For the next three hours all was quiet until Missolonghi, Lord Byron's resting place, came up on our port side. As I turned to glance at this famous town I felt a change in our speed and a tremor ran through the hull. I knew we were about to cut our first mine of the day. It surfaced a minute or two later and we left it to the big fellows to deal with. They had plenty of firepower and would be more accurate than us. Everything was so far, so good. Another hour passed before we cut our next mine and I knew, by the intermittent sound of gunfire, that the Fleet Sweepers were making hay. They were clearing a huge channel that would be doubled in width when they turned back and swept along the markers, which were laid by the trawler every half-mile.

At 1.00pm we sighted the town of Patras, having cut one more mine a mile further back. The narrows were now clearly visible, and I wondered whether the Fleet Sweepers would follow us through into the Gulf of Corinth. My orders, from the Commander aboard *Boscastle*, had been to sweep through the narrows; enter the Gulf of Corinth, pull to one side, take in sweeps and wait for instructions. But about two miles from Patras I saw the BYMS leave the harbour and enter the narrows. Almost immediately there was a loud explosion. I now know that the BYMS had encountered an acoustic mine. The wrecked ship finished up on the far bank. Dinghies and small craft shot out from the beach to pick up survivors. At our speed we were still half an hour from the start of the narrows, and I told Sparks to flash the *Boscastle* to ask for instructions. The big ship was still inside my 'otter' and maintaining a steady four knots. The answer came back 'Carry on'.

By the time we entered the narrows all survivors had been picked up. I made sure of this as we slowly ploughed our way through the bits of wreckage. The whole force followed us into the wider stretch of water beyond, having shortened their sweeps as Peter informed me later. I pulled to one side, took in sweeps and headed for the southern side of the Gulf, to give the squadron plenty of room to turn. The operation was faultless. Each ship completed its turn, took up its position inside the float ahead, streamed the full extent of its sweep, and headed back along the line of markers. As the *Boscastle* re-entered the narrows C-in-C Mediterranean Mine Sweeping Force signalled us: 'Proceed Patras Harbour and wait alongside for instructions from NOIC, Taranto. Well done and thank you!' I have wondered since why the Fleet Sweepers did not hesitate to enter the Gulf of Corinth and turn in unprotected water. I later learned a lot more about our network of intelligence throughout the region and the Adriatic.

We entered Patras Harbour at 4.00pm. It was crowded with fishing boats on all sides. I reckoned it safe to head directly for the southern side and moor alongside a small tanker until we could commandeer a bit of wall space. I reported our arrival to Taranto, which was acknowledged, but no instructions followed. Meanwhile, Peter had discovered a hydrant and, to our joint surprise, fresh water flowed from it. Patras had been badly damaged; partly by the Germans, and partly by one of the warlords who were now operating in the places vacated by them.

Peter, myself and the rest of the crew were all very subdued for the rest of the day. We all felt that the acoustic mine in the narrows had had our name on it, but the BMYS had taken the blow meant for us. The 'knocker' on the bows of the BMYS should have exploded the mine before the ship reached it. 'Knockers' send out a loud underwater pulses that trigger the mine's explosive mechanism. In this case the pulse must have been weak, and as the vessel passed over the mine, the noise of the turning screw would have done the rest.

Nobody felt like eating so Peter delayed our meal until 8.00pm. At 5.00pm I decided to go ashore to try to find some news of the survivors. I was intercepted by a young army Captain coming out of a tent. He waved to me and asked if we could signal our base for transport to ferry the wounded to hospital in Taranto. He said that half of the ship's company of eighteen had been saved and were unwounded, but of the other half five were dead and four others badly wounded. I called to Sparks to send the signal immediately. Three hours later a helicopter arrived to remove the men from the local Patras hospital, which was barely operating due to the shortage of equipment and supplies. That evening a service was held on the beach opposite the wreck. I learned some time afterwards that a memorial service was held on every anniversary, and may even continue to this day.

Peter arranged shore leave, but no one was very interested. Our meal that evening consisted of corned beef, followed by stewed prunes. Some cheese and hard tack pushed the wretched stuff down.

We lay in Patras Harbour for three days waiting for instructions from Taranto. Meanwhile, Peter and the cook searched ashore for additional food to vary our rations, but with little success. As mentioned earlier, the town had been pillaged. The local warlord was called Hermes and it was said that he commanded a force of two thousand men. From time to time, he would terrorise the local inhabitants by marching through the streets at the head of several hundred of his followers. Shops would be looted and girls were seized and raped. If their fathers, or young men protested, Hermes would carve the letter 'H' on the chest of the protester. For some unaccountable reason, a younger man would consider this a mark of honour. In a short while I was to have dealings with Hermes.

On the morning of the third day we received a long signal from Taranto that defined our duties for the weeks ahead. It looked as if we would be in the area for a month or more. We were instructed to sweep the inshore water on each side of the Gulf of Patras, and report our progress at the end of each day. When that was completed we were to sweep the approach to Itea and the Corinth Canal. Itia was the main port in the Gulf of Corinth, but there were several other smaller harbours on that side of the water. If any mines were found at Itia we were to search outside those smaller places as well. The long message ended by saying that a fuel barge was being sent and that it would anchor among the small islands at the mouth of the Gulf of Patras. Its exact position would be signalled to us as soon as it was known. There was an appendix wishing us good luck and saying that the work was to be done in our own time.

This was a great relief. It would have been very difficult to carry out such extensive operations to a set timetable. Peter and I had a talk and formulated a rough plan for the days ahead. We both agreed that it was vitally important to keep the crew exercised by giving shore leave as much as possible. This would mean returning to Patras Harbour as often we could. For some reason, I decided to start by sailing to the south side of the Patras Gulf in the broad channel cleared by the Fleet Sweepers, then to out sweeps and start the search heading back towards Patras. All gear was examined and a departure time set for 6.00am the following day. However, fate was to intervene and impose a short but dramatic delay to our plans.

Having finished our deliberations and swallowed the last of a horrible dinner, Peter played his gramophone and the early strains of a Schubert symphony began its journey through the evening air. It was never completed but was interrupted by the sentry knocking on the wardroom door. He announced the arrival of an army Captain who wished to speak to me. I offered him a drink and was pleased that he asked for a Scotch for, apart from the two bottles I had given to the US base CO at Corsini, the stuff had lain untouched in our wine locker. He told me that his spies had reported Hermes' intention to blow up the olive oil factory on the jetty the next day. This refinery provided the only paid employment in town and, although the drachma was practically worthless as a currency, the factory would be a vital asset as soon as the country recovered.

'We have to stop this,' he said, 'I'll have my chaps on parade with fixed bayonets as soon as he is spotted. Can you help?'

'Can we help? I should say so!' This was better than mine-sweeping. 'Of course, Captain, when do you think he'll arrive?'

'He's been through the town twice before and each time it's been at roughly 11.00am. This gives him time to get back to his stronghold in the hills to celebrate his prizes. He's always followed by his guard of a hundred or so men which enables him to do whatever he likes. My orders have been to avoid conflict with his force as they are a useful addition to our efforts against the

Germans. They hate the Germans, having lost men and territory to them. However, this is different. The factory must be saved somehow.'

It was decided that we would start manoeuvres outside the harbour and, at the signal from the Captain's tent, which would be a Union Jack being waved on a stick, we would head back in at speed. The young army officer left and I called the ship's company to appear on deck. It was still light enough to see by, and the crew quickly assembled. I heard afterwards that it was generally thought that a dire emergency had arisen, but when I explained that tomorrow's sweep was cancelled and gave the reason, a cheer went up. Everyone was sick of minesweeping and corned beef. At 10.30am the next day I was on the bridge, with the ship turning in slow circles outside the harbour wall. My glasses were trained on the army Captain's tent waiting for his signal. I could also see to the end of the main street down which the force would come. Behind the Captain's tent were a number of others that were larger, and they surrounded a thatched shelter that housed a cooking range. Everything about the encampment revealed order and discipline. Presently a shout from someone at the top of the main street warned us of the approach of Hermes.

There they were. A force of rather ragged-looking men, heavily armed with rifles and an assortment of knives and cutlasses. At their head strode a tall figure dressed in spotless attire, consisting of white linen trousers, and a brilliant blue shirt open to the waist. Through the glasses I could see two gold handled daggers thrust into his waistband. No signal yet from the Captain. He was obviously waiting for the moment of maximum effect. When Hermes had reached a point from which he could see the harbour, the Union Jack fluttered open outside the tent, and one hundred and twenty Scots Light Infantry troops marched in perfect formation into the centre of the area above the harbour wall. With kilts swinging and bayonets gleaming in the sunlight, they made an impressive sight. They drilled with faultless precision while we commenced a little gun practice and manoeuvred at speed. I handed over control to Peter as I wished to keep my eyes on Hermes. He did not falter but came on and entered the parade ground. This was our moment. The Bofors crew were at their post. Peter took the ship through the entrance at speed, and the Bofors was trained on Hermes, who stopped dead. At this point I took over control and Peter went forward to the Bofors.

'Full astern both!' I only just managed to take the way off in time before hitting the wall. Hermes and his men were still heading for the factory when Peter and his gunners swung the barrel round and fired two rounds, blowing the chimney off a derelict building just in front of Hermes. That did it.

The ragged army dispersed, ran back up the street and disappeared the way they had come. Peter then trained the Bofors on to Hermes, and kept it there until the Captain left his men, and bravely approached the warlord. An interpreter was sent for, and someone emerged from the Captain's tent. The three of them then went inside, and half an hour later Hermes came out carrying a box of army rations, survival food sufficient for two. He was last seen turning the corner at the top of the street.

The young army officer dispersed his company and, at my invitation, came aboard for another whisky. The factory had been saved. 'It's always best to give them something,' he said, 'That way they think they've won.' It was midday, no time for drinking in my opinion, and so I excused myself by saying that I needed some exercise but inviting him for dinner that evening.

As we were in harbour, the crew had their meal soon after 1.00pm and I asked Peter, as I went ashore, if he could persuade the cook to give us something decent to eat later, owing to the presence of an important guest. We had all admired the coolness of the 'Scotties' that morning, and especially the courage of the young Captain who had walked forward unarmed to meet a man displaying knives with which he had undoubtedly killed and wounded dozens, possibly hundreds of men.

I walked to the top of the main street and turned the corner round which the bandits had disappeared. The view was spectacular. Mountains rose up to form a backcloth to a green plain studded with olive trees. A horse and cart, managed by a girl driver, gave life to the scene. As we passed she said good afternoon in excellent English with only a slight accent. I was astonished and replied raising my cap. She stopped the cart which, when up close, I could see was an elegant two-wheeled carriage resembling a trap. She climbed down and extended her hand saying, 'I'm so glad the navy has come at last. We have been waiting and hoping for so long. The soldiers come and go because the situation with the Germans keeps changing. When the big ships came the other day we all felt safe, and believed that the war would soon be over, but they went away again. It was such a disappointment.' She said all this in a rush, as if she had been saving up the words for the right moment.

'You need to be patient for a little while longer,' I said, 'Our forces are fighting the Germans on both sides of the Adriatic, and we are winning. They will be driven out, you'll see. Half of Italy is now in our hands, and large parts of the Balkans.'

We talked and the pony grazed on the short grass that grew in patches among the stones and scrub. She told me that her name was Amelia Demetropolis and that she had been educated in England. In response to a question of mine she told me that her father was a banker, but since the collapse of the drachma, banking had become a joke. Notes were being printed with denominations of a million and it would take two of them to buy half a pound of coffee.

'How are you living?' I asked, 'Does your father work still?'

'He goes to the bank office in Patras on some days, but only for appearance. The bandits leave us alone because they have been told that they will be rewarded for fighting the Germans as soon as the currency recovers.'

We talked for a time and she invited me to dine with them the following day. I thought for a moment or two. Tomorrow I should be starting the long task of sweeping the inshore waters of the Gulf. Then I thought, Oh, what the hell! 'Yes,' I said, 'I should love to, thank you very much.'

We agreed to meet at the same spot at 6.00pm on the following evening, and parted. I walked on toward the hills. Something had changed in my thinking and in my attitude to authority since being given this lone assignment, which was likely to last for weeks. I felt free to make my own decisions within the framework of the overall task. Corsini was different. There, I took a risk for the sake of a greater cause, but now I was delaying things for my own pleasure, and I did not care. The crew could use the day in attending to some of the many jobs that always need doing aboard. Peter would arrange plenty of leave, and he and cook would no doubt continue to search for fresh vegetables.

But there was one thing I had to do immediately. I must arrange for a set time to receive signals so that Sparks could get more free time. I hurried back to the ship, hoping to find the signalman before Peter arranged his time ashore. He was in the wireless room as usual, and two times were arranged with Taranto for receiving messages. They were 8.00am to 9.00am and 6.00pm to 7.00pm.

'I want to thank you, Sparks, for the long watches you have kept without complaint. From now on I hope you will get plenty of onshore time and, this is important, plenty of exercise.' I left the wireless room and called for cook. 'Any hope of something other than corned beef or Spam this evening, cook? I'd like us to do our best for the army if we can. They deserve our thanks,' I said.

'I've done the best I could, sir. I've opened some of the American ration boxes and found tins of chicken portions and tins of real ham. The two I looked at the other day contained apple pie, which the First Lieutenant said was much appreciated in the wardroom.'

'That's right, cook, the pie was delicious,' I said. 'What's the menu then for tonight?'

'Tomato soup from packets, we've got plenty of that, chicken and ham pie, then plums and custard. Cheese, hard tack and coffee you have in the wardroom pantry, if they're wanted.'

'Thank you, cook, that should fit the bill very well. By the way, have a word with the steward if you would, and make sure he knows it's a special occasion.'

I read for a while until sleep overtook me, and I dreamed of mines coming to the surface and rising into the air like balloons. At 6.00pm Peter came below and woke me up. He was all smiles and said, 'I've discovered the most valuable currency ashore, apart from coffee, and you can buy almost anything, including a camera, with it. It's old motor tyres! Can you believe it? They cut them up and sole their shoes with the rubber.'

We had about a dozen old tyres in the tiller-flat which we used for fenders when alongside in bad weather. Peter said, 'I reckon we could use six of them for currency and save the rest for fenders. We could cut each one in half, and then be very careful how we spend the stuff.'

'Peter, would you mind dealing with the tyre business? They will have to be shared to some extent with the crew. Right now

I can only think about this evening and tomorrow. By the way, I've decided not to sail tomorrow.' He looked surprised to say the least.

Dinner with the young army Captain was a great success. We swapped stories of our various experiences in the past, and the chicken and ham pie went down a treat. The steward excelled himself by wearing a white apron, made from an old torn sheet, and brewed an excellent cup of coffee in the pantry, which was served with cheese and ship's biscuit. The Captain was very impressed with the wardroom. He could not help remarking upon its size and furnishings.

Peter had left a record sleeve on one of the bunks which the officer noticed, and asked if we had a gramophone. It transpired that he liked classical music as much as Peter. The evening finished with a concert conducted by 'maestro' Peter Butcher at the wind-up gramophone. The Captain left us at 1.00am saying that he had not enjoyed himself so much since he left the UK. It is extraordinary how much happiness is gained by giving pleasure to others.

Peter asked me how it was that the soldiers were able to bring their kilts while on active service. I had asked the Captain this question and was told that the 'Scotties' were a garrison force, which meant that their role was mainly ceremonial.

The next morning Sparks brought me a signal giving the position of the fuel barge and an instruction to intercept any craft I suspected of carrying arms. This was a tall order. How would one know? As very few vessels other than Patras fishing boats were seen in the Gulf I decided to concentrate on the sweeping first, and let the other matter rest until the mine search was over.

At six in the evening I was at the appointed place in time to see Amelia in her pony trap emerge from the olive orchard. She waved, and spurred the pony on to arrive beside me in a cloud of dust. The house, a Palladian-style villa, was set among trees and on a slight slope, down which a stream flowed and sparkled in the sun. This banker at least seemed to have escaped the outward signs of war that had scarred so many. 'Amelia, how do you live with money that has no value?' I asked. 'We grow our own vegetables which we trade for flour and fish. My father also gives bank credit notes which can be used after the war when a new currency will have been created,' she replied.

Mr Demetropolis met us at the entrance. He was a short, bald man with a good-humoured expression that lingered on the verge of laughter. His wife, a good-looking woman who was very much younger than her husband, served our dinner. I could see where Amelia's looks came from. The meal consisted mainly of fish, expertly cooked with herbs and spices. Baklava and fruit preceded the coffee which, in contrast to the rest of the meal, was truly awful. Some other substance had been mixed with it to give bulk. I made a mental note to give Amelia some from the wardroom pantry; as Peter did not drink coffee, there was plenty available. We drank a local wine called Mavro Daphne. Daphne was the daughter of the wine grower and had black hair. Thus the wine was called Black (Mavro) Daphne.

Mr Demotropolis practised some of his sense of humour after dinner, and described to me a British invasion. It went rather like this: 'One day a faint smudge appears on the horizon, and we all say, "Ah! Here they come!" but it goes away again. Two weeks later another grey smudge appears and grows larger, and we all say again "Ah! Here they come!" This time it's really them. The grey shape grows into a ship which anchors off the beach. A small launch comes ashore carrying a major and a dog. The major walks about the beach for five minutes, then gets back into his launch and returns to the ship, which goes away. A month passes before two ships arrive; they unload some boxes on to the beach. They are labelled NAAFI. In the night we open one of these boxes and it is filled with toilet rolls and combs! We go back to our houses and drink some wine because the war is over.'

Back aboard I decided that I would persuade the cook to make meals with fish instead of corned beef and Spam. For some reason, sailors rarely eat fish, just as they rarely go swimming. They so often think of salt water as their enemy, and that includes what's in it. We were likely to be based at Patras for some weeks, and there was little hope of finding meat of any kind ashore. The local people were living almost entirely on fish, of which there was an unlimited supply in the Gulf. Large shoals could be seen by looking over the harbour wall. As soon as the first day's sweeping was over I had a talk with cook and Peter.

Amelia had given me her mother's recipe for cooking fish with some herbs. It was agreed that every effort should be made to make fish the staple diet for the time being.

'What about the American rations, sir? Their canned chicken legs and ham are really good.' Here Peter was firm.

'No, no, they are iron rations and are to be kept for real emergencies,' I said. Dinner with the Captain was a special occasion not likely to reoccur.

'I'll try a fish pie, sir, to begin with. That might go down quite well,' said cook.

'Wait, don't serve it right away,' said Peter. 'Dish up corned beef fritters for three days running; by then everyone will be glad to eat fish. Preparation is all.' Wily man!

'I'm getting short of flour, sir. Plum duffs and spotted dick take a lot, apart from suet,' said cook.

'We'll think about that when it's all gone. For now it's important to make fish acceptable, and with the new recipe, with herbs to help, it ought to be possible.'

The conference ended. The rest of the week, and half of the following week, was taken up with sweeping the inshore water on the northern shore. The fish pie was a success. Nobody raved about it, but one of the crew was heard to say: 'Thank God, it was not those bloody fritters again,' as he scraped his plate clean.

'The trouble is,' said Peter as I drank my coffee and filled my pipe, 'fish pie is difficult because he has to make six to feed everyone. They must get used to grilled and baked fish. We can get any amount with a few bits of motor tyre.'

I was not listening. I was thinking about fuel. We must be getting low. At that very moment there was a knock on the door. 'Come in!' It was the Chief. 'We are getting short of fuel, sir.'

'You took the words straight out of my head, Chief. Come in and sit down. Whisky?'

'Thank you, sir, I don't mind if I do.'

The Chief had my fullest confidence, not to say admiration, and I always liked to treat him as an equal and, in some ways, as a superior. I knew little about engines and he was an expert. It was often said that Chiefs were the backbone of the navy just as Sergeant Majors were of the army. We chatted for a while. I assured him that we now had a fuel barge anchored among the islands, so as to be safe from saboteurs and thieves. The petrol was in fifty-gallon drums, which would present a target if on view in the harbour.

'In case there is not a suitable pump on the barge, Chief, have we got one?' I asked. 'We've got two, sir,' he replied. 'But even filling two tanks at the same time, it will take half a day to get two thousand gallons aboard.'

'Right, Chief, I'll make sure we are alongside the barge by noon. The galley will have to be put out of action, so it will have to be cold food tonight.'

The Chief left us. Then Peter and I played some of his records before turning in. The fuel barge was a tank-landing craft, which could carry eight Sherman or Warrior tanks, and their complement of armed men. At the stern were the living quarters for the crew of two, with the engine room below. The tank space was filled with eighty fifty-gallon drums of fuel, and it was presided over by the CO of this floating 'marine garage', a huge red-bearded giant dressed not in navy overalls, but in ragged trousers and a T-shirt. He was later to prove a headache for Taranto, and for ourselves. He was alone and I wondered what had happened to his crew.

With full tanks we made our way back to Patras. We berthed alongside the wall behind a trawler. There remained a small section of inshore water to cover, and one day's work should see the end of operations on the northern side of the gulf. So far no mines had been encountered and this was reported to Taranto in my daily signal. I informed them of my intention to commence sweeping in the Gulf of Corinth, and to leave work on the southern side of the Patras water until last. The signal came back: 'Approved.'

It was late in the day when we took in sweeps for the last time on the northern shore, and proceeded through the narrows to anchor for the night just inside, opposite a place called Nafpaktos. There were only three ports in the Gulf of Corinth, and this was one of them, the others being Itea, at the foot of Mount Parnassus, and Corinth at the start of the canal. No mines were found in any of these places, or in the water between.

The first leg of twenty-five miles took us to the port of Itea. The sweep occupied us for two days. Itea was a well-protected town and harbour, which was situated at the northern end of the Gulf of Corinth. We took particular care in this confined water because it was an important port, serving the hinterland behind. Nights were spent at anchor until we reached this place, and fortunately the weather was calm and the sea smooth. The time at Itea was an experience that I chose to forget. It is only now after the passage of seventy years that I can think objectively about the place.

As we moored alongside the harbour wall, a small brass band struck up with a tune that I vaguely recognised, but it was so badly out of tune that I could not be sure. However, I was gratified that they should take the trouble and was further pleased to see a welcoming committee approaching from the harbour office. In front strode a figure bedecked with chains of office, obviously the mayor. The committee came to a halt above us, and I invited the mayor aboard. He climbed down the iron ladder, and shook hands with everyone in sight. He spoke a little English but with an impenetrable accent that was almost impossible to understand. However, with gestures and signs we managed to communicate. It appeared that there was fresh water on the jetty and, in response to a question of mine, the town would be able to supply us with a limited amount of fresh vegetables and flour.

This was good news indeed. It became apparent that Itea had not suffered the hardship and shortages that had been imposed upon Patras. The surrounding farmers still worked, the Germans had bypassed it, and the warlords left it alone in the main. This may have been for a superstitious reason. The Delphic Oracle at Mount Parnassus still exercised some influence over the more gullible of the population. I decided to stay for several days at Itea and used the time to give all the ship's company enough shore leave to benefit their health.

There was a certain amount of maintenance to be carried out on the sweeping gear and in the engine room. The cook and No 1 would certainly go on a foraging expedition to try to discover what currency was most acceptable to the farmers and shops. Would it be the Allied war currency or old motor tyres? While refuelling, Peter had managed to persuade the Red Giant to give us four tyres from those lying about the deck between the fuel drums. For myself, I decided to make an expedition to the Oracle. I had read about it at school and it would be interesting to actually see the famous example of Greek mythology.

I made the mistake of mentioning this to the mayor the next day when I went ashore to thank him and his committee for their welcome. He at once took over. He organised an escort to accompany me up the hill, with a picnic to be eaten after my visit to Delphi. At midday the mayor, the committee and I set off. The weather was hot with hardly any breeze, and I was sweating profusely by the time I reached the Oracle. While the picnic was laid out on the scorched grass outside, I went into the cave that was home to the Oracle. At the end of the shallow cave there was a hole in the rock about the size of a football, there must have been a space behind it, as an echo came back when you whispered your request or prayer. I forget entirely what I said or asked for. Had I known what was to follow I might have stayed in the cave.

I sat down among the picnickers and was given a glass of something I took to be wine. I was hot and thirsty, and gulped down a draught equal to half the amount in the glass. Ugh! It was Greek brandy, a most noxious and potent liquid. I had barely got it down before the mayor raised his glass in salute again, which I felt bound to acknowledge. Sweet cakes were then passed round, followed by some sort of meat on sweet biscuits, followed by more sweet cakes and more brandy. By this time I was drunk. I now lacked the will-power to refuse these offerings. I do not remember how I got down to the harbour, or how I managed to get down the iron ladder and climb aboard. I only remember having a violent headache and feeling sick. I stayed in my bunk for two days. What a disgrace!

While work went on about the ship, Peter and cook foraged ashore with considerable success. They came back with flour, vegetables and a goose that, together with the one in our freezer, made a meal for the entire ship's company, except myself. I told Peter to inform the crew that I was ill due to having eaten something at the picnic that had upset me. This was roughly true, but, of course, it was the brandy that did most of the damage. I will draw a veil over the next week, which was the time it took me to recover fully.

We swept on down the coast. I did my job and went below. Peter offered to do my watch and leave Leading Seaman Grayham in charge of the sweeping gear. I'm thankful to say that I would not hear of it, and somehow staggered on, until blessed normality returned. I made a vow then and there that I've been able to keep ever since, and that is a vow to say no and mean it!

It took us three further weeks to complete the search on both sides of the Gulf. I was glad that Peter and cook had been able to purchase enough potatoes and greens to last us for two of the three weeks. At one stage the cold store was crammed with vegetables, but even with this facility the stuff goes off in a few days and is often thrown away. Our freezer compartment was very small and the first goose had to be cut up into joints in order to fit in. The cook was doubtful about using it, but he stewed the joints with a little vinegar, and no one complained, especially as the new goose was roasted and was a real luxury.

The currency in Itea was no problem. They were happy to take Allied notes as well as some motor tyre rubber. The month's work in the Gulf of Corinth was finally considered by Peter to be an emergency, and so he allowed some of the American rations to be used as a change from the corned beef and Spam.

The weather was beginning to change as we came in sight of the narrows and what we now considered as our home port. Patras did not actually welcome us, but I knew, and the crew knew, that many good things could be bought there for a few bits of motor tyre. Peter kept one tyre for the wardroom and gave five to the crew to be divided up by the Cox'n. The Chief and Sparks shared half of the large one and that left five for fenders, which Peter locked up with a padlock and chain. I said that no one in the crew would steal a tyre. They were decent men who had been aboard too long to cause trouble of that sort, but the First Lieutenant thought it best to remove temptation. That was about the only occasion on which we disagreed.

As we entered the narrows and could see far down the Gulf, we noticed a vessel about two miles away, in mid-channel. She was larger than a fishing boat of the kind based in Patras or Itea, and was the first boat I had seen in the estuary since our arrival. I remembered the instruction to intercept boats carrying arms. Perhaps this might be such a one. 'Peter, I'm going to investigate,' I said. 'When we are within hailing distance sound "action stations" and close up all guns.'

The distance did not change and so I felt sure the ship had seen us and retreated. Right, that settled any doubts I may have had. I rang down for 'full ahead', and the chase began. Our top speed was twenty-one knots and within fifteen minutes we were near enough to use the loudhailer. They obeyed my order, which was in English, and the ship came to a stop. The Bofors, trained on its bridge, spoke louder than words and we moved alongside. I climbed aboard, armed with two of our pistols and accompanied by a rating with a rifle and fixed bayonet. There were three men on deck and I asked if anyone on board spoke English. They hesitated, and I called to Peter to train the Bofors on to the hull at the waterline. I guessed, and it was only a guess, that they would rather obey orders than have their vessel sunk beneath them. By signs, and my few words of Greek, I made them understand that all on board were to come on deck. One man called down a hatch and a figure emerged who I reckoned was the engineer.

I asked Williams, the seaman with me, to corral the four men in a group in the bows, and ordered Peter to train the small arms on them to keep them covered while I went below. I had no idea whether or not there was still anyone below, but risks have to be taken when you have eliminated all the dangers you can think of. But then I thought again. What was I doing here? Why was I venturing below, without the obvious protection of a hostage? I cursed myself for not thinking far enough ahead and being in too much of a hurry. I turned back and motioned one man to come forward. The pistol was planted firmly into the small of his back and, with him in front and Williams behind, we searched the ship from end to end, including the bilges. Twenty-four rifles were found, one machine-gun of ancient lineage and four boxes of ammunition. The bolts from the rifles were withdrawn and put aboard ML 135. The boxes of ammunition were opened and the contents scattered overboard, together with the rifles and the machine-gun, after having removed the firing mechanism. This was performed by our Bofors gunner who took pleasure in the task. As we let go and headed for Patras Harbour, I remarked to Peter that the guns were almost certainly bound for Hermes and his gang. It was a difficult balance to keep in regard to the warlords. The hostility towards the Germans had to be encouraged, but at the same time they must be prevented from becoming too powerful and a threat to post-war Greece.

Alongside I called the Chief and asked him about fuel. We carried three thousand gallons, but I never let our supply fall below one thousand if I could help it. He reported nine hundred in the starboard tank and fifty-eight in the port tank. Right, that was it. That was my personal red light. Tomorrow we would have to board the Red Giant and fill up. On the way to the barge we would scatter the bolts from the rifles into deep water.

The crew were gradually getting used to fish and at no time did I hear that they preferred corned beef. The Cox'n kept me informed of these matters. The cook was becoming expert in dealing with fish of all kinds, shapes and sizes. His methods were based on the recipe given to us by Amelia. The herbs she sent us inspired him to look for more whenever he was ashore. On our first evening back in Patras he served a baked fish, spiced with herbs, mashed potato and tinned beans. All of this was very acceptable. Peter played his gramophone, I smoked my pipe, and for once I felt free of problems. There was still the southern side of the Patras Gulf to sweep, it was true, but that was almost a straight run with few inlets, if any. The drama on that coast was as yet unthought of, and looking back I'm glad it was so. The long mine sweep off the Gulf of Corinth without any 'trophies' was a tiring and dispiriting business. I determined to spend a few days in Patras after fuelling, before the last operations.

At noon we rounded the island behind which the fuel barge had been anchored, only to find some rubbish caught in a patch of seaweed but no other sign of the barge. This left us with no alternative but to go back to Patras and signal Taranto for instructions. Peter then made a useful suggestion. 'Why not fire the Bofors? If he is near he may reply with a star-shell or something.'

'Good idea, we'll try it.' Sure enough, firing the Bofors produced a result. A foghorn sounded from behind one of the other islands that decorate the mouth of the Gulf, and we proceeded towards it. He was there all right, smugly ensconced in a small inlet, and sheltered to some extent from the sun by some overhanging trees. I could not blame him, though it confirmed my first impression. He was a man responsible only to himself. Our refuelling had used up all forty of the remaining drums of fuel. I told him of the possibility of us remaining in the area, and asked him to signal Taranto for orders. He looked at me with a strange unfocused expression and did not answer. I felt very uneasy about him and made a mental note to call Taranto myself that evening. I did, only to learn that he had failed to answer any of their signals. I informed Taranto that I now had more then enough fuel to finish the work and leave a large reserve. They replied to this by asking me to contact him in person, and pass on their order for him to return to Taranto immediately.

This was a confounded and unnecessary chore. One that wasted fuel and time in making another trip down the Gulf just when I wanted a few quiet days in harbour for a general 'make and mend', plus exercise for everybody. Ah, well! There was no choice and we left at 8.00am. The Red Giant received the order with his usual blank expression. I wondered, not for the first time, whether he was quite sane. I hoped never to have to see the man again.

We stayed alongside in Patras for five days before beginning our last task. I met Amelia on two more occasions. On one afternoon I rode with her in her pony trap, and enjoyed a delightful wander through the countryside. Among the olive trees, on the banks of the stream that tumbled down the slope near her house, she spread a picnic so different from the last one I had endured. Cheese, bread, jam and little cakes washed down with spring water were all that a picnic should be. Our acquaintance did not become an affair and was bounded by kisses and a promise to write.

The crew spent their portions of motor tyres wisely, or foolishly, according to their own needs. I bought a Voigtländer camera with which I hoped to photograph exploding mines. Peter found several recordings of the Berlin Philharmonic. This put him in a good mood for weeks. Altogether the five days proved useful and a tonic to everyone. Even being back on 'bully beef' failed to arouse a complaint. Vegetables with an unlimited fresh water supply compensated to a large extent.

At 8.00am of the sixth morning after our holiday began, we were at the start of our final sweep. The water on the southern side was crystal clear, which was an indication of its unfrequented state. In comparison with the rest of the Gulf it was shallow, in some places less than three metres at a distance of two hundred yards from shore. I did not expect to find any mines here. How wrong can you be? Within five minutes we cut our first mine. I called to the lookout on the bows to be extra vigilant and we exploded the deadly weapon with two shots from the Bofors. We were sweeping on both sides and this mine was on the seaward side.

At this point Sparks appeared with a signal received just before 8.00am. 'Proceed as soon as possible to fuel barge and repeat the order to return to Taranto.' That bloody man! I hated abandoning a sweep before it was completed. This would mean hauling in and restowing all the gear when I was on my marks with everything set. On the other hand, we were very near to the islands and the barge, and there would never be a better opportunity than this. Peter was still in a good mood, and made no fuss about hauling in. An hour later we were in sight of the barge. The order from Taranto was passed once more. This time the Red Giant spat over the side and said, 'Bugger Taranto. OK, I'll go when I'm ready.'

This time I resolved to finish the day's sweep in spite of the fact that Sparks was on duty all day as was usual when sweeping. If any more orders came during the day I would ignore them if it meant another encounter with the Red Giant.

Earlier in this narrative I briefly mentioned a 'miracle' that would occur later in the account. We are now about to experience the only event in my life that can be explained in no other way.

We returned to our task in the Gulf, and I tried to forget the time wasted on the Red Giant. There was a good seven hours' sweeping time left in the day. I was approaching my mark for the start, which was a headland in line with a ruined building, and I called to Peter to 'out sweeps'. For some reason, known only to him, he always let the port sweep stream before the starboard one. The first bit of gear to go down is the 'kite', which is towed immediately under the stern and keeps the ship end of the 'sweep wire' submerged at the right depth. The 'otter', which is similar to the 'kite' and keeps the sea end of the sweep wire submerged, is then lowered into the water and the wire paid out from the winch, then checked according to the width of water intended to be swept. I waited to hear the splash of the 'kite' as it went over. Nothing. No sound, and no 'otter' streaming away on the port quarter.

'Peter, what the hell is happening?' I asked. 'I'm nearly at my start point and both sweeps should be out by now!' I was really annoyed by then. 'Take over, Cox'n, I'm going aft. Keep her steady on this course at four knots, I'll be back before we reach my marks.'

As I arrived Peter was struggling with the 'kite winch', which seemed to be jammed. Then a shout from the 'mine lookout' on the bow, 'Mine, sir! Mine under the hull!' and, almost instantly, a full-sized 'moored mine' popped up from under the stern less than three feet from the ship's keel and stern gear.

Had the 'kite' been down and suspended only six feet from the stern, it would have collided with the mine. There was no possible chance of a collision being avoided. We would have been blown to bits! The water was so clear that I could see the deadly horns sprouting from the mine casing like toadstools. It drifted astern and a moment later the winch came free.

Years later, in 2006, I visited Peter Butcher not long before he died. He had forgotten most of our service together, but he did remember the 'miracle' and we talked about it for much of that evening.

Before returning to the task of sweeping the southern side of the Gulf, I would like to add that the 'kite winch' worked perfectly for the rest of that day and, although it was later examined by engineers in both Malta and Bari, no fault could be found with it, nor any reason for it jamming. It never jammed again.

In a chastened mood we cleared out to safe water, streamed both sweeps, and headed to a position that, I hoped, would cover the mine that had so nearly been our executioner. During the rest of the day we cut and sank several mines, hoping that their number included the brute that had missed us. For the remainder of our work on the southern side of the Gulf we encountered no more mines, and I wondered why there had been a nest of them at the top end. It was very odd indeed. I reported the incident to Taranto in my nightly signal that evening. I have wondered since whether I should have held a small service of thanksgiving for the ship's company, on the foredeck.

Ten more days work in the Gulf saw the completion of our assignment in those waters. The task, apart from initially covering the Fleet Sweepers, had never been to guarantee completely clear waters, but to investigate and report. If we cut mines in the process, that was all to the good.

We were still living on corned beef and Spam, eked out by the occasional raid into the American rations. Some days I hardly noticed what I was eating as the affair of the jammed winch, and work in hand, filled my thoughts, making everything else seem totally unimportant. I believe that this was also the case with others on board. Peter was certainly very quiet.

We left Patras for the last time on the morning of the twenty seventh day in Greek waters and the evening saw us berthed alongside in Taranto. I was a long time in the NOIC's office where he listened with great attention to the story of our near disaster. I asked him if the fuel barge had returned, and he told me that it had docked two days before. Apparently the base had ordered the Red Giant to report immediately, in person, to the office, saying that a car would be sent. The car had been a little late, which resulted in the NOIC receiving a signal from the Red Giant that simply said, 'Where is car?'

The NOIC was concerned about the state of our 'kite winch' and said that it should be thoroughly overhauled by the engineers in Malta. He authorised us to proceed to Malta as soon as the new hands had joined. 'What new hands, sir? I'm not expecting any changes,' I said. 'Then call at the Drafting Office on the next floor down. They will give you all the information you need.'

Oh, God! There was always something. I did not want to lose any of my crew. We had an expert ship's company. Every man was experienced and knew his job well enough to perform it blindfolded. These were the thoughts that ran through my mind as I went down to the floor below. In one way the news was worse than expected. I was to lose a seaman who had been granted compassionate leave, owing to trouble in his family back in the UK. His relief would be joining at the end of the week, but, and here was the great shock, I was to lose Peter Butcher! He had been promoted and given command of a BYMS to operate in waters around the UK. I was glad for him, of course. He deserved promotion and a command of his own. His expert knowledge of minesweeping gear alone would qualify him to be CO of a BYMS. I climbed aboard with a heavy heart.

'Peter, congratulations, you damn well deserve it, but I can't say I'm happy. I don't want to lose you. Where am I going to find someone of your experience and knowledge?' We were standing on the bridge of 135 looking out over the silver sheet of sea that was the Gulf of Taranto. There was scarcely a ripple on this calm evening. The ripples were in my head, if they were anywhere; ripples of doubt, ripples of regret. I had grown to admire Peter with his quiet ways, his apparent lack of humour, disguising his utter reliability. He never once let me down in anything, and took all of his responsibilities seriously and without question. I have wondered since whether I ever let him down. I expect that I did, but I hope not.

We had to wait a week in Taranto Bay for his relief but only three days for the replacement seaman. The man's name was Lavender. I remember this name because he gave us some trouble later. He was an ordinary seaman with absolutely no experience, and very little sea time behind him. After Peter had interviewed him and introduced him to the Cox'n, Peter came into the wardroom looking gloomy. 'The Cox'n will have trouble with that one, of that I feel sure, he said. 'The man seems to have learned nothing during the six months he's been in the Service.' I groaned, 'Six months, is that all?' but Peter wasn't listening, he was getting out his gramophone.

We played records all the evening, the same seven, over and over again. As he pulled down the lid and stowed the records he said, 'I'll leave this, sir, and the records. My dad and I have a huge collection at home, and I'll be seeing my mother and father soon.' I had to swallow hard before I could answer, 'Thank you, Peter. You have taught me to appreciate music in a new way. I used to just listen without knowing or caring about how it was put together. Now I have a request to make. For the last few days left to us as a team, I would like you to use my Christian name, like the other COs of the flotilla, as you are now, or soon will be, a CO yourself. My first name is Richard, but I'm called Dickie and so, if you don't mind, it's Dickie from now on.' We shook hands and drank a toast to his new appointment.

The next few days passed all too quickly. With his usual conscientious attention to duty, Peter saw to it that the ship was stocked with water, fuel and food before he left. The whole ship's crew saluted him from the upper deck as he stood on the wall and waved to us. He was liked and respected by all of us. Beside me stood his relief, a man different from Peter in every way. In the wardroom we discussed his last experience. To my great relief he had served as First Lieutenant to Phillip Fellows, SO of the Third ML Flotilla, who like John Peel, my predecessor, was returning home, having served his time abroad. His ML was temporarily taken out of commission, the crew disbanded and drafted to other vessels. My new First Lieutenant was called James Swinson. He was tall, good-looking and possessed a ready sense of humour that made light of things that others thought serious. He lacked Peter's concern for detail, but made up for it by having good relations with the crew. You could not help liking him because he was such good company. His knowledge of minesweeping, though not as complete as Peter's, was perfectly adequate. James and Leading Seaman Grayham also got on well, especially after Grayham recounted the story of the jammed 'kite'.

CHAPTER 8

❋

Adventures in the Adriatic

1944–45

The day after Peter Butcher's departure we left for Malta. The engineering department there had been authorised to carry out a further thorough examination of the jammed winch, and to renew it if necessary. On arrival we berthed in Sliema Creek and waited for instructions to continue on round to Grand Harbour. The engineering there was second to none in the Mediterranean, and dealt on a daily basis with mighty problems and very big ships. We had to wait for three days, during which time I lectured James on the importance of exercise for the crew, and a whole host of other practices that had become part of our routine on board. Poor chap. I think that I overdid it, and so I took him up to the Officers' Club and signed him in. The meal and the evening were a success; I had been lucky in his appointment, and I knew it.

Our week's stay in Malta was quiet. It produced nothing but six yards of dress material, which I bought in the hope that I would see Ljerka and her parents again. Terka was an expert dressmaker who made clothes for herself, her daughter and a neighbour. Other than that, much seemed familiar: rats still lurked in the holes and cracks among the rocks at the edge of Sliema Creek; Maltese housewives still shouted at their children in a mixture of their own language and English, which was to the listener like coming across a daisy in a bed of nettles; and the wives at the Naval Club still complained that the seniority of their husbands was being ignored. I would be glad to leave the island. Furthermore, our tanks were now filled with the disgusting 'treated seawater', which did duty for fresh water on this arid rock. Malta was my least favourite place in the Mediterranean.

Both James and I stayed at the Naval Club for the week. The crew had the choice of staying on board, moving ashore to the Seamen's Mission or to one of the cheap lodging houses that were plentiful on the island. Finally, at last, the message came through to the club that ML 135 was now ready to be collected from the dockyard in Grand Harbour. I asked for a report on the winch, and all other bits of equipment that had been serviced. The base engineers could find nothing wrong with the kite winch. It had been tested many times by the expert engineering staff, who did little else but service minesweeping gear. They examined, cleaned and tested both winches and gave me a written report. No faults. The miracle was now set in stone.

I left Malta without telling anybody, intending to signal NOIC, Taranto, on the way in. When within flashing distance, Sparks signalled them to ask for permission to berth alongside. The answer came back, 'Proceed to Bari and report to Commander MS, Adriatic.' Oh good. We were back in the domain of Sharky Ward. As no arrival time had been ordered, I decided to stop for the night at Brindisi. It was approximately one hundred and fifty miles from Taranto to Bari, and Brindisi was a convenient break point.

We arrived there in time for cook to do a little foraging before dark. He came back with half a small pig that he had bought in exchange for some of the olive oil that the Cox'n had thoughtfully acquired in Greece. The oil was plentiful, if not to say abundant, in the Peloponnese and could be bought for almost nothing. In Italy it was expensive, and the further north you travelled the more expensive it became. Malta had proved a poor place for shopping. Every item of food was priced at an exorbitant rate ashore, and the base had little in the way of luxuries to offer. We did, however, manage to obtain a large quantity of flour, which was something we had been short of for a considerable time. Cook served up gammon steaks for dinner, with fresh greens and tinned potatoes. It was a banquet in comparison with what we had lived on for the past three weeks. Fish had been fine for a while, but sailors seemed to need their meat.

After the meal I hauled out Peter's gramophone with the object of trying one or two pieces of classical music on James. He did not respond, and seemed deep in thought. Eventually I asked him if he was worried about something. He told me that he had had two complaints from the Cox'n about the new hand, Ordinary Seaman Lavender. Apparently the man was untidy, and even dirty, spilling food and failing to do his share of the chores. 'I've seen him once, sir, and given him a caution, but it has made no difference. Today the Cox'n said the men are getting restive and there is a bad atmosphere in the fo'c'sle, which I'm not used to,' he said.

I was alarmed at this news. ML 135 had always been an efficient and, as far as I could tell, a happy ship. It was amazing that one bad hand could upset all this. I could put him on a charge, and stop his leave for a time. There were, in fact, a number of penalties that could be levied, but punishments were difficult to enforce on a small ship without the means that are available on a large warship. Petty Officers, Chief Petty Officers, Masters-at-Arms and Warrant Officers: all of these were part of a disciplinary force whose job it was to see that orders were carried out and discipline maintained.

'Tell him to report to the wardroom at 8.00am tomorrow before we sail. I want the Cox'n and yourself to be present. We will do it in style, in the hope that a bit of ceremony will be effective. If we fail, I'll get him drafted. I will not have relations among the crew spoiled for the sake of one man,' I told James. It is often the case that one or two of the others will side with the culprit, and the whole edifice of trust and good intentions can be undermined. 'No, we can't have this, James. Sharky Ward will shift him if necessary.'

The Cox'n marched Lavender into the wardroom. 'Stand to attention! Off cap!' he cried, and having delivered those orders, stood to one side so that the man faced me and the First Lieutenant. We were both sitting behind the table, on which was a Bible and a pair of handcuffs. It was precisely 8.00am, and the crew could be heard above stowing ropes and fenders and preparing the boat for sea.

'Do you know why you are here?' I asked.

'No!' said Lavender.

'No, SIR!' came from the Cox'n to Lavender.

'No, sir!' said Lavender.

'You are here because you are not doing your share of work in the fo'c'sle. You are leaving it to others to clear your mess. Furthermore, you failed to obey orders from the Cox'n, on whom the smooth running of the ship depends. You will obey him at all times, without comment or complaint. Do you understand?' I said.

'Yes,' replied Lavender.

'Yes, SIR!' the Cox'n ordered the seaman.

'Yes, sir!' said Lavender.

I finished by saying, 'You see these handcuffs? Think carefully before you say or do anything in future. I do not wish to call for the Military Police.'

'On cap! About turn! Dismiss!' ordered the Cox'n.

'Thank you, Cox'n,' I said. 'I'm sorry you've had this trouble. If he does not improve we will get him drafted.'

An hour later James and I drank a mug of cocoa, on the bridge, and tucked into ham sandwiches. Another raid on the American rations must have taken place. It was a fine morning, the coast was slipping past us at fourteen knots, and I was glad to going back to Bari.

Porto Vecchio was empty. The Third ML Flotilla had been reformed under a new SO, and had moved north to sweep the waters off Manfredonia. I reported to Sharky Ward and gave him an account of the miracle. I think that he was impressed, especially upon hearing that Malta had found no fault with the winch. He had a job for me and this was to be a night sweep. We were to sweep the inshore water along the eastern side of the island of Vis. Our support vessel, HMS *Calypso*, was anchored some fifty miles south of Vis, among the islands. The area of the mainland opposite was largely clear of the enemy, but 'Jerry' still occupied the land further north. It was therefore necessary to 'darken ship' and carry out the operation at night. There was to be no unnecessary talk or noise.

Two days after my talk with Commander Ward we sailed from Bari, in time to reach Vis in complete darkness. There was no moon, and low clouds obscured the stars. Now began one of the most eventful nights of my time at sea. Vis loomed ahead and appeared to stand out of the sea like a platform above the water. Tall cliffs faced us on this western side but, as we approached the southern end, the land flattened out and became indistinct. I had no marks to go by, and used the southern tip as my starting point.

'Out sweeps!' I ordered, and heard the splash of the starboard 'kite' and 'otter', then the port 'kite' and 'otter'. A few minutes later I felt the shiver go through the hull as the load was taken, and we started to pull. For an hour all went well. The ship moved through the water like a ghost. No lights and no sound but the soft purr of the engines.

Suddenly I found it impossible to keep on course. The ship's head was wandering from side to side. 'The wheel won't answer, sir,' came the call.

'Stop both!' I ordered and called for James as quietly as I could, 'James, the steering has gone. Rig the manual steering arm urgently. I'll try to keep the hull clear of the sweep wire and 'kites'!'

By alternately using the port and starboard engines and the screws, I was able to keep a rough course. There we were, off the enemy coast, unable to steer and trailing sweep wires on both sides. It was not a pleasant situation. I could hear occasional firing on the mainland, and hoped to God that we'd not been spotted from the island.

The manual steering arm was a heavy bar, about eight feet long, requiring at least three or four men to manage it. At one end there was a spanner-type opening that fitted over a boss midway between the rudders, and managed them both together. It was an awkward and cumbersome arrangement: an extension to the boss had to be fitted first so that the bar could be manhandled on the deck, there being no room to swing the arm below in the tiller-flat. I whispered to a seaman to give No 1 the hand-bearing compass. To maintain silence I employed him as a runner between James and myself on the bridge.

When the four men on the bar were able to swing the bar, I gave James a course from my bridge compass, and between us we were able to maintain a fairly accurate heading. If I saw us wandering off, on my bridge compass, the messenger would run in his bare feet and tell the First Lieutenant to correct by the necessary number of degrees. It was to be a long and painful night before we could finish the sweep, and miraculously we avoided fouling our sweep gear when we stopped.

Gradually James and I, together with men on the bar, got into a rhythm and became a team. But, after two or three hours, the men had to be changed and we had to form a new partnership again. This was trying and time-consuming, and it was midnight before we were halfway along the length of the island. At this midway point there was a sudden burst of gunfire, and then a huge explosion, which appeared to come from the other side of Vis, on the seaward side. This was followed by two more explosions in quick succession, and then the unmistakable crackle of more gunfire. Star shells began to go up, and the sky was filled with flashes of light and white hot debris being hurled aloft. An almighty battle was taking place only a mile or two away.

By the time we reached the northern end of Vis, and had begun our turn to sweep south, the fireworks subsided and then suddenly stopped. No further sound, or light, was heard or seen. This was uncanny. Sporadic firing usually went on for some time after an engagement. I knew that there were E-Boats, and even a German destroyer, operating in this part of the Adriatic. There were also F-lighters, slow, heavily armed vessels similar to a barge. In my mind I prayed that such a force had not met with, and destroyed, some Allied shipping, but I was later to learn that the opposite was true.

We rounded the southern end of the island at first light, hauled in our sweeps and set course, as fast as we could with our crippled steering, for Bari. An amazing sight came into view as we headed north along the western side of Vis. Masts and bows of sunken vessels were showing above the water, and further on there were even more masts. In all, I counted fourteen masts and topsides sticking out of the sea ahead of us. It was a truly amazing spectacle. Again, I prayed hard that they were not ours.

At this point I must describe a most unique officer, whose exploits outshone every other CO in the small ship's war against Germany. His brilliant leadership, and tactical ability, gained him victories that became the stuff of legends. His name was Lieutenant-Commander Timothy Bligh RNVR. He commanded a flotilla of D-Boats. These boats were the same length as ML 135 but broader in the beam, more heavily armed and they were faster, with a top speed of thirty knots. They carried two torpedo tubes, one on each side of the foredeck.

On the night of our sweep he was informed that a convoy of twelve German vessels was ten miles ahead of him proceeding north along the western side of Vis. With all lights masked and sound reduced to a minimum, he led his five D-Boats quietly inshore of the German force, and into the shadow of the cliffs. Before coming between the cliffs and the convoy, he detached one boat and sent it far out to sea and abeam of the Germans. At a signal from Bligh this boat started firing at the convoy, which immediately replied. The D-Boat then dropped a smoke float and soon after that, another one.

Smoke floats give off a brilliant orange flame at the base of clouds of white smoke. From a distance, the smoke floats would have given the impression of two ships on fire. Every one of the German force brought all guns to bear on the burning patches on the horizon, while Bligh led his force forward abeam of the German ships. At a signal from him, the D-Boats opened up with everything they had. The larger vessels were sunk with torpedoes, and the rest by gunfire. The German force had consisted of three E-Boats and four F-Lighters escorting five supply ships. All were destroyed, without Tim Bligh losing a ship or a man.

There were many other victories to his credit, including the surrender of a German destroyer. During the last few days of the war the destroyer was at the head of the Adriatic and was taken by Bligh. It was anchored in a thick fog and Bligh had himself rowed over to the ship, called to the officer on watch in German, asking for permission to come aboard to speak to the CO. This was granted. After a long conversation, Bligh was able to convince the German CO of the hopelessness of continuing hostilities, and of the need to preserve life on both sides. For this brave and unusual act he was awarded the KBE (Knight Commander of the Most Excellent Order of the British Empire). His other decorations included the Distinguished Service Cross and Bar, the Distinguished Service Order, the OBE and fourteen mentions in dispatches.

I met him once. I had to go aboard his ship one day, fully expecting to see a weather-stained, blue-eyed hero of the sea. Instead I met a slim, rather girlish figure with pale delicate features, and soft wavy brown hair. After the war he became Principal Private Secretary to two Prime Ministers, Macmillan and Home.

Two or three days after peace was declared Bligh married a Wren Officer in Malta. Small ships from every part of the Adriatic and beyond seemed to 'develop defects, and the urgent need for repairs in Malta'. The numbers attending his wedding could not be counted. Those who could not get inside, waited and cheered him from outside. I don't think Malta had ever witnessed such a scene before. The occasion was further enriched by the knowledge that the war in Europe was over.

It has been my intention to keep episodes in this narrative in chronological order, but it is an indication of the influence of Tim Bligh that I have broken the rule and jumped ahead. We now return to the remainder of my story.

At 5.00am cook served up soup with cheese and pickle sandwiches for all hands. It had been a difficult night and we all needed the cheering sight of food and the warmth of a good soup. Fortunately, the weather was calm, because a broken swell would have made the task of steering by hand almost impossible. The best speed we could manage was eight knots, and darkness was falling by the time we sighted Bari Harbour. I signalled NOIC for assistance, and a small tug towed us into Porto Vecchio. They explained that Bari dock was full and that we would have to wait a week before repairs could begin. Cook had provided dinner halfway across, and all hands turned in as soon as we berthed, leaving only one sentry on watch, who was to be changed every two hours. James and I had been compass watching for thirty hours, and our bunks were all that we needed.

Ship's company turned out at 8.00am. Cook once more did us proud. Plates of stewed pork and beans came down to the wardroom, where the steward also made us toast and coffee in the pantry. I then went to the base to report to Sharky Ward, giving him a full account of all we had heard and seen. I did not know if he had yet received news of Tim Bligh's victory, but he listened carefully to all I had to say. He was pleased to note that we had found no mines along the eastern shore of Vis, as the area was clearly being considered for some future operation.

James arranged shore leave for the crew, one watch at a time. The watch on board cleaned ship and paid attention to their own 'make and mend'. I put my feet up and read some week-old newspapers that I'd found at the base. Thus ended an eventful two days.

The Chief appeared in the doorway and asked if he could have a few words. 'Of course, come in, Chief, sit down. A drop of Scotch?' 'Thank you, sir, I don't mind if I do.' He always said 'I don't mind if I do' when offered a drink and I would miss it if he ever forgot.

'Sir, I'm worried about the steering, and sorry for all the trouble you have had over the other side. I feel that it's my fault,' he said. 'I've examined the system from end to end. There is nothing wrong with the slave cylinder, which is the usual cause of trouble, but I found two leaking joints. As you know hydraulic systems depend on completely airtight pipe work, and our steering process is old, and has had a lot of work. When we go into dock I want to make a strong request for the whole network to be scrapped, and replaced by Reed's steering. This is a purely mechanised system that cannot fail, except by wilful damage. It is not quite so sensitive as the Lockheed, but far more reliable. I don't think that you'd notice any difference on the bridge.'

'Have you had experience of Reed's, Chief?' I asked him.

'Yes, I have, sir, we had Reed's steering on a BYMS back in the UK, and never had a moment's trouble,' he said. 'You see there is nothing that can go wrong, provided that the moving parts are kept clean and lubricated.'

'You've convinced me, Chief, I'll do my best, but you know what base engineers are like, they'll argue "black is white" if they're short of stock,' I told him.

'Yes, sir, but we can try, and hope for the best,' said the Chief.

The talk then passed to other things: wives, families, the state of things at home, the shortages, the bombings that our loved ones were enduring. 'Let's all hope for the second front, sir,' he said. 'Perhaps if we hope hard enough it may happen soon. I had a letter from a mate of mine a month ago and he's seen signs of it. I can't say more.'

I always enjoyed talking to the Chief. He was a man of limitless common sense, backed up by real knowledge of his calling. He was good at his job because he loved it, and had taken the trouble to learn. I looked at my watch; it was 3.00pm.

'Right, Chief, I'll go now. No time like the present. You have inspired me,' I told him. 'If they want to talk to you I'll signal from the base, or better still I'll send a runner, Sharky Ward will lend me one of his ratings.'

With that we shook hands, and I set off for the Bari dock. They were certainly busy. Two armed trawlers and a destroyer were being serviced. Both divers were in the water examining the rudders of two other vessels. With difficulty I managed to get the attention of the head engineer, a Warrant Officer with years of experience behind him, judging by his grey hair. I was in luck; they had no Lockheed parts but did have a complete Reed system suitable for a BYMS. Although made for a BYMS, it could, with slight modifications, be fitted in an ML. The work would take two weeks, but could not start for eight days. I walked back in high good humour, thinking how good it would be to give Chief the news.

The following day, leaving No 1 to organise fuelling and watering, I reported to Commander Ward to give him the engineer's information. He instructed me to turn the vessel over to the base, and while repairs were taking place, I was to store all codes and confidential books in his office. The whole ship's company, including James and me, were granted two weeks' leave. The wireless room, wardroom, engine room, galley, tiller-flat and fo'c'sle were to be locked, with the keys being handed over to Warrant Officer Hughes.

I returned to the ship. When we reached the Porto Vecchio Harbour wall, the fuel tanker driver was rolling up his hose and stowing the huge 'NO SMOKING' signs that were always displayed on the jetty when fuelling was taking place. I thanked him and he pointed to 135 with his thumb.

'You've got a right one there, sir,' he said. 'Nearly had us all up in flames.'

'What! What do you mean?' I cried.

'One of your crew was smoking, not three feet from a hose joint. Your No 1 saw him, and sent a rating to walk casually by and snatch it from his mouth. Otherwise the idiot might have thrown it on the ground,' he told me.

I was appalled. The entire harbour could have been set ablaze, and especially ML 135 with all the men inside it. In the wardroom,

James told me the whole story. Ordinary Seaman Lavender, of course! In spite of all the notices, in spite of all the warning lights, in spite of the galley stove being doused, this man climbed to the jetty and lit a cigarette. Right. This was enough! He would have to be removed from the ship at once.

I went straight back to Sharky Ward's office and reported the entire history of Lavender during his time aboard, ending with the horror that had just occurred. 'I want him off my ship, sir,' I said. 'He is a danger to others and a constant menace to the smooth running of the vessel.'

Commander Ward reached forward and pressed a bell. A voice answered from a voice-pipe, 'Sir?' 'Phone the Military Police and tell them to send a Red Cap to ML 135, in Porto Vecchio, and arrest Ordinary Seaman Lavender. He is to bring the man to my office. His effects are to be packed and sent after him. This is for immediate execution!'

'Thank you, sir,' I said. 'We have no way of dealing with serious matters of discipline. Small cases we can manage, but without Petty Officers or Chiefs we have no way of enforcing punishment. I don't want the man punished in this case, I just want him off my ship.'

'Lieutenant, don't worry. Come into the bar,' said Sharky. We drank a toast to a happier ship. Sharky told me that Lavender would be drafted to the first warship that was a man short, and meanwhile he would be kept in the small barracks used by men on passage. I realised just how fortunate we were in the Third Flotilla, to have a man such as Commander Ward in charge of our operations. He understood the problems of small ships and made life easy for us wherever possible.

The whole sorry business was over by the time I was back on board. Both the Cox'n and No 1 were looking more cheerful than I had seen them for days. James and I enjoyed the evening. I played some records, which James pretended to like, and we both turned in feeling relieved that we had emerged on the right side of a bad situation. Although for a time we would be one crew member short, I knew that Sharky would replace him as soon as someone became available.

The next morning at about 10.00am there came a knock on the door. It was the sentry who told me that a US soldier wished to speak to me and that she was in a Jeep on the jetty. 'She?' I said. 'Yes, sir, a girl member of their armed forces, like our WAAFs. I don't know what they're called,' he replied.

On the harbour wall above stood a very pretty girl of about nineteen, leaning against a Jeep. Behind her was a second Jeep, also with a girl driver. I motioned for her to come aboard, and she handed me an envelope containing a short note. As far as I can remember, it read something like this: 'From – CO 10th US Fighter Squadron, Corsini. Thank you, Captain, for everything. I see you guys doing a lot of walking and so I hope you enjoy a ride now and again. Good luck. Signed JF Franklin, Colonel.'

'Does this mean that the CO is giving me a Jeep?' I asked.

'Yes, sir, that's what it means, I guess,' she replied.

'Are you sure?' I said.

'Yes, sir, there's another Jeep waiting to take me back, so I reckon it's for you to keep all right,' said the girl.

'Good Heavens! Do you come with the vehicle?' I said.

She laughed, and perhaps blushed a little, I don't fully recall, but I do remember that she was exceptionally attractive.

I scrawled a note of thanks saying that I was overwhelmed by such generosity, and that my crew and I would enjoy the Jeep whenever we were in harbour. I ended by saying that I would remember him and his brave pilots long after the war was over. I watched the two young soldiers drive away, waving as they did so.

Well, here was a turn-up for the books, and no mistake. Not only did ML 135 now have a Jeep to its name but, most importantly, a pile of blank 'work tickets' which the girl had passed to me on leaving. The 'work tickets' were officially printed slips that enabled a person to obtain petrol from any Allied fuel depot. You merely had to fill in the amount required.

This gift from the CO of the US fighter squadron did more than I could ever have done to repair the damage caused by Seaman Lavender. We became a proud ship once more. The Cox'n and one of the hands painted it navy grey, with an anchor on the windscreen and ML 135 on each door. In future, we would not have to carry our supplies back from the base. Everything, especially heavy hawsers, could be thrown in the back of the Jeep. It was such a luxury.

The very next day we had occasion to use the Jeep in this way. I noticed fishing boats being pulled up on to high ground, all along the shore. Not one of them was left near the tidemark, with some being carried inland on trailers. This meant only one thing; the Bora was due, possibly within the next twenty-four hours. The Bora is an exceptionally strong wind that hurtles down the Adriatic, sweeping all before it. Only vessels of several hundred tons, with powerful engines, can deal with the conditions it creates. I had experienced the fag end of one when in HDML 1297. We had ferried a high-ranking officer to Preveza, but that was only the 'left over' bit of sea. The Adriatic fishermen had a sixth sense about the weather. It seemed that they always knew, before the Met Office, when a Bora was on its way.

I instructed James to hurry to the base at once. He was to draw from stores two eight-inch hawsers each of the same length as the six-inch ones we already had. These ropes would have been impossible to carry back without our Jeep. The Cox'n drove, and petitioned for what we needed, with a big smile on his face. The afternoon saw a huge drop in the air pressure. A quiet, tense feeling pervaded the atmosphere, as if we were wrapped in cotton wool. I told James to arrange one-hour sentry watches through the night, and that they could be kept from the wheelhouse and not the open bridge. The new eight-inch hawsers were rigged. A second anchor was laid, upwind of the main anchor. Extra fenders were hung between our stern and the wall. All hands were warned to have their oilskins to hand. I turned in at 11.00pm, but still nothing had happened. I closed my eyes thinking of the big storm off Ushant so long ago.

At 6.00am a great noise like a tree falling made both James and me leap out of bed. This was followed immediately by a near hurricane-force wind, which struck the side of the ship causing an almighty jerk through the hull as the hawsers took the strain. We both struggled into oilskins and went on deck. The anchors were holding, and the eight-inch ropes were doing their job. As yet there was no rain so I told the sentry to keep watch from the bridge. For now everything that could be done, had been done, so James and I went back below. I called the sentry, from the voice-pipe, to instruct him to call me immediately if he became worried about anything.

By 8.00am the wind had reached its peak and remained at a constant strength for some hours. Green water poured over the sea wall in huge waves, much of it hitting our quarterdeck. The steward fought his way aft with breakfast. He made us coffee and toast in the wardroom pantry. So far so good; I was just about to light my pipe when the sentry called down the voice-pipe. My immediate reaction was, 'Oh, my God, here we go!'

'Yes, sentry, what's the trouble?' I asked.

'No trouble, sir, but there is a man struggling along the jetty and waving to us,' he told me.

I dived into my oilskins and rushed up the wardroom ladder to the deck, stubbing my toe on a ring bolt as I did so. A bedraggled figure extended a boat hook towards me with something on the end. It was a sodden envelope held on by an elastic band. I pulled it off, and the man at once turned and ran back, through the spray, to the road. Below again, I removed my wet oilskins, dropped them in a heap on the tiller-flat deck and went to the wardroom. I carefully dried the envelope with a towel and gently opened it. Whatever message was inside must be important. I spread the paper on the table. It read, 'Take all precautions, strong winds expected.' I could think of no reply to this missive. I might, however, frame it and hang it in the wheelhouse.

The Bora lasted a further twelve hours, then stopped quite suddenly. It did not die down gradually, as gales do in UK waters, but just stopped as if it had been switched off, although there was nasty broken sea left behind in its wake.

For the few days that remained before we were towed round to Bari, the crew enjoyed the novelty of having their own transport. They were supposed to only use it for essential trips to the base, but both James and I knew that joyrides into the countryside were taking place. We did not say anything, it was better that way, and I trusted the Cox'n not to let things go too far. I did tell him, however, that I wanted exclusive use of the Jeep during the first few days of our general leave, after which he and the crew could use it for pleasure. James would have to make his own arrangements with the Cox'n. He was not a member of the ship's company at the time of the Corsini affair, and therefore had no claim to its use.

The tow round was without incident, and it was a relief to hand over responsibility to someone else for a while. Having carried out Sharky Ward's instructions, I packed a few clothes and set off for Fasano and the family that had made me so welcome before. I feared that there might be others staying there and that I would have to stay in a different part of the rest camp. But even if this happened I could still enjoy the company of Ljerka, my little wartime daughter.

The Jeep ate up the miles like a thoroughbred. It was obviously in good order. With its coat of navy paint, it looked new and was a vehicle to be proud of. I was in luck: Terka and Charles had no guests. A Wren officer who had been staying with them had left the day before. I arrived in the early evening and, before everything else, I took them for a joyride to the coast and back.

Terka was delighted with the material I had brought from Malta. She thought that there would be enough to make two dresses for Ljerka. But after measuring it carefully against her daughter, she realised that there may be just enough for three frocks. She then served a meal of spaghetti and meat sauce, followed by a home-baked cake and some fruit. When I asked her what meat was in the sauce she told me it was rabbit boiled with tomatoes and herbs. It made me realise that people such as the Ebenspangers were used to making much out of very little, and are rarely defeated by anything, except perhaps by illness.

For example, while Terka ran the home, Charles, along with the few possessions he had brought out of Yugoslavia, had set up a trading business buying and selling small articles, making a little profit each time. Their object for their future, after the war, was to emigrate to Canada and settle there. They managed it and on their way there stayed for two nights with my parents. However, that is a story for another occasion.

After the meal we drank the local wine, sang many songs, some in Serbo-Croat, some in German. I did my best to remember English folk songs such as 'D'yer Ken John Peel?' and the 'Ash Grove' for their benefit.

The days passed happily and all too quickly. Ljerka and I swam once, and ate one of Terka's picnics on the beach. It was on the way back from this trip that I remembered a duty. Ljerka had spent a short time on board 135, and had been cared for, and made much of by the crew. She had become a mascot, and her photograph was pinned up in the wheelhouse where she had slept. I must certainly take her back to meet them again, but they would, at that time, be dispersed around Bari and nearby places. This was a problem. I would ask James to take charge on the day the crew were due to return, and I would ask Commander Ward for permission to take a day off. This proved unnecessary in the event as the work was not finished on time, and 135 remained in the engineer's hands for a further three days.

Not knowing this, I took Ljerka on the long ride to Bari and the Officers' Club, where we would have lunch and, hopefully, find James. Fortunately, when we arrived I spotted him through the window having his lunch. We shared his table while I told him the whole story of the rescue. I told him of how Ljerka, after being separated from her parents prior to the evacuation, had stayed with us aboard ML 135, was looked after by the crew and that she had become their mascot. Of course, he agreed at once to my request. I was proud of my wartime daughter; she was sitting upright in her chair and looking as if she had lunch out every day. I left her in the care of James while I went to the base in the hope of seeing Sharky. Again, I was lucky. He was eating a sandwich in the bar. He readily gave permission for my extra day and imparted a bit of unexpected news.

'Beale, my engineer tells me that the modification he had to make on the BYMS steering gear must be replaced by fitting the authentic part,' he told me. 'In all other respects, the BYMS system is the same as the installation for an ML. If anything went wrong in future Reed's would not replace it, or guarantee the present work. They have a full-time agent in Malta. You will leave for the island as soon as work here is finished. The proper part is to be fitted, and the assembly passed by Reed's. I cannot have any boat under my control taking unnecessary risks when sweeping.'

The fact that I was able to leave a child of eight in the care of a stranger, and in a club populated almost entirely by grown men, illustrates the huge difference between attitudes in those days and in the Britain of today. The social climate was simply different. I had left Ljerka with James with complete confidence, and it would not have occurred to anyone to question this. In fact, I think James was quite sorry when I called for her. I found them playing noughts and crosses.

The ride back to Fasano delighted the little girl who had probably only been in a car but once or twice in her life. She kept looking round at the passing country and pointing things out to me. There is nothing like a Jeep for viewing the terrain.

The three days of leave I had left were filled with many happy moments. Good simple food, wine and song enriched the evenings, and the days rushed past like dreams made real. We explored the hills and valleys and forgot the war. I tried to get Terka to come with us, but she always refused saying she had too much to do. I soon realised that she was happy in her work and did not wish to leave it. She kept six hens that she had trained to come into the kitchen to lay their eggs. The stone sink was supported on brick plinths with the space between laid with straw on which the obliging birds deposited their contributions to the household rations. This idyll in the hills ended with tears and a song of parting. Ljerka and I set off for Bari having explained to her parents that the crew wanted to say hello to their 'mascot', and to take another photograph.

Ljerka spent an hour on board as the crew returned, one or two at a time, from leave. I went to the engineer's office to get the keys for 135 only to learn that the work was not yet finished and another three days in dock would be needed. I was glad of this because it would give James and the crew a fairer share of the use of our transport.

When the goodbyes had been said and another picture had been taken of Ljerka, I bundled her into the Jeep for James to drive her back to Fasano. I thought that my First Lieutenant would enjoy driving her back, which he did. Meanwhile, the crew went back ashore and continued their leave. No one was sorry about this, as minesweeping is not the most enjoyable of occupations. I had told no one except James that we were going on to Malta after Bari. It would be a pleasant surprise for the men, as they never minded being at sea.

James and the crew made good use of the Jeep during the three days' bonus leave. One morning James and the cook penetrated far into the farmland east of Bari, and returned with seven chickens, plucked, drawn and ready for the oven. I asked what they had paid with, but they would not tell me. I suspect it was petrol.

The passage to Malta was marked by calm sunny days and two meals of roast chicken and American ham. However, Malta was not my favourite place, and this time was no exception. It was full of heat, unpleasant smells and bad water. The water question was the real horror. We had left Bari without topping up our tanks, as there had been a queue waiting for the hydrant and so after two days in port we were forced to take on two hundred gallons of the terrible Maltese stuff. When I suggested to the crew that they cleaned their teeth in beer, nobody laughed.

Reed's agent and his assistant were highly efficient. They did the work on ML 135 in Sliema Creek so there was no need to go round to Grand Harbour docks. James and I ate at the Officers' Club, which saved the larder aboard. I bought several more lengths of material, which I thought might appeal to Terka, and hoped that she would use some of it for herself for a change.

When the work was finished at the end of the second day, it was too late for trials at sea unless there was no alternative, because the agent said he preferred to test everything in daylight. That suited James and me. I returned to the club and consumed a vast amount of excellent curry, for which the chef was rightly famous.

At 10.00am the following morning we were found outside Grand Harbour breasting a heavy swell at speeds varying from two knots to twenty knots, turning at full helm, half helm and very little helm. At noon the agent pronounced the test satisfactory. He then gave me a certificate to that effect, and a warranty. During the test the Chief had spent the whole time with the agent. He was now an expert with a lot of literature by his side.

As soon as Reed's agent was ashore, I set course for Taranto, where I reckoned to spend the second night. It is approximately 350 miles to the head of the Gulf and the port where I hoped to ditch the awful water, and to fill our tanks with something a lot more palatable. As it turned out, we did better than that. By early evening we were passing close to the Sicilian coast, about five miles south of Syracuse. This was a well-known stretch of water and I took up the glasses to renew my acquaintance with the country ashore. The steward had just brought up a welcome mug of tea, and a chicken sandwich, making it seem like we were engaged in yachting, not war. My eyes travelled along the shoreline to the cove of deep water with overhanging trees, in which I had anchored just before the fall of Syracuse. That seemed a long time ago now. A large ship was anchored in the cove, obscuring most of the country behind, and immediately a thought struck me, 'What if she was fresh out from the UK? She would have plenty of really good water!' Supply vessels were constantly arriving and leaving.

We closed the small inlet and saw that it was a large naval vessel known as an assault ship. They were heavily armed and carried landing craft and the soldiers that manned them. Their huge superstructure belied the fact they were no longer than a destroyer, but their beam is much greater. It was worth a try. Her paintwork was new, and not faded like most craft in the Med. Her water tanks would have to be enormous to accommodate the crew and the army personnel. Altogether things were looking more hopeful. As we drew near I heard voices, or at least one voice,

'Lef', right, lef', right, lef', right, about turn! Lef', lef', lef', right, lef', about turn!' Good Heavens! It was Ordinary Seaman Lavender in full kit, rifle and tin helmet, marching up and down the quarterdeck to the commands of a Chief Petty Officer!

Through the loudhailer I asked for permission to come alongside. After a minute or two an officer appeared with two ratings, who took our lines. 'Welcome aboard,' he said. 'What can I do for you, sir?'

I ventured the question of water with some hesitation, but my doubts were swept aside. 'Of course, sir. We've tons of the stuff fresh from the Helford River. We don't have the army aboard now, so help yourself. We dropped them in Malta, and picked up that specimen to replace an injured hand.'

Lavender's punishment drill continued, and after leaving James to deal with the watering problem, I went over to the Chief. 'I see you've got Ordinary Seaman Lavender, Chief,' I said. 'I wish you luck, he used to be one of my crew for a short time, but we had to lose him. I'm sorry you've been lumbered.'

'Defaulter! Defaulter, halt! Stand at ease! If you move more than one inch, your time out 'ere will be doubled! 'E'll be alright, sir, when I've finished with 'im. 'E just don't know the time of day!' said the Chief. There was not an ounce of anger or ill feeling in either the Chief's voice or expression. He had probably dealt with dozens of Lavenders over the years, and made good sailors out of them, and possibly better sons and husbands. I thanked the Chief for his attempts to improve the human race, and turned back to the Officer of the Watch.

'I'm grateful, sir, for the water,' I told him. 'We've been carrying that ghastly stuff from Malta, which No 1 is now getting rid of. Tonight we can enjoy the taste of cold Cornish water, a luxury not to be missed.'

An hour later we were on our way, dipping our ensign in salute, as we went. James and I toasted each other, and the Assault Ship officer, with mugs of water as we stood on the bridge, and waved to our benefactor. The liquid was really quite delicious.

We gave Taranto a miss and pushed on to Bari. What with water tanks filled with fresh water from the UK, and brand new Reeds steering, I felt rich and rather smug. Porto Vecchio was full of vessels, but they were ours. The Third ML Flotilla had returned, leaving our usual place free. It was a welcome break to go aboard one of the other boats and swap stories with them.

Twenty-four hours later the whole force was underway, and heading for the islands south of Vis. It was an awkward sweeping ground that had been allocated to us, and I estimated that two weeks' work would be necessary. At night we were to anchor in the lee of the nearest land suitable. On the first Sunday the SO signalled us to remain at anchor and enjoy a day's 'make and mend'. One of the boats had damaged some gear, and needed time to make repairs. I decided to do 'Captain's Rounds'. That is an inspection of the entire ship, in company with the relevant heads of departments.

It was essential to look after the bilges, especially the engine room bilges, as fuel was likely to collect there, thus endangering the vessel. Unbeknown to me, the Chief had lifted the floorboards ready for my inspection. I stepped straight off the ladder and into a black hole, barking my shin on a cross beam. The wound was deep, and needed stitching. Fortunately, we were near our support vessel, HMS *Calypso*, which had an MO aboard and a sickbay. We went alongside, and the wound was quickly dealt with. Next door to the doctor's surgery was a large compartment containing six beds. The beds could be screened from each other with a chintz curtain. Over the door was a sign simply saying 'Rose Cottage'. Four of the beds were occupied by patients and all of them had venereal disease (VD). The medical officer told me that VD was the most common ailment he dealt with.

The sweeping, like so many that we had performed, was exploratory and no mines were found. The next Sunday I visited *Calypso* to have the stitches removed. The wound had healed well, so I expected no further trouble with it. The MO was ashore when I arrived, but his assistant was present. This man was what the navy calls 'a sick bay artificer'. They are unqualified, but possess a rudimentary knowledge of matters medical.

When I entered the surgery he was reading a comic. I showed him my leg. He agreed that it was time for the stitches to come out. He went to the steriliser and took out five hard-boiled eggs, some of which still had traces of bird manure on their shells. It was with some trepidation that I observed this procedure. The eggs were carefully placed on, what I assumed to be, the operating table, then he went back to the steriliser, fetched the forceps and removed the stitches! A week later I noticed that the area round the gash had gone soft. The base MO at Bari said it was cellulitis and it was a year before the leg healed properly and returned to normal.

During the few days we had in Porto Vecchio I was able to pay a visit to Fasano. I gave Terka the fabric that I had bought in Malta. She was delighted with it. After dinner we sang songs and Ljerka insisted on climbing on my knee. The Jeep was a joy to drive. On the way back I reflected upon our Cox'n's wisdom in the safeguarding of our prize possession while we were away among the islands. He had secured the wheels with a chain, plus an enormous padlock drawn from the base, the very sight of which would have discouraged any would-be thief. He had also removed the distributor cap.

Our next call was to Ancona. The port had only just fallen to the Allies, and firing could still be heard from the countryside behind the town. We carried out the usual search of the approaches, and found nothing. But we were in for a surprise once inside. I stopped at the entrance and considered the aspect before me. The harbour was empty of all shipping, except for local fishing boats. Should I go across the centre and berth near them, or around the edge close to the wall? There were no guides that I could see, so I went through the centre and tied up to the dirtiest fishing boat I could find because it seemed most unlikely to disturb us by moving. The lines were quickly made fast by our crew, and I was just leaving the bridge when a ragged figure appeared out of the vessel's only hatch and spoke to me in perfect English, 'Would you care for a gin?' he said.

I was staggered. What? Who was this man? 'Are you English?' I asked him.

'As English as you are, I expect. Come below,' he said. I followed this strange man down to his small but beautifully equipped cabin. The vessel was in fact an MTB powered by three Rolls-Royce Merlin engines. A dummy structure had been built over the basic hull, which left her looking, from the outside, like a fishing boat. There was even a wheelhouse on deck.

'I'm going home, done my stint here, and the port has fallen so there's nothing more for me to do,' he told me.

We had a long talk over a drink, and it turned out that he had been 'mine watching' in the Adriatic for two years. It was on the intelligence he had provided that all minesweeping operations in the Adriatic were based.

This 'ragged fisherman' with an English public school education, was good company. He showed me over his boat, and the various disguises that had been employed throughout his time there. The MTB wheelhouse had been encased in what could only be classed as a 'shed', with a window facing front. Lengths of fishing net were hung about the deck to dry, as was the custom among Italian fishermen. There was a stone jar lashed to the base of a rudimentary mast, with a string of onions suspended above. The upper deck was littered with odd bits of carpet, and the sides of the MTB were hidden behind a covering of clapboard. I asked the skipper what would happen to this outer shell if he were to drive the vessel at speed. An MTB is capable of 38–40 knots. He assured me that the disguise had been tested at high speed, and the outer skin was double-layered and bolted right through the hull.

'Why do you need such speed?' I asked.

'This boat is crammed with mine reports, codes and confidential information of all kinds to enable me to do my job, and be able to communicate with any warship or base. If there was ever a danger of falling into enemy hands I have to be able to outrun any other pursuer,' he told me.

'Where do you get your fuel for the Merlins?' I enquired.

'That is something I can't answer, it's top secret. I speak Italian, if that helps,' he said.

'Doesn't the slow running of the engines damage them over a long period?' I asked.

'That is a problem I solve in a number of ways,' he replied, 'I give them all a burst at full power from time to time, when the horizon is free of all other shipping.'

'When do you leave for the UK?' I asked, to which he answered, 'As soon as my relief arrives. I thought that he'd be aboard you. The war, in these parts is coming to an end, and he'll only be a kind of caretaker.'

I was sorry to leave this interesting man and invited him aboard 135 for a meal, but he thanked me and declined. He apparently had friends ashore with whom he spent some of his evenings, with one of the other fishing boats keeping an eye on his vessel while he was away. 'Can anyone get below?' I queried. 'Not without an axe,' he said. 'The wheelhouse is also secured against anything but an attack with explosive or an axe.' I bid him goodnight and climbed back aboard 135, reflecting that my war had been pretty mundane compared with his.

Our next meal was a matter of simply filling the space caused by hunger. We were back on corned beef. This time the cook had made a shepherd's pie with the stuff, which helped a little, but I blessed the wardroom pantry where the steward dished up a couple of omelettes filled with onions. The super spy next door had given me half a dozen eggs and some onions, saying that he could get all the eggs and onions he needed from his friends.

James and I played records that evening and later, when lying in my bunk, I went over the events of the day, especially my encounter with the 'fisherman' alongside. I came to the conclusion that not all of Italy had been under the heel of Mussolini, but that was only a guess. Ancona was a medium-sized town, about the size of my home town, St Albans, in the UK. In peacetime it must have been an important port, judging by the warehouses and idle cranes lining the wharf.

We stayed in Ancona for five days, which gave time for James and the cook to make several successful forays into the countryside. They returned with 'real' meat and some chickens!

There were two kinds of meat, sheep and goat, with enough for two meals for the whole ship's company. I never knew how they paid for it, but I suspected that it was with petrol from our 'ready-use supply' kept for the two auxiliary engines that provided power and light.

I had been expecting to be sent back to Bari, but instead received a signal that had a surprise at the end of it. We were ordered to proceed to a bay a few miles south of Trieste, anchor there and wait for further orders. The bay was a calm, well-sheltered anchorage called Pirano, which we found without difficulty. The water was still warm, and I had several swims while waiting for the new instructions. As before, no one in the crew joined me over the side. It has always puzzled me that sailors have such an objection to sea bathing. Even James had a distaste for it.

The aforementioned surprise arrived in a signal on the night of our second day in the bay. We were ordered to rendezvous with the cruiser Orion, and sweep ahead of her into Trieste Harbour. A time and place for the meeting was given. HMS Orion was the ship in which my youngest brother was serving. He had not long left school, and must have joined the Navy aged seventeen. The war was nearing its end in Europe, so his time in the navy was restricted to about a year. In that short time he rose to the rank of 'Leading Seaman', and was the best helmsman on board, as I learned later. I had not seen him for several years and hoped to do so after the sweep into Trieste.

The co-ordinates given in the signal put the rendezvous position immediately outside Pirano Bay. It would be possible to see the Orion long before we met, which was an advantage. We left the anchorage in good time, and cruised about in open water, until we could see the cruiser on the horizon. I judged that she would be in position in thirty minutes given a speed of sixteen knots, which was the normal cruising speed for destroyers and above. I had observed this when keeping company with one of them from time to time. I waited for fifteen minutes before streaming port and starboard sweeps. As we took the strain, and felt the pull of both sweeps, HMS Orion entered the space between them. Both 'otters' were running smoothly on the surface, and I prayed that they would stay that way. My usual speed with both 'otters' streamed was four knots, which might be difficult for the cruiser, so I risked the speed of five knots and hoped for the best. The distance to the centre of the inner harbour was eighteen miles, therefore the passage lasted three and a half hours. I swept as close to the wharf wall as I dared before turning to port, and hauling the sweeps out of the path of Orion, who dropped anchor as soon as we were clear. This surprised me as I was expecting the ship to go alongside. We headed out for open sea and commenced winding in both sweeps. The Orion flashed, 'Thank you and goodnight.'

To which I replied, 'From CO ML 135 to HMS Orion. Request permission to visit my brother Leading Seaman Donald Beale.' The answer came back at once, 'Approved. Welcome aboard.' I then decided not to take 135 alongside Orion, but to do the thing in style, as Nelson would have done, which would be to launch a tender and be rowed across by a rating. Our small dinghy actually had an inboard engine – a four-horse power Stuart Turner two-stroke. My predecessor, Johnny Peel, had been responsible for this luxury, and we were the only boat in the flotilla to boast a powered dinghy. Now that we also had a Jeep, it looked as if we were getting too big for our sea boots!

The Stuart Turner started without trouble, which amazed me, as it was often the very devil to get going. I brushed my uniform, took one of the crew and set off. It was a long way across the harbour and I began to wish that I had not embarked on this foolish stunt. At last we reached their companion ladder and I climbed aboard. It was a thrill to be piped aboard this great ship and be saluted by the Officer of the Watch. He thanked me again for the successful operation and motioned my brother to come forward. 'I will leave you two to talk,' he said. 'Good night.'

Don greeted me with a remark guaranteed to deflate any ideas I had of my own importance, 'Hello, I saw you coming across. I thought it was two men swimming!' Don had certainly grown since I last saw him. I left a schoolboy back in the UK and here was a man, strong, tall and good-looking. If the war had lasted another year he would certainly have been commissioned.

We talked of home, our parents and of Tony, our middle brother. He was a Gunnery Officer in a frigate in the Pacific who had, during his time as a rating, survived a Russian convoy to Murmansk. We couldn't talk for long as Don had duties to perform, and I had a small ship that I was responsible for. It was a pity that we could not have spent an evening together, but neither of us thought that way then. We were both members of His Majesty's Navy, and that was all.

When, to my surprise, the little dinghy's engine started on the first pull of the handle, I realised that the gods were smiling on us that evening. The Stuart Turner motor rarely started when it was hot, and it would sometimes be necessary to wait for up to an hour for it to cool down. After the respectful treatment I had received aboard Orion, it would have been spoiled completely if my crew member and I had been unable to leave. Certainly we had oars, but it was a long way back to 135.

As soon as I was back aboard I signalled, 'Operation completed. Request instructions.' The reply followed quickly, 'Return Bari.' This concerned me. Our home port was three hundred and fifty miles away, and I knew that we were getting low on fuel. We had managed to acquire some from a tanker, when working with the Flotilla in the islands, but they rationed us, and we had left with tanks only half full. I consulted Chief and we worked out an economical speed, which was eight knots. If in doubt, I would go into Pescara or Ortona on the way. These small ports had been explored by the Flotilla while I was away on other jaunts. We made it, just, and two days later we entered Porto Vecchio to find the rest of our flotilla berthed in their usual places. We had only enough fuel left for two hours' running, a risk that I swore I would never take again.

The weather was becoming colder, but not markedly so. Warm winds still came up from the south, but when they were not blowing, cold air from the Carpathian Mountains in the north lowered the temperature. There was a general feeling of 'waiting for the end' in the air. The urgency had left the scene and it seemed as if we were being given tasks merely to fill up time.

An Italian opera company came to Bari. They were giving *Lucia di Lammermoor* again on the day I arrived back, and there were two days left before they took the production to Ancona. I realised, as I entered the auditorium, that I was lucky to have got a ticket.

For several days the base left us alone, and the Flotilla socialised, as the term goes today. That is to say that officers and men visited each other's boats, and a considerable amount of liquor was consumed. Our Cox'n had once more taken the usual safety precautions with our Jeep, and I drove it to Fasano. This was to be my last meeting with Terka, Ljerka and Charles in Italy. I stayed for two nights and spent time teaching Ljerka some English phrases, and she in turn helped me to learn Italian. This little girl, who was now nearly nine, spoke three languages fluently, Italian, German and English. I knew that she would go far in life if they ever managed to get to Canada, as was their hope. It was hard saying goodbye not knowing if we would meet again, but it had to be done. I drove back, sad and thoughtful.

The odd dead days lingered on, and it was hard to find enough work for the crew when they were not ashore. All the men continued to enjoy our Jeep and made many trips into the surrounding countryside. I had most of my meals at the Officers' Club, and on one occasion met an RN Lieutenant Commander with whom I shared a table. He was very interested in the 'doings' of small ships, and wanted to know what sort of war we were having. He was good company. He enlightened me on much that I did not know about the workings of really large warships, such as battle cruisers and above.

One day I very stupidly told him about our Jeep. He asked if he could borrow it. That, sadly, was the last day of our ownership. In the evening he drove it out of town, promising to return it the next morning, but it never arrived back. We heard later that he had smashed it beyond repair by hitting a tree at speed when on his way back to Bari after a party. The Cox'n was really angry, ostensibly with the RN Lieutenant Commander as a substitute for me, who was most to blame. I did not know if the Lieutenant Commander was injured in the accident, and lost touch with the whole matter soon after. Fortunately, we were given a commission that was to take us away from Bari, the day after the loss of our transport. You can't think of small losses when you have important work to do.

I was summoned to Sharky Ward's office, where he briefed me on what was to be an unusual mission. It was known that a German destroyer was present somewhere in the head of the Adriatic. Most other enemy craft had surrendered by this time, and we had heard news that the Allied Forces were within striking distance of Berlin. Lieutenant Commander Tim Bligh would try to locate the destroyer and attempt to persuade the CO to surrender, thus saving lives on both sides. My job was to take 135 to the edge of the scene and stand by, ready to pick up survivors if hostilities started.

I returned to Porto Vecchio to find it empty. The Third ML Flotilla had left to go I knew not where. We proceeded at once to the main harbour to take on fuel and water. Nightfall found us on our way. I was given a time and an approximate position, as the exact location of the destroyer was not known. The sea was calm. Cook served up a decent meal of soup and a shepherd's pie made with American ham and vegetables.

During the morning watch the sun shone brightly on to a glassy sea, when a shout from the forward lookout warned me to look over the side. I thought that he was referring to a floating mine. 'Port twenty midships!' I looked and saw that it was the naked body of a young German sailor. The only article of clothing he wore was a cap band round his neck, with the name of his ship on it. The body was swollen, and he had clearly been dead for some time. Strangely enough, his youthful face was still unmarked. I could not stop to pick him up and identify him, as I had to be in time and in the right place for Tim Bligh's daring attempt.

We reached the area in fog. Cold air coming down from the north meeting the warm sea was a perfect recipe for fog. I was in the right area, but there was no sign of anything. We cruised in a circle for half an hour, when I heard the unmistakable sound of engines. Tim's engines, I hoped. I followed the sound, and the fog grew thicker. One bank of fog looked darker than the rest. It grew even darker as I watched it resolve into a long grey shape.

'That's her!' from the forward lookout, and there was the destroyer, a sinister grey shape coming and going in the mist. We were close; it was the fog that made the distance seem greater. I stopped, glanced behind me, and saw a dinghy being rowed toward the German warship. Later, when a full account of the exploit was made known, I realised that I had been late to arrive. Tim Bligh had found the German vessel with his radar, had closed the destroyer and, using a loudhailer, asked for permission to come aboard. His near faultless German no doubt persuaded them to agree. I waited for more than an hour until Tim climbed down into his dinghy, and the German ensign was lowered. The young seaman who rowed the dinghy saw us, and passed close. I lowered our ensign in salute to a brave and clever man. Tim's D-Class ML then became visible for the first time, and I watched as the tender was hauled aboard, and the two figures disappeared below.

In my own estimation I had failed: I was late, and that was unforgivable. If firing had started before permission to board had been given, I should not have been there to rescue anyone. The fog was an excuse but only a partial explanation. I had failed, and the thought could not be avoided. In a dismal frame of mind I set course for Trieste. It was the nearest harbour, and I had no reason to report the surrender of the destroyer as Tim Bligh would have done that already. 'Sufficient for the day,' as they say.

CHAPTER 9

✳

War's end and beyond

1945

Trieste Harbour was deserted. The *Orion* had left, and the few fishing boats were crowded into one corner. Lights were on in the town, and along the quay, revealing a heavy fall of snow on the quay and on the roofs of the warehouses that lined the waterfront. It was obvious that the enemy was no longer present. The inhabitants must have been aware of the expected fall of Berlin. The sight of the lights made me realise that the war was nearly over and that the surrender of the German destroyer had been an important sign of this fact. This was not a night for gloomy introspection, but a time for rejoicing.

When peace was finally declared, James and I would go into the mess deck and celebrate this momentous event with the whole ship's company. In a better mood I headed for the dock wall, keeping as near as possible to the track we had steered when ahead of the *Orion*. The snow on the dockside was over a foot thick, and it obscured the bollards and all means of tying up. Cold air funnelled down into the town, bringing with it occasional flurries of snow. We secured temporarily to an iron ladder while some of the crew dug in the snow looking for the bollards, which were quickly exposed.

Cook did us proud with a piping hot stew for everybody, with chunks of his own baked bread, made from the flour we had obtained in Malta. James and I drank a toast to the master tactician, Lieutenant Commander Tim Bligh, who had just crowned his amazing career with an outstanding act of bravery. During the night I was woken by a call from the sentry through the voice-pipe. It must have been about 2.00am. 'Sir, there is a man on the wall asking for hot water.'

I thought it was an odd request at this time of night, and could see nothing else for it but to investigate it myself. I bundled into my trousers and greatcoat, and went up on deck. Standing there in the snow above me was a figure in Italian battledress. In the light of my torch he looked somehow familiar. When he spoke my suspicions were confirmed. In good English, with only a slight accent, he asked if he could have some hot water, then he held out a bucket for the purpose. The man was one of Popski's private army, one of the men who had held a conference in my wardroom on HDML 1297 all that long time ago. A lifetime it seemed. There were three other figures with him on the wall.

'Of course, but where are you spending the night?' I asked.

'Right here, sir, on the jetty,' he said.

'You can't do that, bring the others aboard, and you can sleep in the gangways', I told him.

He thanked me but refused by saying, 'We only need hot water, and will use our sleeping bags. We are quite used to snow.'

The sentry roused the cook, apologising for spoiling his sleep. Cook had a machine for rapidly heating water, and he was the only one allowed to use it, as it ran off spirit. We had some 'safari jars' that were vacuum-lined. Each held a gallon and they were filled and passed up to the wandering soldier of fortune. The next morning the jars were handed back down to the sentry, who told me later that he saw them shake the snow from their sleeping bags, then vanish into the town. I did wonder what exploits of theirs had contributed to the fall of Trieste, and what their next objective was to be. Peace would surely have no attraction for such men.

Trieste Harbour was cold and uninviting, and the town, being partly under snow, promised little either. I decided to sail for Ancona, and to do so at once. I had heard nothing from Bari. I intended to let sleeping dogs lie, and wait for them to make a move. The Chief consulted with me over the various fuel gauges, and we considered that there was sufficient fuel to reach Bari, even if we broke the journey and went into Ancona.

What a change had occurred there! It had turned into a festival city. Bunting flew from lampposts and trees. The harbour was crowded with craft of all shapes and sizes, among which I recognised our fuel tanker from the islands. So that was all right, as it carried petrol and water, we could top up with both. A band was playing somewhere ashore as we tied up next to two of our Flotilla. Officers and men greeted old friends while music served as a background. James arranged one-hour watches for sentries, and gave leave to everyone else who wanted it. Most of the crew preferred to visit their mates in other boats, and it said a great deal about our cook that he stuck by his post, and kept everyone fed while this jollity was going on.

The day after our arrival was spent in fuelling, general cleaning and overhauling of the ship and gear. Most went ashore in the evening to sample the delights of Ancona. The following morning peace in Europe was declared. Within minutes of the announcement the town exploded in a cacophony of sound, sirens, car horns, ship's foghorns, anything that would make a noise. This went on all day, and at night a fireworks display lit the heavens. Star shells, tracer bullets and Very lights added to the display of the real fireworks, such a rockets. For some hours after dark order, both aboard and ashore, seemed to have disappeared completely. In company with other officers I went into town, and sampled various cafes and bars, going from one to the other, looking for the best place to eat and drink. Early on in our search, we stole a female clothes dummy from an open shop window, and took her with us. In the restaurant, we sat her down, and spoke to her from time to time, especially when a waiter was in earshot. I was then, and still am, surprised at the speed with which a town reverts to normal trade as soon as the enemy departs. Shops and markets would open to start trading, people would appear in the streets, this happening even while tanks were still on the outskirts of town, provided, of course, that the tanks were in retreat.

The celebrations overwhelmed usual procedures and interfered with the memory. I cannot now remember whether or not we received a signal to sail to Malta, but we did soon after the affair with 'the lady of wax'. At the same, time dozens of small ships, from every part of the Adriatic and beyond, were en route to Malta for Tim Bligh's wedding. I doubt if Malta had ever seen a wedding to compare with that one. With, or without permission they came. Defects real and invented were the excuse made so that they could be there. The result was that the church was so packed that all the windows were blocked from outside by the numbers of people peering through. The road outside the church was so crowded that traffic had to be diverted.

It was noticeable that seamen of all ranks were present. This was not an occasion for officers alone, even though the bridegroom was a Lieutenant Commander. Ratings from Ordinary Seamen to Petty Officers were as much in evidence as commissioned personnel. There can surely be very few men and women in history who have been admired equally by people of all stations in life.

After the wedding celebrations had died down, none of the officers of the Third ML Flotilla knew what to do, or what was to happen next. All our boats were moored stern-to in Sliema Creek. Work of some sort had to be found to keep the crew busy for we were still in the navy. Service had to go on, even though the war had stopped.

A few days later a dreadful rumour spread through the boats to the effect that we would not be sailing our ships home to the UK, but that officers and men would be returning by other means. I went up to the base determined to find out if this was true. 'Sit down, Beale. Yes, I'm afraid, it's true,' I was told.

I was aghast and could think of nothing sensible to say. The Engineer Commander offered me a drink, and then I found my voice. 'Sir, we have lived and worked in these vessels for many months. They are not like big ships such as destroyers and above, they have become our homes, and the thought they would be broken up, or left to rot in some foreign port is unbearable.'

'They are to be sold to the Italian Navy, which is now under my direction. They will not be broken up or left to rot,' he said.

'Sir, can I ask the reason for this policy?' I asked him.

'You can, Beale,' he said. 'The fact is that the Admiralty will not finance the cost of the fuel, which would be considerable. However, if it will help to lessen the disappointment you can choose something from your boat to take as a souvenir.'

I think he expected me to ask for something small like the watch bell or the bosun's pipe, but instead I decided to do better than that without any hope of getting it, but it would be interesting to see how shocked he would be. 'Thank you, sir. I would like the ship's wheel from the bridge,' I said. 'For so many hours, days and months, I have stood by that wheel, and can think of nothing else that I would want.'

There was a silence and I waited for the explosion. He poured us each another gin and tonic, drank a little, put down the glass and leaned back. 'All right, Lieutenant, I'll have my shipwrights take it apart for you and pack it for transit to your home in the UK. Will that do?' I was, as the modern saying goes, gobsmacked. I stuttered my thanks as well as I could, and left the office. You may like to know that the wheel is still in my house to this day.

Another blow waited for me on the ward room table. It was in the form of a signal from the NOIC informing me that I would be going home via 'Medloc'. This was a long-distance train from Marseilles to Calais. This news was bad enough, but there was still worse to come. I was to be in charge of a draft of two hundred ratings all going the same way! There would only be one Chief and one Petty Officer to help me.

The passage to Marseilles would be by the next vessel bound for the UK. This would be notified in due course. Why could I not stay on that ship and reach the UK in that way? I had two hundred ratings to look after, that's why. Bloody hell. I was furious and lost all interest in my ship, in the navy and much else. OK, I thought. If that was the way they wanted things to be, I would spend my time on doing a bit of smuggling to take my mind of this disgrace.

I would go to the gold and silver market in Malta, but first I went to the Pay Office. I drew out two hundred and fifty pounds of the money that had been stacking up for several years while I was in the Mediterranean. During this period I had only drawn small amounts of cash occasionally. I bought ten gold sovereigns at seven pounds each. I tied them in a corner of a handkerchief that I kept in my top pocket during the journey back to England. Sovereigns are quite small and are thinner than a pressed coin of today. In France and the UK they were worth twenty-five pounds each. I was told this by someone in the Officers' Club who had just come out to relieve an injured officer who had broken a leg. I then purchased a diamond that I pressed into my shaving soap. Thus equipped, I was ready for the overland marathon that I knew would take at least two days in a railway carriage. I had heard dreadful reports of this lark. My mood was entirely black.

Returning from one of my moody 'moochings' around the markets of Malta, I climbed aboard an empty ship. The crew and the First Lieutenant had left. There was a note on the wardroom table. It read, 'Sir, as you know we received our draft orders some days ago and to await transport. This arrived soon after you left. A tanker is taking us, and the crew of two other boats, to Marseilles. I don't know what happens once there. Sorry to miss you. The crew and I thank you for everything that as CO you did for the boat and for us. We wish you good luck and a happy future.'

The note was signed by all the ship's company. As I put down the sheet of paper, footsteps sounded above and a civilian appeared in the hatch. 'Sir, I am a caretaker from the dockyard,' the man said. 'My instructions are to live aboard until she is handed over to the 'Eyties' (slang for Italians). I will sleep in the wheelhouse where I've already put my gear.' I had no idea how this man would manage about food, but that was his business not mine. I was pretty sure that the business of caretaking was his profession, and he had done it many times before.

I showed him where the heads were, and got down to the matter of packing. This took some hours. I had to go ashore again. I bought two more navy-style green fibre suitcases from the base store that was just about to close down. These cases were good value, bound in leather at the corners and edges, they looked smart and were very strong. It was dark by the time I finished. Standing on the jetty I looked down for the last time on HMS

ML 135. In my mind I thanked her builders and designers, men who had created a vessel that could meet emergencies and could adapt to so many situations. I then called a garry and went to the Officers' Club, where I intended to live until the horrible organisation called 'Medloc' took over.

I did not have to wait long. Two days later found me on the dockside in Grand Harbour standing by a draft of two hundred ratings while a Chief called a roll. This he did by making each man shout his name, which was checked against a list. In the afternoon we boarded a small merchant vessel bound for Marseilles. She had been fitted out for the purpose and was part of the 'Medloc' plan. Bunks for the two hundred were provided, and a large galley installed. The heads had been increased to twelve, with washbasins of the same number. There was a small cabin that would sleep three officers, with a similar one for Chiefs and POs. All this had been done in order to save the cost of fuel. Surely there must have been other warships beside MLs and MTBs that would be made over to the Italians. It was more than six hundred miles to Marseilles, which meant two nights at sea given a speed of ten knots, which is what I remember; I know I went into the wheelhouse and checked our course and speed with the Captain.

Other arrangements had been made at Marseilles. French army huts had been taken over and fitted out for two hundred men, like the merchant ship. The Trans-Europe train, as it was known, was unable to keep to any sort of timetable, which meant the waiting time in Marseilles was a matter of pot luck. I did, however, learn that there would be a minimum wait at Marseilles of two days. I attended the calling of the roll once more, informed the Chief of my intention not to wait there, and set off for Nice via the local bus service that had just restarted.

In Nice I booked into a large hotel that had been taken over by the Americans. The rates were extremely cheap, and were obviously being subsidised by the US government. It was pleasant to move among our Allies whom I had always found to be generous beyond belief and good company. At breakfast I ordered bacon and egg, with fried bread, tomatoes and a sausage. I sat looking out to sea, and waited with my mouth watering for the feast to come, and there it was. The waiter placed before me exactly what I had asked for; it looked a splendid sight.

He was still standing behind me as I raised my knife to cut the bacon. A hand appeared holding a small jug, and hot maple syrup was poured over my breakfast. By the time I had recovered from this vandalism the waiter had left. I tried to call out, but no words came. Several Americans came into the room at this point and sat at the table next to me, because both were near the window. I felt that I could not make a fuss in front of them, and so I tried to eat it but gave up after several attempts. Fried egg and syrup is not a delicacy I would care to repeat or recommend. Toast and marmalade repaired my palate somewhat, and the coffee was good.

In the town shops were open and there were few signs of damage. I bought a Leica 3c camera with four of my sovereigns, and sat on the beach and admired the sea and the girls in bikinis. It was as if there had never been a war.

I idled away another day and returned to the dreaded 'Medloc'. One night was spent at the ex-French army barracks in a hut even smaller than the cabin aboard the transport from Malta. The next day brought news of the train. Another muster of the draft was held, and this time five men were missing. What do I do now? I thought. I would do nothing. That was the answer. I had absolutely no interest in, or feeling of responsibility for, this operation beyond reporting the loss of five men to the temporary

NOIC down at the docks. I did this, and quickly left before he could think of any other task for me.

That evening we boarded the train and began a horrible journey that took four days in all. We were shunted into Spain for two days and remained in a siding. A long carriage fitted out as a galley had been added to the others, and another, containing toilet facilities, was connected to the end of the assembly. It was quite inadequate and a long way from some of the carriages. There were prearranged stops where the men could get out to stretch their legs. But unfortunately there were others that were impromptu, and at these stops one dared not disembark because there was the possibility of the train departing without warning.

There were no bunks, and some ratings climbed on to the luggage racks to sleep. Most, however, including myself, just dozed sitting upright in our seats. The journey was not quite a nightmare, but it was certainly a bad dream. At Calais, the draft was met by officials of all kinds: gendarmes, POs and two Naval Warrant Officers. I was glad to hand over to them, and so was the Chief. The gods had not finished with me even then. A runner from the navy handed me an order.

It was a long message instructing me to remain on the train, which was still in the station, and proceed to Rotterdam. Once there, I was to locate a trawler named Lindisfarne, which was berthed in the main dock, and to bring her back to the UK. I would be met in the Thames near Tower Bridge and escorted to a berth in London docks. This was more like it. This particular delay was quite to my liking and my spirits rose for the first time since Malta.

From the train window I noted the cleanliness of the streets and houses of Rotterdam as we passed through the suburbs. Of course, there was bomb damage, and gaps showed among the buildings, but a sense of calm and order was noticeable. I saw women leaning out of windows to clean outside walls with long brooms. The Dutch were getting on quickly with the peace and I hoped that I would find England doing the same. The trawler was a large minesweeping vessel and in very good order. Everything was shipshape and polished. The crew had clearly been with her for some time as all routines were running smoothly, but there were no officers. This was a mystery that I never solved, and no member of the crew volunteered any information. The CO's cabin was well appointed with an adjoining heads and washroom, where I was able to remove some of the grime and dust that I had accumulated during the long journey from Marseilles.

I asked the Chief, who like all Chiefs was the salt of the earth, what was their best cruising speed. He said ten knots, but he would be happy at twelve, and that they had full tanks. I went into the chart house and everything was in perfect order, like the rest of the ship. Charts, tide tables, parallel ruler, dividers all were there laid out ready for use.

I had a rudimentary wash and shave after which the steward brought me a meal. I found a bottle of beer in the CO's cabin. After the meal I called for the Cox'n and told him to be ready to leave at 6.00am, and I then went ashore for some exercise. It was warm early summer weather, which helped me in making the decision to complete the passage in daylight. I purchased four bottles of vintage Bordeaux wine and returned aboard. The bunk was spacious and comfortable, with a mattress and pillow. At 5.30am I was called as requested, and exactly at 6.00am the Lindisfarne slipped away from the wall, headed for open water and home. We maintained a constant twelve knots and arrived within sight of Tower Bridge at three minutes after 6.30pm. I was lucky in this because I had not done a proper calculation of the tide movement before setting the course. I had merely looked up the tides for the day and done a bit of guesswork. The sun was shining when we entered the mouth of the Thames and passed south. I was glad to be coming home in a ship, even if it was not my ship. The riverbanks on either side were busy behind with people and traffic of all kinds. Many small craft dotted the inshore water on both sides of the river and a number of cargo vessels and two tankers passed me, heading for the Estuary and the open sea. As the river narrowed I could see many ruined buildings inland, with piles of building rubble littering parts of the foreshore.

About five cables short of Tower Bridge two launches approached us, and one of them came alongside. It was HM Customs, wouldn't you know, and even a five-year war, involving the whole of Europe and the Far East, had failed to impress them, it seemed. Two men climbed aboard, one with a clipboard. They spent a long time below with the crew, while the helmsman and I tried to keep the ship in one place with one engine at slow ahead and astern.

At last they came to me and asked, 'Anything to declare?' I showed them the four bottles of Bordeaux. The man with the clipboard did some calculations. The duty they were to charge me came to half the price of the wine. I was outraged. Years away from base trying to do my bit, which was not much compared with the army, and then to be charged duty on four paltry bottles of wine. I knocked the neck off each one, and threw them over the side. They left saying they were only obeying orders. Which is what every Nazi said when interrogated by the Allies.

I realised afterwards that I had been a bit two-faced for I had a diamond in my shaving soap, four gold sovereigns in my top pocket and a Leica 3c camera that I had entirely failed to mention to them. The other launch led us to a convenient berth. I said goodbye to the crew and the Chief, then went ashore. One of the ratings carried two of my three cases and left me waiting for a taxi near a bus stop. It was a pleasant surprise to find that there were still taxis running after my long absence, and what must be a shortage of petrol. I was lucky that a taxi arrived after only a few minutes. The driver took my three cases and asked for my destination. 'Driver, can you suggest a really good hotel in the West End, but not a posh expensive one like The Ritz or Claridge's?' I asked.

'I can, sir,' he said. 'I suggest the Mayfair. It's very good, but not cheap, though it's not dear when you compare it with Claridge's or The Ritz. I've had many customers recommend it.'

'That'll do me nicely. The Mayfair, it is.'

I had made up my mind way back on the 'Medloc' train that if I ever reached English soil, which at the time seemed doubtful, I would not go home in my present state. Instead I would book into a decent hotel and clean myself up.

Bowling along the Embankment in the evening sun was a delight hard to describe. If it could be compared with anything else, it was as if waking from a dream to find that it had in fact been real. Familiar places and 'objects' kept jumping into view causing me to exclaim out loud, 'Oh, look! It's still there, amazing!' One of those objects was the wreck of a sailing ship that had been abandoned, high up on the foreshore, near Blackfriars Bridge.

The Mayfair was all that the taxi driver had said it would be, and more. I think that they must have been used to returning service people. As a matter of course they took a suitcase full of dirty washing and my uniform, promising to return everything by breakfast. I had a hot bath with a bewildering selection of scented soaps, soft towels and toiletries, which prepared me for a civilised and idle evening. My spare uniform had been laid out on the bed while I was bathing. Some ghostly part of room service had entered my room without me hearing a sound. I looked at the jacket, and was not reassured. It too needed valeting in a big way. I found a clothes brush in one of the drawers and did the best that I could with it. At least I had a clean shirt and pants, but I was in fact down to my last one of each.

Dinner was a dream, one that I had not expected, come true. I had not tasted rump steak for several years, and in the taxi I had thought that steak would be off the menu in these hard times. It was definitely on the menu, together with new potatoes and asparagus, followed by a trifle. A half bottle of Bordeaux completed the dream.

After dinner I was about to phone home when, with my hand on the receiver, I changed my mind. It would be an exciting surprise for my Mother if I arrived with my Father the following evening. I would telephone his office, and arrange to return home with him.

With that settled I sat down and read the day's papers. That too was a minor luxury, as the best that Bari Officers' Club had offered were seven days old. The wireless played a large part in everyone's lives in those days, as it did for me that evening. I lay in bed, yes bed, not a bunk, and listened to Tommy Handley, and other programmes, right up to the late news, before falling asleep with the wireless still on. Some time in the early hours I awoke and switched it off.

Breakfast found me resplendent in a beautifully valeted uniform and polished shoes. All the dirty washing had been laundered and ironed. The Mayfair rose to dizzy heights in my estimation as I sat down. The waiter arrived almost at once with news of the lack of bacon and the abundance of eggs. 'I'm sorry, sir, we have no bacon, eggs, yes, we have plenty of eggs,' said the waiter. 'May I suggest an omelette or kippers?'

'Kippers! Yes, kippers. That'll do nicely. I'll have a pair of kippers,' I replied. Toast and coffee followed, and then I looked at my watch. It was 10.00am. In half an hour I would phone my Father. It was then that I remembered I was supposed to report my arrival in London as soon as I landed. The instruction was in the message I received in Calais, which also included a number to ring. I had completely forgotten this order, and phoned at once.

A voice, which sounded official, first awarded me two weeks' leave, and then ended with the statement that confirmation and details of my new appointment would be sent to my home address. I hoped that it would not be minesweeping, but I really did not care. England and home was all that filled my thoughts. It is a strange fact that while I was away I did not miss my family or home. ML 135 was my home, and the crew my family. I wonder if this was the same with other service people.

It was now 10.30am. Now for it, so I dialled the number. 'Could I speak to Mr Beale, please? I'm his son.' Father was clearly shaken and there was a pause before he spoke, then in firm voice he said all the usual things: 'Good Heavens! That's wonderful! When did you arrive?' When the preliminaries were over he said that we must celebrate with lunch.

'Where would you like to go, old man?' He often called me 'old man'. Fathers did in those days.

'Oh, anywhere, Father, you choose,' I told him.

'We'll go to the Café Royal. You've never been there, have you?' he said.

'No, I've never been there. Far too posh and expensive for my pocket,' I replied. We agreed to meet at the Café Royal at one o'clock.

I went to the reception desk and asked directions to the nearest bank that would change my sovereigns. 'We'll do that for you, sir,' said the receptionist. 'Our rate is slightly higher than today's bank rate.'

I had no reason to distrust the hotel, especially after their good offices in regard to my clothes. I received twenty-six guineas for each of my four gold sovereigns, paid my bill, which was very reasonable, piled my three cases into a taxi, and set off for the Café Royal. There they made no fuss about taking care of my luggage. I then reported to a Naval Pay Office to draw some of the money that had been accumulating to my credit while I was away.

Armed with £300 in my pocket, I turned my attention to Father, the Café Royal and home. Our meeting was probably a mirror of all the others at that time, but I could see that Father was as moved as I was myself. We did not embrace. Men didn't in those days. We shook hands and laughed in pleasure. I cannot remember the meal. The occasion was too important to pay much attention to anything else.

However, something did happen in the restaurant that I do remember. A large party was seated at a table near us, and was headed by the father, or host, who did the ordering. My Dad ordered a bottle of Beaune to go with our meal, and the other man ordered Champagne. The Beaune was uncorked and tasted.

'Fine. That's fine. Would you take the chill off it, waiter, thank you?' said my Father. The gentleman at the other table called the waiter over, and asked him to take the chill off the Champagne! I laughed, silently I hope, but my Father did not laugh. 'You shouldn't laugh, old man,' he said. 'We all do silly things to begin with. He will learn, as we all have to at some stage.'

I have tried to bear this in mind ever since, though not always successfully. If I'm to be fair to myself, it was the waiter who made me laugh. His face was a study in gloomy resignation. 'The chill orff, sir? The chill orff? Very good, sir!'

I also remember that the meal finished with a cigar and liqueurs.

Father had parked in a nearby side street; you could park anywhere in London in 1945, and he brought it round so I could load my cases. I spent the afternoon at the firm, meeting people on the staff whom I had known briefly during the three months I had worked there prior to being called up for training.

My homecoming was a huge success. I thought that my Mother would never stop laughing and crying at the same time! It was then that, for the first time, I looked closely at both my parents. Mother had not changed a great deal, although her forehead was creased with lines, but Father had shrunk and his face was thin and pale. Three sons at sea, a Russian convoy and a rotten telegram announcing serious injury were quite enough to worry the flesh from the coolest of humans. However, I learned that Phillip Fellows, our one-time SO, had called upon my Father at his office in Holborn and given him news of me, an act of kindness that was typical of the man. I remembered that he had asked for the address before leaving Bari.

My dog Simon kept trying to say his piece. I didn't know at this stage if he remembered me, but by the following morning he made it plain that he did. It was still daylight when the greetings were over, the evening was warm and so we sat in the garden over sandwiches and tea. The talking lasted for hours and it was midnight before we went to our beds. I learned that Tony was ashore at the naval base at Greenwich. He had been given the rank of Lieutenant Commander, and placed on the reserve. It was expected that he would be discharged before the summer. My youngest brother, Donald, would be home any day soon.

I lay in bed thinking hazily of the years gone by. One memory that kept recurring was that of the corpse of the young German sailor that floated by as we headed north. I made a vow that I would try to marry a German girl in a small effort to repair relations. By some great good fortune I was able to keep this promise.

I awoke to the sound of birds singing in the trees at the bottom of the garden. Simon was curled up at the foot of the bed. Mother had obviously put him there, so I decided to test his memory. Before breakfast we went for a walk and I pointed to my heel, which was the signal that he was to walk to heel. He did so at once and I felt reassured. Every day that went by he further demonstrated to me that he had forgotten nothing.

The days were spent doing odd jobs about the house and long walks with Simon. I shot several rabbits for the pot that delighted my Mother who was an ace at cooking rabbits for the table. Rationing was still at its height; fresh meat, butter and petrol were the hardest things to obtain. All of these could, of course, be bought on the black market, but that took money and know-how to track them down.

The appointment and leave confirmation duly arrived. It was better news than I had hoped for, or could have expected. I was appointed Divisional Officer at the training camp in the Malvern Hills. What could be better? The first thing I had to do was to buy some sort of car for I would probably be able to come home occasionally, so transport would be essential. I bought a battered Hillman Minx for £50, which turned out to be a headache. It constantly went wrong in minor ways, but always ran again after I'd messed around under the bonnet.

The training camp was based around a beautiful ivy-covered country house. I was given a handsome room, with an adjoining bathroom and toilet. There was a pantry for the preparation of breakfast, but best of all, I was allotted a Wren steward to make my bed, and keep the room tidy. Was this Heaven? It seemed like it. Furthermore the duties were so light they were absurd. They consisted of hearing defaulters, and dishing out minor punishments once a week; marching in front of the Division on the parade ground every other Sunday; and to give two lectures on minesweeping each week. That lot would not strain an invalid.

Main meals were taken in the Mess. At the camp there was one other Division with its CO, and an RN Commander in overall charge, but who was rarely seen. The ratings, of which there were one hundred in each of the two Divisions, lived in huts, with their own Mess and necessary facilities. Two Petty Officers and one Chief were attached to each Division. There was a NAAFI, an assembly room and a volunteer band. Four instructors lived out but came in each day to teach the basics of seamanship and gunnery. It was in this 'Penal Settlement' that I spent the next three months.

The Hillman finally packed up completely after the second journey home and I bought a Vauxhall from a local garage. Trouble with the Hillman before its demise meant that I had to spend one free weekend at the training centre. I was therefore able to watch the other Division on the parade ground.

The only incident worth recording during my whole time at Malvern happened that weekend. The Divisional Officer seemed to me to be a bit of a show-off, and I had thought so right from the outset. This Sunday confirmed my view, though I tried my best not to laugh, in accordance with my new resolution. The ratings were marching in four ranks, in line abreast, with their officer marching in front. At one point he turned and marched backwards to see if his men were keeping in a straight line. He tripped and fell. The men did not stop; they marched over him, managing to avoid his face and other sensitive areas of his body. It was a scene worthy of a Chaplin film.

The Vauxhall cost me £90 and did me very well for two years. To be able to go home on alternate weekends was a blessing that was enriched by returning to a comfortable room with someone to look after it. Breakfast was always a joy because the table was by a window that overlooked the well-wooded slopes of the Malvern Hills. A boiled egg, toast, marmalade and coffee, served by a Wren steward, started the day in fine style. A couple of lectures were a small price to pay for such comfort. The lectures went well. I found that delivering the information came naturally to me, though I doubt that anyone listened.

One morning, ten weeks after I had entered the gates of this, my last appointment, a letter arrived terminating my service in the RNVR at the end of that month. It required me to report to Naval HQ, in Whitehall, for confirmation of my discharge. On my last day I thanked the kind Wren and wished her a happy peacetime life. I particularly sought out the Chief and the two POs. 'Well, gentlemen, I'm here to say goodbye, and thank you for the excellent way you have kept order during my appointment,' I said. 'Coming from small ships it's an education to see how it's done when there is a Chief and POs on the strength. Goodbye and good luck.' It was with these words that I made my departure from the wartime Navy.

As the car hurried through the country roads of late summer, I could not help reflecting on the good fortune bestowed on our family. So many had died that we might live. My two brothers Don and Tony were now home, and I looked forward to the new life to come.

I have decided to finish this memoir in a way that may – or perhaps may not – surprise you. A few days after the drive back from Malvern, I went down to a pub called The Round House, reputed to be the oldest inhabited house in England, but then they all make that claim, don't they? It is by the lake in St Albans, and was a favourite meeting place for my school friends who had survived the war. Some were still in uniform. It was 8.00pm, and Simon was with me as usual. It was a riotous evening. The place was packed to the rafters, with people surging back and forth between the garden and the bar. There was much singing and many of my friends were present. Simon had a hard time keeping sight of me between people's legs, but he somehow managed to keep close to me, and was made a fuss of by those who knew him. Three times the landlord tried to close the pub, and finally managed it at about 11.00pm. Feeling tired, a little drunk, but happy, I drove home in the warm night air.

Bed was more than welcome; it was a womb to crawl into. I gathered up the blanket and instantly fell asleep. Then much later I woke with a start as if I had been shaken, and sat upright. What was it? Why had I wakened so suddenly? I switched on the light and looked at my watch. It was 2.30am. Oh, my God! I had forgotten Simon for the second time in his life!

I literally hurled myself out of bed and into some clothes, raced downstairs to the garage, and drove like a lunatic to The Round House. There was nothing about. The roads were empty, the moon shone brightly. My heart pounded, and I think I prayed. As the car topped the rise leading down to the lake and the pub, I intentionally threw away all hope. Of course, he wouldn't be there. I must accept that he was lost or even dead. Dozens of cars had pulled away from the area at closing time, and any animal would have been lucky indeed to have survived the traffic chaos.

With a sick feeling in my stomach, and lead weight in my chest, I turned into the last straight of road within sight of the pub. The moon at this spot was obscured by trees and so I switched the headlights on to full beam, and there he was! There he was, sitting in the middle of the road, immediately opposite the pub door, waiting for me. He had positioned himself so that he could look up the road to see me coming back. I gathered him in my arms and we drove home, with his head in my lap. It was 3.00am.

Timeline

Brief timeline of the war at sea in the Mediterranean 1940–45

1940

June	Richard Beale (RB) commissioned into the navy.
11 June	Start of the siege of Malta.
28 June	Battle of the Espero Convoy. Italian convoy attacked, destroyer *Espero* sunk.
July	RB on HMS *Collingwood* to begin naval training.
3 July	British fleet attacks French fleet in harbour in Algeria at Mers-el-Kebir.
9 July	Battle of Calabria. Encounter between fleet forces escorting large convoys.
19 July	Battle of Cape Spada. HMAS *Sydney* sinks Italian cruiser *Bartolomeo Colleoni* off Crete.
September	RB goes to Chatham to wait for a ship.
12 October	Battle of Cape Passero. One destroyer and two Italian torpedo boats sunk, cruiser HMS *Ajax* seriously damaged.
11 November	Battle of Taranto. British air attack on Italians anchored at Taranto.
27 November	Battle of Cape Spartivento. British fight back an Italian interception.

1941

January 1941	RB in Scapa Flow on the *Arethusa*.
6–11 January	Operation Excess. British convoy to Malta. Italian torpedo boat *Vega* sunk, British destroyer HMS *Gallant* disabled.
25 February	Operation Abstention, Allied assault and occupation of Kastelorizo thwarted by Italian forces.
26 March,	Suda Bay, Crete. British cruiser HMS *York* sunk by explosive motor boats launched from Italian destroyers.
27–29 March	Battle of Cape Matapan. Fleet action. Regia Marina lose three cruisers and two destroyers during the night.
16 April	Battle of the Tarigo Convoy. Italian convoy attacked and two Italian destroyers lost along with the British HMS *Mohawk*.
8 May	RB receives his commission as a sub-lieutenant on HMS *King Alfred*.
20 May–1 June,	Battle of Crete. Series of actions supporting army in Crete, nine British warships sunk by Axis air attacks.
21 May–1 June	Battle of Crete. Royal Navy loses three cruisers and six destroyers to Axis air attacks.
24 May	*Bismarck* and *Prinz Eugen* sink HMS *Hood* at the Battle of the Denmark Strait.
24 May–27 May	German battleship *Bismarck* hunted down and sunk.
July	Operation Substance. British convoy to Malta. British destroyer HMS *Fearless* lost to air attack.
September	Operation Halberd. British convoy to Malta. Transport ship *Imperial Star* sunk by an Italian aerial torpedo.

8 November	Battle of the Duisburg Convoy. Axis convoy destroyed and Italian destroyer *Fulmine* lost.
7 December	Japanese attack on Pearl Harbor brings US into the war.
13 December	Battle of Cape Bon. Italian convoy attacked.
17 December	First Battle of Sirte.
19 December	Raid on Alexandria. Manned torpedoes attack British fleet; two battleships sunk in harbour.

1942

22 March	Second Battle of Sirte. British convoy and escort attacked by Italian fleet; all four cargo ships sunk during later Axis air strikes.
15 June	Operation Harpoon. British convoy resupplying Malta attacked by Italian cruisers and aircraft: four merchantmen and destroyers HMS *Bedouin* and the Polish vessel ORP *Kujawiak* sunk.
15 June	Operation Vigorous. British convoy attacked, it is driven back by the Italian fleet.
15 August	Operation Pedestal. British convoy resupplying Malta is attacked; nine merchantmen sunk by Axis E-boats, aircraft and submarines; but vital supplies, including oil, delivered
14 September	Operation Agreement, the Allied assault on Tobruk which is repulsed by the Axis forces.
November	Operation Stone Age. British convoy reaches Malta undisturbed.
8 November,	Start of Operation Torch, the Allied invasion of Vichy-controlled Morocco and Algeria.
2 December	Battle of Skerki Bank. Italian convoy attacked and destroyed.
11 December	Raid on Algiers. Manned torpedoes attack Allied shipping, two steamships are sunk.
8 November	French ships attempt to defend Moroccan neutrality at Casablanca.
20 November	End of Siege of Malta.

1943

16 April	Battle of the Cigno Convoy. Failed British attack by two destroyers on an Italian transport, the Italian escort *Cigno* is sunk, the British destroyer *Pakenham* is scuttled.
3–4 May	Battle of the Campobasso Convoy. Successful British attack by three destroyers on Italian transport *Campobasso* with the escorting destroyer *Perseo*. Both *Perseo* and *Campobasso* are sunk with no loss to the British.
9 July–17 August	Invasion of Sicily with Allied landings in Operation Husky.
3 September	Operation Avalanche, the start of the Allied invasion of Italy.
8 September	Start of Dodecanese Campaign, the failed Allied attempt to invade the Dodecanese Islands
9 September,	Start of the Allied landings at Salerno in Italy.
2 December	Air raid on the port of Bari by German forces.
10 December	RB badly wounded in an explosion on board ship.

1944

22 January	Start of Operation Shingle, the Allied landings at Anzio in Italy.
23 January	RB assumes command of ML 135 until the end of the war.
9 June	Allied Tenth Destroyer Flotilla (comprising UK/Canadian/Polish ships) engages and defeats remnants of the German Eighth Destroyer Flotilla off Brittany in the Battle of Ushant.
5 August	Start of Operation Dragoon, the Allied landings in southern France.

Index